I think that [Tillich] has been the only theologian who has made possible theological thinking in a contemporary and realistic way in our history. He was the only one with courage enough to face the secular consciousness and society of the 20th century.

Thomas J. J. Altizer
Obituary for Paul Tillich
Time, October 29, 1965

Altizer assured Tillich that he, more than any other theologian, had "opened the confrontation with the real world. You fathered us, here we are." Tillich became so excited that his wife took him home; they agreed to talk the next day. That night he suffered the heart attack from which he died.

Obituary for Paul Tillich
Life, November 5, 1965

The last paragraph of your article on Paul Tillich is badly misleading.... Professor Tillich delivered a brilliant lecture the evening before his heart attack, went to a reception for a short time, spoke only briefly with Professor Altizer, and invited him for cocktails the next day....

As his last lecture proved, Professor Tillich was not excited about the "God is dead" movement, although he was interested in it as in all theological developments. His eyes were toward the future, to a new age in which systematic theology would be seen in the context of the history of religions.

Jerald Brauer
Letter to the Editor
Life, November 26, 1965

IMMANENCE AND FANTASY

Paul Tillich, Thomas Altizer,

and the Dialectic of the Sacred

In The Horizon of the Infinite, vol. 1

CHRISTOPHER D. RODKEY

Immanence and Fantasy

Paul Tillich, Thomas Altizer, and the Dialectic of the Sacred

In The Horizon of the Infinite, vol. 1

Christopher D. Rodkey

Barber's Son Press
York, Pennsylvania

Published by

BARBER'S SON PRESS

York, Pennsylvania

© 2025 Christopher D. Rodkey
Original dissertation © 2008 Christopher D. Rodkey

Scripture quotations are from New Revised Standard Version of the Bible, copyright © 1989 National Council of the Churches of Christ in the United States of America. Used by permission. All rights reserved worldwide.

ISBN: 978-1-7347188-7-4

Also available:
In the Horizon of the Infinite, Volume 2:
Intersubjective Transcendence: Mary Daly and the Baptism of Imagination (ISBN 978-1-7347188-8-1)

No part of this book may be used or reproduced in any manner whatsoever without written permission. No part of this book may be stored in a retrieval system or transmitted in any form without the prior permission in writing from the publisher.

10 9 8 7 6 5 4 3 2 1

TABLE OF CONTENTS

IN THE HORIZON OF THE INFINITE
VOLUME 1

List of Abbreviations	*i*
Publication Credits	*iv*
Preface *Immanence and Fantasy*	*v*
Introduction to the Two-Volume Work *In the Horizon of the Infinite*	1

PART 1
PAUL TILLICH
AND THE DIALECTIC OF THE SACRED

Chapter 1 Paul Tillich's Post-Christian Theology	25
Chapter 2 A Pantheon of Theisms in Tillich	47

PART 2
THOMAS ALTIZER
AND THE GOSPEL OF CHRISTIAN ATHEISM

Introduction to Part 2	85

Chapter 3 93
Altizer's Christological Project

Chapter 4 117
Transcendence and Immanence in Altizer

Chapter 5 143
The Dialectic of the Sacred

Bibliography 161

Index 197

Author 210

LIST OF ABBREVIATIONS

Paul Tillich (1886-1965)

BR	*Biblical Religion and the Search for Ultimate Reality* (1955)
CE	*Christianity and the Encounter of World Religions* (1963)
CB	*The Courage to Be* (1952)
DF	*Dynamics of Faith* (1957)
EN	*The Eternal Now* (1963)
FR	*The Future of Religions* (1966)*
HCT	A History of Christian Thought (1968)*
IH	*The Interpretation of History* (1936)
IRR	*The Irrelevance and Relevance of the Christian Message* (1996)
LPJ	*Love, Power, and Justice* (1954)
MH	*The Meaning of Health* (1984)
MB	*Morality and Beyond* (1963)
MSA	*My Search for Absolutes* (1967)*
MTD	*My Travel Diary: 1936* (1970)*
NB	*The New Being* (1955)
OAA	*On Art and Architecture* (1987)*
OB	*On the Boundary* (1966)*.
PEX	*Political Expectation* (1971)*
PE	*The Protestant Era* (1948)
PEX	*Political Expectation* (1971)*

PPT   *Perspectives in 19ᵗʰ and 20ᵗʰ Century Protestant Theology* (1967)*

RPT   *The Recovery of the Prophetic Tradition in the Reformation* (1950)

RS   *The Religious Situation* (1962)

SS   *The Spiritual Situation in Our Technical Society* (1988)*

ST1   *Systematic Theology, Vol. 1* (1951)

ST2   *Systematic Theology, Vol. 2* (1957)

ST3   *Systematic Theology, Vol. 3* (1963)

SF   *The Shaking of the Foundations* (1948)

TC   *Theology of Culture* (1959)

UC   *Ultimate Concern* (1965)*

TOP   *Theology of Peace* (1990)*

WR   *What is Religion?* (1969)*

*Published posthumously.

Thomas J. J. Altizer (1927-2018)

AM   *The Altizer-Montgomery Dialogue* (with John Montgomery, 1967)

CA   *A Critical Analysis of C. G. Jung's Understanding of Religion* (1955)

CJ   *The Contemporary Jesus* (1997)

DH   *The Descent into Hell* (1970)

GA   *Genesis and Apocalypse* (1990)

CG   *The Genesis of God* (1993)

GN   *Godhead and the Nothing* (2003)

GCA   *The Gospel of Christian Atheism* (1966)

HA   *History as Apocalypse* (1985)

LDG	*Living the Death of God* (2006)
ME	*Mircea Eliade and the Dialectic of the Sacred* (1963)
NA	*The New Apocalypse* (1967)
NG	*The New Gospel of Christian Atheism* (2001)
NGT	*Nature and Grace in the Theology of Saint Augustine* (1951)
OM	*Oriental Mysticism and Biblical Eschatology* (1961)
RT	*Radical Theology and the Death of God* (with William Hamilton, 1966)
SEG	*The Self-Embodiment of God* (1977)
TP	*Total Presence* (1980)
TNC	*Toward a New Christianity: Readings in the Death of God Theology* (ed., 1967)

Mary Daly (1928-2010)

AG	*Amazon Grace* (2006)
BGF	*Beyond God the Father* (1973)
CSS	*The Church and the Second Sex* (1975)
G/E	*Gyn/Ecology* (1978)
O	*Outercourse* (1992)
PL	*Pure Lust* (1984)
Q	*Quintessence* (1998)
W	*Webster's First New Intergalactic Wickedary of the English Language* (with Jane Caputi, 1987)

PUBLICATION CREDITS

The original dissertation was archived electronically:

In the Horizon of the Infinite: Paul Tillich and the Dialectic of the Sacred. Ph.D. diss., Drew U. UMI microfilm no. 3340963. Ann Arbor, MI: ProQuest, 2009.

Parts of this dissertation have been published in the following, either in the course of writing or after its completion:

"Is Bad Theology Good Philosophy?" *Bulletin of the North American Paul Tillich Society* 31.2 (2005).

"Paul Tillich's Pantheon of Theisms." *Models of God and Other Ultimate Realities.* Eds. A. Kashner and J. Diller. Dordrecht: Springer, 2013.

"The Nemesis Hex: Mary Daly and the Patriarch with Good Ideas." *Retrieving the Radical Tillich.* Ed. R. Re Manning. New York: Palgrave Macmillan, 2015.

"Thomas J. J. Altizer," with J. Pearl. *The Palgrave Handbook of Radical Theology* Eds. J. Miller and C. Rodkey. New York: Palgrave Macmillan, 2018.

"Mary Daly." *The Palgrave Handbook of Radical Theology.* Eds. J. Miller and C. Rodkey. New York: Palgrave Macmillan. 2018.

Preface

Immanence and Fantasy:
Paul Tillich, Thomas Altizer, and
the Dialectic of the Sacred

In the Horizon of the Infinite, Volume 1

This dissertation, *In the Horizon of the Infinite*, was completed and defended at Drew University in the autumn of 2008. The project was directed and advised by Robert S. Corrington; Catherine Keller and Chris Boesel served as readers; and Jeffrey Robbins acted as an external reader. As I was completing the work, both Thomas Altizer and D. G. Leahy (1937-2014) offered critical feedback, and later, Gabriel Vahanian (1927-2012) would offer the critique that the dissertation had "too much Altizer and not enough Vahanian!" Since its completion, the dissertation has been offered contracts to be published and pieces of it have been previously published, but its entirety has never been published as a whole work because of a variety of reasons: the death of an editor, the death of a publisher, the change of ownership of a publisher, unreasonable financial demands from a publisher upon my affiliated academic institution, family demands, and professional conflicts. Since its writing, though, while a few copies sat in libraries and in Syracuse University's Altizer archive, *In the Horizon of the Infinite* has been cited in other dissertations and books and is listed in a recent work highlighting scholarship on Mary Daly.

To offer some context around the work's completion: the week of my dissertation defense began on Monday, September 15, 2008, when Lehman Brothers declared bankruptcy, and the Dow Jones Industrial Average fell by 200 points. On Tuesday, the U.S. federal government announced a bail-out of American International Group, Inc., or "AIG," for $85 billion. Panic ensued, and money market funds lost nearly $200 billion within the course of hours, and banks skyrocketed their interest rates.

Driving home from my oral defense on Wednesday, September 17, I heard on the radio that the markets had crashed again by 550 points. Rumors of bailouts circulated to stabilize and rebound the market by the end of the week, but this simply set up the coming disaster two weeks later, when the Dow lost another 780 points, triggering a global economic catastrophe. By the end of the year, the Dow was down by 34%—and it would shrink even more by the Spring of 2009. During the week of graduating with my Ph.D. at Drew's fall commencement, the Dow closed at its lowest in five years, which was hardly the end of the damage, and the U.S. government began coordinating global bank bailouts.

But driving home from my oral defense, I had the feeling that *something had changed*. And things *were* changing—for me, at least. Just a few weeks later, during the course of a single weekend, I graduated and I was ordained as a pastor in the United Church of Christ. I had just bought a house and I started a new job, but within months my wife would be laid off from her job and shortly thereafter, suffer the first of two miscarriages.

Everything *was* changing. Within weeks, the United States would elect Barack Obama to the presidency, largely to his self-proclamation of being a "change candidate." Change, however, came in different forms and was not always or necessarily better than the status quo.

The decline of the economy signified a changing religious landscape, that the American economy of the early War on Terror years had shown itself to be a hall of mirrors—evil doctrinally predicated upon ecclesiastical Christianity in the United States. The nature of practiced religious faith was changing, and the American public would look for deliverance from the unlikeliest of sources in the face of financially and morally bankrupt institutional systems, for better or for worse. Writing now in 2025—once again, *in media res*, amidst another economic crisis—while the American middle class never recovered from the 2008 economic collapse. If our stock market numbers look higher today—at the time of writing, they are, though they are in decline—it's because we want to believe it so. We are more financially, morally, and spiritually bankrupt than we were in 2008; we play this ritual dance of denial because the horror that would be to come points us toward the kingdom of implosion that only John of Patmos could see and hear more clearly.

These crises, and *crisis democracy* itself, are distractions from the true crisis, which is the death of God as known as the inevitable decline of inhabitable earth. When Nietzsche asked whilst declaring the death of God, "How could we unchain this earth from the sun?", the horror of the present moment ought to stand plainly before us. While our American culture argues First Things, our first *thing*—our habitat, our planet—is slowly dying the slow death of divine decomposition.

Amidst such doom and gloom connected to the completion of this dissertation, why revisit this dissertation now, fifteen years later? I am regularly asked for the dissertation by those newly interested in the works of Tillich, Altizer, and Daly, but there is apparent renewed interest in both Tillich and Altizer among Christian scholars. No other academic project has explored the relationship between Tillich and Daly as deeply as this dissertation. And further, reading Altizer with Daly, and interpreting Daly as an important voice in the tradition of radical theology, has become among radical theologians an accepted interpretation of the canon. Although Mary Daly wasn't exactly a theologian, she should be included as part of the "tradition" (for lack of a better word) of the death of God theology.

Fifteen years later I believe that I made a crucial error in this dissertation, which was to read too unitary of a line between Tillich and Altizer. Tillich clearly had an influence upon Altizer—and undoubtedly, upon Daly as well—but today I recognize that it is *Karl Barth* who influenced Altizer in a much more dramatic and forceful way, if one is to take the whole of Altizer's work seriously. In my own defense, however, Tillich *was* a clear influence upon what would become the death of God theology and its legacy as a whole, particularly upon Altizer. On this count I believe my project remains relevant. Yet Altizer's theology owes to Barth a distinct and unique way of Christian thinking and theologizing which Tillich did not fully embrace—and I suspect that Tillich's rejection of Altizer's earlier ideas were not only that Tillich didn't understand Altizer (as I suggest in the dissertation) but that Altizer was approaching Christianity from a Barthian perspective. While Altizer's theology is Barthian filtered by multiple other influences, such as Norman O. Brown Mircea Eliade, and American jazz, my estimation is that Tillich did not understand those other influences, either. A worthwhile future project could be to present and re-interpret Altizer as an experiment to reconcile Karl Barth and Tillich's constructed rivaling legacies within contemporary Christian thought.

Yet Tillich's influence upon Altizer, and Tillich's impact upon American theology should not be downplayed. Today we may now speak of Tillich's impact upon African American, feminist, and queer theologies, as well as defining the academic study of religion itself in the United States. Some have argued that Tillich alone shaped how Continental philosophy was received and initially interpreted in North American philosophy departments. I hope that making this dissertation more accessible to the public adds a contribution to the larger ongoing academic conversation about Tillich's influence and importance. My framing of how to approach Tillich from a radical perspective—by going back to St. Anselm's ontological argument—is a novel approach that opens new ways to think theologically.

The long journey of publishing this dissertation eventually led to what would later become *The Palgrave Handbook of Radical Theology*, which I co-edited with Jordan Miller. *The Palgrave Handbook* has fulfilled its mission to establish a central starting point for researchers and interested students of radical theology. I gently point the reader to that resource as an introductory text.

After the 2008 dissertation was completed, Altizer continued to write, and radical theology continued to develop. He also continued to publish; his later books were *The Call to Radical Theology* (2012), *The Apocalyptic Trinity* (2016), *This Silence Must Now Speak* (2017), and *Satan and Apocalypse* (2017). Altizer died in Pennsylvania on November 28, 2018, claiming to have been working on an ongoing project on Catholicism; I suspect, based upon conversations with him, that his direction of thinking would point toward a radical Mariology. Mary Daly stopped publishing after *Amazon Grace* was published in 2006, and she died on January 3, 2010, in Massachusetts. To date, no other works of hers have appeared posthumously, but a massive and ongoing archive of her writings and correspondence exists within the Sophia Smith Collection of Women's History at Smith College's library.

* * *

The dissertation, *In the Horizon of the Infinite*, is here distributed into two long volumes: *Immanence and Fantasy* and *Intersubjective Transcendence*. The contrarian titles are intentional. Revisions presented in these new additions are mostly cosmetic. Tom Altizer and Mary Daly are discussed as if they were still alive, which was the case at the time of writing; however, I changed a few matters of fact or history made after 2008.

One glaring missed detail I want to highlight is that *In the Horizon of the Infinite* does not adequately address some of the significant moral issues connected to Daly's work related to transphobia. In fact, after her death on January 3, 2010, a few major newspaper obituaries focused upon her legacy as being solely her promotion of transphobia. While this is unfortunate, it isn't undeserved, either. In fact, some of the transphobic roots of Daly's thoughts extend right back to Paul Tillich's lesser-known writings on technology. This is addressed somewhat in *The Palgrave Handbook of Radical Theology*, and I will explore this in the opening pages of the second volume, *Intersubjective Transcendence*.

All this being said, in this work I am enacting Daly's own theological method of "pirating," which is how she took useful ideas from patriarchal figures—like Tillich. This is to say, not outrightly dismissing ideas based upon the moral failures of those who wrote them down because useful ideas are, in fact, *useful*, but also because exposing these flaws and taking them seriously is revelatory of both the author and their times.

April 4, 2025

Introduction

In The Horizon of the Infinite, Vols. 1 & 2

Immanence and Fantasy: Paul Tillich, Thomas Altizer, and the Dialectic of the Sacred

Intersubjective Transcendence: Mary Daly and the Baptism of Imagination

> *Transcendence is no longer the issue.*
> *But healing the web of life is.*
>
> Nelle Morton[1]

Outline of the Dissertation

This dissertation is an investigation into the radical aspects of Paul Tillich's thought and how he influenced a younger generation of theologians in the 1960s, in particular Thomas J. J. Altizer and Mary Daly. Thomas Altizer is perhaps the most representative theologian of the so-called "Death of God" theology movement; Mary Daly is the most infamous of radical feminist theologians of the last portion of the 20th century. Through this research project I will show the complex ways in which Tillich's ideas manifest themselves in new contexts that both forwarded and betrayed his theological and philosophical enterprise. In doing so, fruitful directions for new theological discourse emerge.

This dissertation will not go into substantive detail about the history of the "Death of God" theology, though the academic and religious freedom issues that emerged from Altizer's early publishing will be discussed. For my readers who are not familiar with this movement, let me say that it was in some ways an artificial "movement" of young post-Tillichian theologians, mostly assembled by University of Chicago theologian Langdon Gilkey. The names most associated with this movement in North America include in addition to Altizer, Gabriel Vahanian, William Hamilton, Harvey Cox, Richard Rubenstein, and Paul

---

[1] Nelle Morton, *The Journey is Home* (Boston: Beacon, 1985), 216.

Van Buren.[2] In the second volume, I will make a case for Daly to be considered among this group of thinkers. Even though each of these theologians had very different backgrounds, agendas, and theologies, they were all at once Tillichian and post-Tillichian. They all took Tillich with utmost seriousness, and most understood his theology as moving Christianity into a new religious paradigm, by which, ironically, most of them radically departed from Tillich. The title "death of God theology" has since waned; today this particular strand of North American theology takes the title "radical theology"—theology following the *radical* Tillich.

This dissertation will, again, examine the radical aspects of Tillich's theology. Among Tillich scholars, "the radical Tillich" is not always the most popular incarnation or constructed representation of Tillich, even though a radical Tillich is, we will see, clearly part of his complex layers of personae. Similarly unpopular and somewhat unexplored is his influence upon the radical theological thinkers of the 1960s. Although the "Death of God theology" was an intense, short-lived movement, its legacy is often unacknowledged and trivialized.[3] This dissertation will enter a discussion of this radical theology, primarily around the themes of transcendence and immanence in the thought of Tillich, Altizer, and Daly. As mentioned before, framing the trajectory of conversation in this way will open, I hope, what will be a new constructive direction.

This project is presented here as having three "parts" spanning two volumes: *Transcendence and Fantasy*, volume one; and *Intersubjective Transcendence*, volume two. Parts 1 and 2 are included in the first volume, and Part 3 is included in the second volume.

In Part One we meet Paul Tillich and enter an introduction to his massive system of theology. For Tillich, the question of God is an important question or problem, but the answers are never clear; we consider the various models of divinity proposed by his system and his critics. For example: was Tillich a pantheist, a pan*en*theist, an atheist, or an ecstatic naturalist? No clear answers emerge, but within the traditional posing of the question of transcendence and immanence in God arises

---

[2] There are others, to be sure. The English incarnation of this radical theology has a different history, although Tillich is also at the center of this trajectory as well. That incarnation is most often associated with Bishop John Robinson and Don Cupitt.

[3] Cf. Mike Grimshaw, "Did God Die in *The Christian Century*?", *Journal of Cultural and Religious Theory* 6.3 (2005): 7-23. As an example of this trivialization, see Russel McCutcheon's parenthetical reference to radical theology in his review essay "A Gift with Diminished Returns," *Journal of the American Academy of Religion* 76.3 (2008), 755.

Tillich's idea of self-transcendence. Self-transcendence, we will see, suggests a new kind of immanence.

Part Two introduces and explores the most important "death of God" theologian, Thomas J. J. Altizer. Altizer's theology takes Tillich as a "springboard" and, as a whole, is in some aspects an elaborate criticism of Tillich. Taking the radical aspects of Tillich—the atheistic, ecstatic, and immanental Tillich—Altizer constructs a kenotic Christology that, over the first fifty years of his writing, discloses a Hegelian diachrony that historically pours God out from Creation to incarnation to resurrection, where resurrection is the final fusion of God in an enfleshed immanence. As enfleshed Godhead creation is perpetuated by *us*, piercing through the "Nothing," and is initiated by *the thinking itself now occurring*. In Altizer is a shift away from *being-itself*, Tillich's ontological name for "God," to *thinking-itself*: from *esse-ipsum* to *reputo-ipsum*. But in the *thinking of Godhead* is an implicit immanence of reality—the reality in which we all live and either *think* Godhead or *drown* in the Nothing. As an apocalyptic ethics, I will show, the immanence of life-itself, or *vita-ipsum*, must precede thinking or being.

Part Three (in volume 2, *Intersubjective Transcendence*) introduces and explores another radical theologian deeply influenced by Tillich at the end of his career, Mary Daly. Daly's feminist system of thought is structurally more similar to Tillich than Altizer's theology, but Daly, over time, intentionally sheds any likeness of Christianity in her theology or philosophy. In fact, she rejects the whole notion of "theology" for an "Elemental philosophy"—an *Elemental* philosophy, it should be noted, which seeks to construct a forward-looking return to pre-Socratic, non-patriarchal philosophies of the Elements. As a "meta-ethics," as she calls it, her philosophy points toward a morality system that posits life before and over death, suggesting that the lust for death is what perpetuates false religion in the world.

That false religion is *patriarchy*, the over-arching religion in which Christianity participates. *Life*, however, is a prerequisite for being, or for thinking, and is implicit in her formulation of *esse-ipsum* as *be-ing* or *Metabe-ing*. The Elements are elemental, immanental, ultimate and intimate reality. The immanence of the Elemental is perpetuated by the *telos* of the "fifth essence," or *quintessence*, the life that permeates everything. Life-itself, "*vita-ipsum*," is ontologically prior to being; the *necessary* being or *be-ing* is the ground, fountain, and symbol of the self-transcending nature of women.

Out of this discussion I will conclude with a radical phenomenology of theology, or what I call a *metatheological* direction of thinking. I will argue that theology, as a task, centers around the practice of constructing and creating reality; Tillich points toward this in a brief discussion in the transcriptions of the introductory lecture of his *History of Christian Thought* course, and Altizer and Daly explicitly do this as well. It might be easy to say, as some have, that Altizer represents the last of the theologians because of this reality-creation implicit in his work.[4] In fact, the kind of thinking that Altizer and Daly do are so foreign to modern Christian theology that it might be nonsensical to even call it "theology," just as Daly has rejected this title herself, preferring "philosophy." I suggest, on the other hand, that Altizer and Daly point toward the fact that we are all theologians; some of us suppress our theological impulse, others relegate it, but we all have the potency to *think Godhead*, to *think Elementally*, to think being. Few of us are aware of these powers and even fewer have the courage to create, which is the courage to be: the courage to be ourselves—magical, human beings.

Metatheological Thinking at the Edge of Language

Among the many themes that these thinkers share is a shift of attention to the central importance of language for theology. To make a generalization about the death of God theology movement, theology is a language-event. All of the death of God theologians wrote in some way about this theme; however, the one who has written the most about theology as a language-event is Paul M. Van Buren. Van Buren (1924-1998) was a descendent of U.S. President Martin Van Buren, an Episcopal priest, a student of Karl Barth, and longtime professor at Temple University. His later work is generally regarded as one of the most important systematic theological treatments of the Holocaust and in his work he blazed new trails for the work of Jewish-Christian relations.[5] I employ Van Buren here because no other radical theologian has so systematically explored the theology of language, and his theology will yield a fruitful discussion to contextualize the rest of this dissertation.

---

[4] See, for example, Mark C. Taylor's forward to *LDG*, "Forward: The Last Theologian," *Living the Death of God* by Thomas Altizer (Albany, NY: SUNY UP, 2006): xi-xvii.
[5] Ellen Charry, "Heart of Integrity," *The Christian Century* 122.4 (22. Feb. 2005), 31.

Van Buren's lesser-known 1972 book, *The Edge of Language*, is a meditation on linguistics and the importance of language for a contemporary Christianity. "Our human language is not simply a collection of words," he writes, "but our distinctly human way of going about the...business of life." If language is not considered to be a key component for discerning the meaning and structure of religion in human lives, then, "we should indeed be far removed from the possibility of understanding [Christianity] or any other religion." To employ a linguistic analysis of religion is a somewhat dangerous task, as to do so is to risk a "new or different Christianity."[6] That is, a *radical Christianity*.

Van Buren views the central crises facing churchly Christianity (writing in the late 1960s and early 1970s) as including new forms of secularisms and atheisms emerging in culture which challenge the validity of Christian faith. Luckily for Christians, however, the question of *atheism* is linguistic, and van Buren is up for the challenge; he writes that the "central thesis" of *The Edges of Language*

> will be that religious discourse, in its most crucial and characteristic utterances, those in which the word 'God' is likely to be employed, takes place upon the edges of language, at the farthest reaches of our rules for, or agreements in, the use of words. This particular linguistic behavior, then, may be thought of as speaking at the frontiers of language, a way (certainly not the only way) of behaving when we have reached the point at which we want to say the very most that our language entitles us to say, where we want to say as much as possibly be said. When the religious use of 'God' is understood as a case of walking language's borders, the nature of the puzzles engendered by this talk will become more comprehensible[.][7]

Religious language, along with jokes, metaphysics, poetry, and love-language, according to van Buren, all occur at *outer limits* of language. But language for expressing any conception of 'God' permeates all other

---

[6] Paul Van Buren, *The Edges of Language* (London: SCM, 1972) 2. He continues: "This is true of any subject: to accept a new description of X is to see X in a new way, to have a new understanding of X. But if I understand X in a new way, then X is to that extent different for me from what is was before.... To this extent, at least, my analysis will be far from 'pure' description" (3).
[7] Ibid. 4.

language at the very *edge* of language: pushing the edge to its own limits and into a state of flux.[8]

Christians have, however, become lazy in the arena of God-language. Most Christians, including pastors and theologians, never take the risk to venture into the more dangerous regions of language—that is, the *edge*—reflecting a deep ambiguity regarding the word *God*. Used in these common terms, *God* is "the name of we-know-not-what, and the effects of his agency."[9] Being used as the name of a "something-or-other," the use of the word "God" by modern religious people suggests that the word's meaning "would indeed be explained by pointing to or otherwise defining its bearer." *God* has become a label for a thing.[10] Even while Christians have become lazy in their use of God-language, the laziness emerges as a *fatigue* against the difficulty of approaching the *edge* of language.

As a central example of the problem and nature of God-language at the edges of language, van Buren takes a statement which most Christians can agree upon within safe realms away from the edges of language: *God loves us*. The "difficulty with this position," that is, that 'God loves us,'

> is that it consists in maintaining that no conceivable event can be incompatible with the claim that God loves us. This results in a contradiction: for we cannot, without contradiction, say that God makes a difference in this world, and also that whatever happens in this world, God still loves us. The reason for this conclusion is that to affirm one thing is to deny its opposite. To affirm God's love…in this world is to deny that no difference in the world results from God's love. This challenge of falsification is destroyed to show that a non-falsifiable claim cannot also be a claim about the state of affairs in this world. This claim that God loves us, no

---

[8] Cf. Nicholas Lash, "For God Read Red Ink," *Frontier* 16 (1973), 56.
[9] Van Buren explains: "Religion has led men to 'speak *of* God' and to 'speak *to* God,' a God who, it is said, acts, loves, and judges, and also therefore seems to be a personal agent in the world. However, it is notoriously the case that neither this agent nor the effects of his agency can be distinguished. If God is an agent, then his agency seems to have no ascertainable effects upon the course of this world," citing, for example, Psalm 79 (Van Buren [1972], 16-17).
[10] Ibid. 18. I would go so far as to suggest that given the *ambiguity* of any sense of "God," the atheist would be right to reject the linguistic nothingness of "God." We will see later that Tillich makes a similar move in his argument against "theological theism."

matter what happens, is unable to stand up to the challenge and is therefore hollow.

To accept this criticism, but also to answer it directly, is to accept the model of language which it assumes. The model derives from those areas of discourse in which to assert that of X is so is to deny that X is not so. The point is a logical one *and in logic it works*.[11]

To this end, language about God, when it is authentic and thought through to its full logical ends, is *self-subverting*; which is to say, it is on the *edges* of language. The problem that rises regarding language, then, van Buren writes, "places us in a circular situation: the very language in which our problem is presented is also the only tool we have for solving it." As an element—if not *the* element—which constitutes what it *is* to be human, language is a puzzle for which there can be no *escape* or *answer*. "Words are so centrally and inextricably a part of our [lives]," van Buren writes, "that there is no Archimedean point from which the puzzle can be unraveled." It is "[o]nly as linguistic beings can we set out to understand what our language is for us," to which he adds, "[o]therwise, we have literally nothing to say." [12]

Before moving further, van Buren considers a basic problem at the center of language, namely, the question of how words' meanings are relative to their own and our own contexts. Although words are part of our lives, he writes, some words appear to be divorced from "the context of human life," such as words in "spelling lists, grammar books, and dictionaries," but even these words have one or more practical applications to our daily use of words. Words are usually used as "words-in-action," that is, existing "in the context of people doing things together." *In other words*, words are tools: words do not only *simply* communicate simple and complex ideas, record memory, etc., but words also build and destroy buildings, friendships, nations, and social structures. Words are so connected to our lives that "[t]o imagine a language in its actual use is to imagine 'a form of life,' and to learn a language as it is actually used is to share in a way of life." [13] van Buren's argument that humans are naturally connected to language is not only a philosophical anthropology but an argument for

---

[11] Ibid. 27-28, ital. add.
[12] Ibid. 45.
[13] Ibid. 46-47.

language's relevance to our cultures (and our cultures' relevance to ourselves).

Language, however, is not "ontologically prior," but language is *existentially* or "logically prior." In other words, "we do not first have concepts and then the words for concepts." He explains that even if someone does not know *the word* for a thing, he or she could still describe it or learn the proper word for the thing from someone else. When our experience pushes us to invent a new word or words to describe something (which, van Buren says, is "unusual") "we have to stretch our language and come to new agreements about what to say"—in this sense, one should be careful to differentiate and not confuse *concept* with *word*. Language, as a communal phenomenon, always has two characteristics: first, language is *public*, and second, language is *contextual*.[14]

First, language is public—not only in the sense that certain kinds of language are acceptable outside of closed communities, but that in the sense that "in learning a language we begin to share in a form of life." Language is a convention which is publicly agreed upon and is the means by which one "relates to the world" with others: "it is...the distinctively social way of being in the world." This is not to say, however, that language is a *static* phenomenon, that "extra-grammatical rules" must be 'followed' to break the form of language and effectively communicate from one's own, or to someone else's *context*.[15]

Second, language is always contextual in the sense that the meaning of words is contingent upon the person and location(s) of the one using the word. "Failure to attend to the context of words," van Buren writes, "results in a failure to see the context of meaning."[16] As such, language helps to *construct our reality* (or *realities*), as, he writes, "[t]he only world we have is the one we can speak of." By this van Buren means that to understand a German person, one not only has to study the German language but also how she individually employs the German language for her own use. Similarly, systems of language emerge among 'tribal' communities: one speaks differently when speaking in the "geological

---

[14] Ibid. 50-51. Van Buren explains: "[I]t would be incorrect to say that Helen Keller first had the concept 'water' and then discovered a word to go with the concept. We who have the word can say that she felt the water, but it is difficult to say what the water was for her before she had the word, for our language, with which we settle such puzzles, is designed for usual cases" (51).
[15] Ibid. 51, 52.
[16] Ibid. 53-54.

world, the chemical world, or the astronomical world." The English language, according to van Buren, has recently become more infiltrated with scientific language—therefore, he concludes, the more that scientific language is integrated into English, the further removed we (in the present) become from "pre-scientific" humanity. As such, today's language is more concerned with the idea of "fact" as factuality "concerned with empirical data" than a few hundred years ago. To this end, van Buren writes, "the world is what it is for us as we speak of it."[17]

Van Buren, at this point in *The Edges of Language*, raises some relevant objections to these points. The first objection, he writes, is that "religion cannot be encompassed by language, since religion points to a reality that surpasses language." In other words, van Buren wonders whether language can contain the dimensions, size, or weight of an idea such as religion. "In the strictest sense," he writes: "we do not have to warn ourselves to keep silent about that of which we cannot speak: we have no choice in that matter! It might seem, however, that religion is the living refutation of this argument, being the case par excellence of an experience which surpasses language." van Buren cites that the same conditions apply for other abstract ideas, such as beauty, justice, love, etc.[18] Therefore, I interpret this objection as an appeal to Plato's *Phaedrus*, recognizing the Forms as that which occurs at the limitations of language, as well as a limited experience of the soul's pre-corporeal life and memory.[19] Van Buren, however, refutes this objection by claiming that such an argument would assume that non-verbal communication has no *logical* connection to language. Since religious experience is ultimately experienced by a local self, the experience is a human one; and therefore, such an experience must be connected to language.[20] (This begs the question of the self's role, in relation to the epistemological claims, to *religious experience*. An interesting case study here would be John Wesley's famous experience of his 'heart strangely warmed' as a legitimate category of revelation.)

---

[17] Ibid. 57-58.
[18] Ibid. 61-62.
[19] Cf. Plato, *Phaedrus*, trans. Alexander Nehamas and Paul Woodruff (Indianapolis: Hackett, 1995) esp. 246A-250D (p. 30-39); Paul Tillich, "Symbols of Eternal Life," *Harvard Divinity Bulletin* 26.3 (1962), 3.
[20] Van Buren (1972), 62. He explains further, that if this objection stood, "[a] single element in seeing, hearing, or feeling is isolated from the larger context of our lives, as though what we then went on to do with this pre-verbal and therefore pre-reflective something were no part of the original" (62-63).

The second objection is that "the heart of religion, not being a matter of words at all, cannot be adequately described by a linguistic analysis."[21] In other words, van Buren asks, even if language has a *logical* relationship to the religious, can a linguistic examination of religious language really *work* as a methodology, if so much of religious experience could be considered non-verbal experience? Like the Forms described in the *Phaedrus*, van Buren says, there is a difference between language *of* something and language *about* that same 'thing': "language *of* love," for example, is different than "language *about* love." Understanding love requires knowledge of both uses of *love*.[22] So-called "non-verbal experiences" encompass these kinds of experiences, and, as such, are then not *really* non-verbal. Van Buren explains:

> ...[I]n a strict sense there are no non-verbal experiences, if by that is meant experience about which nothing at all is or can be said. If there were, nothing at all *would* be said about them, and even that nothing can be said about them. That we have experiences which we cannot describe is not denied, but description is not the only use of language. If, therefore, we reckon within only that of which we can speak, we are not omitting anything of which something can be said, which is very close to saying we are not leaving *anything* out. This applies to those experiences of which we say are indescribable or that they are not expressed in words.
>
> ....
>
> ...[I]f it were further claimed that religions consist of more than can be said, that claim could not be supported, for if there were some "more," and if that "more" could be spoken of, than nothing whatsoever would be said of it, not even that it is a "more" beyond speech. It seems reasonable, then, to begin by saying that whatever can be said about religion will be said in human words, that here...language is our principal tool for understanding a religion.[23]

Even if a religion claims that it cannot be contained by words, it can in fact *talk about* religious phenomena with words. If we limit our religious

---

[21] Ibid. 61.
[22] Ibid. 62-64.
[23] Ibid. 66-67. He adds: "I can quite well imagine a religion in which there are no doctrines, and hence nothing is said," but one could still communicate the premises of faith and practice (or lack thereof) verbally to others (65).

language for description or indicative purposes, however, such language must be thought impossible. To the contrary, though, authentic religious language should *not* limit itself to the "safer" grounds of description and lend itself to its own edges.[24] Therefore, van Buren argues, "it makes sense to attempt to understand a religion such as Christianity, in any of its various forms, as a linguistic enterprise, and that when we try to understand religion as a linguistic behavior, we are entering the subject by the front door, not crawling in a basement window."[25]

Finally, van Buren turns to specifically examine the God-language employed in the Christian traditions. Obviously the written word, as well as the theological and philosophical conception of 'word' (as the *logos*), is extraordinarily important in the Christian religion, for example: the emphasis on the written scripture and the expulsion of certain ways of speaking, thinking, preaching, praying, singing, etc.—all of which also "exclude a certain way of living."[26] The most problematic of all religious language for the Christian, however, is the use of the word "God." *God* at first glance, however, is a word that operates in the same way as any other word in the Christian tradition, except that it is *the primary* term contextually located at the center of Christian belief.[27] As many Christians believe that "Christianity stands and falls with its doctrine of God," a closer look must be taken at this word.[28]

Van Buren determines that the Christian use of *God* is incoherent, but this incoherence does not point toward a contradiction but an affirmation of the inability to define the word. "Christian talk about God," van Buren writes, "begins the abstracting process... of the self-revealing God, the God of the biblical authors," etc. The use of the word *God* by "skeptical analysts" miss the point of the word God for many Christians, that Christians have affirmed the abstraction and incoherence of their word *God* "themselves from the beginning." To believe otherwise is a "biblical or doctrinal" literalism, which is not different from that of the "skeptics," who treat religious language on the level of description—far from the *edge* of language.[29]

---

[24] Ibid. 68.
[25] Ibid. 67.
[26] Ibid. 69.
[27] Ibid. 70-71.
[28] Ibid. 72.
[29] Ibid. 72-73. He adds: "[t]he difficulty with the position can be demonstrated briefly by considering what sense could be made, on the linguistic grounds considered, of the concept

God-talk, when authentic, according to van Buren, occurs at the *edge* of language, where language points toward the dynamism of its *current* limitations. There God-talk is self-subverting, and breaks down its own form(s). Van Buren clarifies:

> ...[W]e may speak better of the edges of language rather than its limits. We can go so far out on the platform of language, but if we try to go further, we fall off into a misuse of words, into nonsensical jabbering, into the void where the rules give out. We can, if we are so inclined, walk right along the edge of language, or stand teetering on one place on its circumference. We can, on the other hand, find this a silly place to stand and choose to confine our life to the no-nonsense areas as well within the edges of language, where the rules are clear, their application is undisputed, and language is safely unproblematic.
>
> The safe, central area of language is the part we know best, where we are so familiar with the rules that misunderstandings hardly ever occur. Or to put it another way, here is where the rules work so well that we scarcely notice them. Where we begin to wonder about how to use a word, or whether the rules we have been following will allow us to go a step further, there we are coming to the edges of language. We are approaching the point at which language breaks down, where it ceases to be language because we can no longer do anything with it.[30]

To put it another way, he further writes:

> The feature of our language which I want to describe is connected with the fact that we sometimes extend the application of words, stretching their use from the range within which they work straight forwardly, out into areas in which they work less clearly. A word works least ambiguously on what I...call its home-field.... To this stretching, however, there is a limit, not always sharp, beyond which we are unable to use the word and still be understood, and beyond which we ourselves cannot account for what we are doing with the word. Beyond some point, the use of

---

of a God who speaks, a God whose word is supposed to have been addressed to, and heard by human beings" (73).

[30] Ibid. 83; cf. E. L. Mascall's review of *The Edges of Language*, *Downside Review* 91 [1973]: 70-71), where on this topic Van Buren is brought into conversation with the Canadian theologian Bernard Lonergan (70).

the word become extraordinary, no longer rule-governed or ordinary.... I shall speak of this employment as laying along "the edges of language."[31]

This model of language, while certainly influenced by Ludwig Wittgenstein and Anthony Flew, is very similar to Tillich's writings on the dynamics of form.[32] For Tillich, in sum, form is stretched by *theonomous* content; however, theonomy eventually becomes *autonomy* and/or *heteronomy*, which stagnates in content and form. Eventually, a new theonomy dialectically rises out of stagnancy, shattering the old form to create a new boundary on the limitations of the form, etc. To this end, language at the 'center' is stagnant and used without risk; there also is safety in terms of the language. At the edges of language, according to Van Buren, language becomes *dangerous*: here language requires risk, courage, and ambiguity. Meditation or use of language 'on the *edge*' can require an openness to not only babbling incoherence but requires an openness to stretch the very form of language—like a Kierkegaardian leap into the unknown.

This kind of stretching, however, "is extremely rare in any time, especially ours."[33] Nonetheless, one does not necessarily have to break the formal rules of a language to experience or express the edges of language. The use of "metaphors, parables," proverbs, and wisdom literature in the Christian tradition almost always involve "speaking in paradoxes, stammering,...silence," and even obscured theological discourse (as in the case of the writings of Saint Paul.)[34] To accept this feature of language does not necessarily have to *other* religion, but instead, it acknowledges religion's connection to the often abstracted and obscured location of human experience. "Frontiers are in fact a frontier of our language and our humanity," van Buren explains, "to exclude them [frontiers] is to place artificial and undesirable limits on our freedom."[35]

This kind of "stretching" of the "limits" is also a necessary occurrence for the sustained or sustaining continuance of a living religion. This is not to say, at the same time, that linguistic border-stretching is "a sufficient condition" for religions or Christianity.[36] If religion were strictly

---

[31] Van Buren (1972), 83-84.
[32] Cf. ibid. 78n-84n, 74.
[33] Ibid. 99.
[34] Ibid. 110, 111.
[35] Ibid. 101.
[36] Ibid. 115.

a linguistic practice, it would not be genuinely religious—without practices, texts, traditions, communal anomalies, etc.—but instead it would be language game. Instead, as occurring in Christian practice, "the word 'God'...marks the final limit of [the Christian's] language." Although the word *God* is a "name," such naming of a limit would include the belief "that there is such a being" as that God. It should not matter to a Christian, according to van Buren, that her language is incoherent when naming God at the *edge* of language, since *God* should be used as "the final speech-act at the limit of language," and at this *edge* "the categories of coherence...do not apply." Furthermore, he adds, that such "distinctions between coherence and incoherence" not only break down for the Christian at the edges of language, but such distinctions are shown to be themselves "incorrect."[37]

According to van Buren, the use of language on the edges of language, like language in the 'center' of language, is "learned behavior," and as such, the use of *God* by the Christian "is also a learned use, and therefore it can also be mislearned, or misunderstood." Beyond this, just as there is a proper use of *God*, there are in fact strictly improper uses of the word: for example, naming God as an "object."[38] Still, for van Buren, this line of inquiry acknowledges that 'proper' usage of *God* is marked by its incoherence, and this feature of religion—especially Christianity—is perhaps the largest target for skeptics of the faith. The nature of God-language is for van Buren a salient component of the Christian religion, as the position of *God* on the outer reaches of language locates *God* as "a religious way of indicating that one longs to say all that could possibly be said on some matter of great concern" is "just barely but legitimately within our language."[39]

Finally, this linguistic analysis of religious language for van Buren points to a new understanding of how the categories of transcendence and immanence ultimately break down for Christian theology. He writes:

> Those who have toyed with a religious use of "transcendence" have perhaps not seen the proper logic of 'God.' They seem to have failed to see the word 'God' as a speech-act acknowledging the limits of speech, and turned elsewhere for a word that would do justice to their longing to say more than is possible with a clear

---

[37] Ibid. 132, 133.
[38] Ibid. 136, 137.
[39] Ibid. 144–145. Van Buren explains: "The wobbles of those who balance on language's outer edge are taken by [literalists, both theistic and atheistic] to be a sign of clumsiness" (40).

use of words. As rational men they have perhaps felt uneasy with the stumbling gait of walking language's frontier, have also wanted to use something more than the vague word "mystery," and yet do something more than taking the way of silence. It may be hoped that further reflection on the logic of 'God' will offer a better way. If it is realized that religious utterances are more adequately describes as language at the limit of its use than as assertions, then it may be seen that the word "transcendence" could also be used as an edge-marker. Since such a use would not pretend to "go beyond" or even to "point beyond" language, however, the spatial connotation of the word makes it a misleading synonym for 'God.'[40]

Elaborate philosophies and concepts for explaining the Godhead in religious discourse—such as transcendence, immanence, theism, atheism, pantheism, pane*n*theism, animism, paganism, etc.—are always limiting terms which do not necessarily "point beyond language" and use special analogies to explain themselves. Even panentheism, which, at first glance seems to "point beyond language," actually, in the end, describes God as a *both/and* of classical theism and pantheism and is constrained by the limitations of these two ideas.

Van Buren on St. Anselm's Use of Language

Shortly after the publication of *The Edges of Language*, van Buren put his theories to the test in a major essay in the journal *Religious Studies*, turning to an examination of St. Anselm's religious language in the *Proslogium*. "Although," van Buren wrote, "I cannot prove the ontological argument, Anselm's argument points to the logic of the use of the word 'God.'" Van Buren's argument will hinge upon two things: first, what he believes to be the larger *point* of the *Proslogium* and "the difference between the uses of the verb 'conceive.'"[41]

The first point is straightforwardly stated for van Buren, but I will return to it later, as this point highlights the importance of the second. Simply stated, Anselm's *Proslogium*, famous for its so-called "ontological argument," is not really an 'argument' in the sense that the argument proves anything not already accepted as a given in the first place. Instead, the *Proslogium* is then a meditation of 'faith seeking understanding': As

---

[40] Ibid. 147-148.
[41] Van Buren, "Anselm's Formula and the Logic of 'God,'" *Religious Studies* 9 (1973), 279.

such, Anselm's goal "was to understand that which he already believed as a faithful Catholic." Anselm was searching for an explanation of God which helped him better understand the Catholic religion, church, and doctrine at once.[42]

The second thrust of van Buren's argument is a close examination of Anselm's language, which he identifies as a kind of *praise*. Recognizing that Anselm would have been a monk at the Abbey of Bec for eighteen years at the time of writing the *Proslogium*, van Buren writes that based upon the daily office used at the time, Anselm would have literally recited the entire Psalter over nine hundred times.[43] Bearing this theory in mind, van Buren maintains a similarity in the language of the Psalms and the *Proslogium* will emerge. "Given these circumstances," he writes, "it is not difficult to identify the ancestry" of Anselm's "famous formula":

> "I will praise the name of the Lord most High." (Psalm 7:17)
>
> "Who is so great a God as our God?" (Psalm 77:13)
>
> "Who is he among the clouds that shall be compared unto the Lord? And who among the sons of God that shall be like unto God?" (Psalm 89:6, 7)
>
> "Thou, Lord, art the Most High for evermore." (Psalm 92:7)
>
> "The Lord is a great God and a great King above all gods." (Psalm 23:3)
>
> "Great is the Lord, and greatly to be praised; there is no end of his greatness." (Psalm 145:3)
>
> "Great is the Lord, and greatly to be praised in the City of our God." (Psalm 48:1)

Van Buren remarks: "And so indeed, Thou art that than which nothing greater can be conceived!"[44]

---

[42] Ibid. 279.

[43] Ibid. 279. Cf. David Klemm, "Open Secrets: Derrida and Negative Theology," *Negation and Theology*, ed. Robert Scharlemann (Charlottesville, VA: UP of Virginia, 1992), 9.

[44] Van Buren (1973), 281. Van Buren notes that this list of Psalm quotations is taken from "the sixteenth-century Psalter of *The Common Book of Prayer*, as being closest to the *Vulgata* which Anselm would have known, with some emendation to bring citations closer to the Vulgate texts" (280 n. 1). He also mentions that while there are certainly many other

In the *Proslogium*, the topic of discussion is "that than which nothing greater can be conceived," which van Buren refers to as X.[45] The first problem which emerges for van Buren here is that Anselm switches "back and forth between the use of his formula X as a name and its use referring to the presumed bearer of that name." Van Buren explains further, commenting on the *Proslogium*, chapter four:

> Anselm—good Augustinian that he was—never seemed to have contemplated any other view of the workings of our language than the notion that it consists of name-tags. God…has the name 'X'…. Now the fool's position is that although Anselm may have had an unusually interesting name-tag (or name of a property in hand), there just wasn't any bearer to which to tie it. To this Anselm replied that the fool could understand the name, and that he would have to agree that a name together with its bearer is—in some sense of the word 'great'—greater than a name without any bearer…. It may well be that if we think of God in Anselm's sense of that word, we are in fact thinking of a god who exists in such a way that we cannot logically think of him as ever coming into or passing out of existence.

"This point," van Buren notes, "only underscores the peculiarity of the logic of 'God'; it hardly establishes what Anselm wanted to prove."[46] The logic of *God* for Anselm, according to van Buren, is a *fuzzy logic*, which can only be accepted by either the easily-convinced (perhaps, the 'fool?') or one who already believes.

Next, van Buren writes that there "appears to be a confusion of predication, in that Anselm's X predicated something about us as well as about God;" in other words, the ontological argument argues less about God's existence or nature but is more insightful about explaining Christian beliefs about humanity. "Surely," van Buren writes of Anselm: "he is making two claims: (1) that God is so great, that (2) we cannot conceive of a greater." To this, "two subjects and two predicates are being confused," namely, "[t]here is the subject God…with the predicate of a unique way of being," and "there are ourselves, we human beings, without a predicate about our limited conceptual powers." Again, Anselm's statements about

---

scriptural passages which could be cited here as well, the point remains that none would have had the frequency in repetition as the Psalms (280 n. 2).
[45] Ibid. 279.
[46] Ibid. 281.

God, then, are about the human condition, rather than God's condition(s): "nothing has been established," van Buren observes, "about the existence, however special, of God."[47]

To this end and as mentioned before, van Buren turns to Anselm's "puzzling" use of the word "conceive." If Anselm claims "that we *conceive* of that which nothing greater can be *conceived*," van Buren argues, *two different uses* of the word 'conceive' are employed. The first *conceive* is a "weak conceiving": it is a conceiving that the 'fool' does to conceive that there is no God, a conceiving that may or may not be factual or based upon fact, such as the idea of a square circle. The second conceiving is, conversely, a "strong conceiving": a conceiving "of that which may or may not be the case but could at least possibly be the case." In this strong conceiving, "[n]o contradiction is contained in X; what we are asked to think of might possibly be the case."

The second conceiving "exerts a particular pressure on the first, which reveals a difference" between the two conceivings. Van Buren explains that "[t]he second use seems to guarantee that there be no laziness in our original efforts at conceiving," in other words, we are to "[c]onceive until you can reach no higher, Anselm urges us; conceive until it would be impossible to go further." This second conceiving "juxtaposes the logical limit to, and the actual enterprise of, conceiving."[48] He clarifies:

> Anselm's formula confronts us with the limit not just of our thinking, but of our linguistic conventions for speaking of thinking, whether about greatness or anything else. At the limit of the rules for the use of the verb 'conceive,' we come to the limit of our thinking itself. At that point the rules give out. Not fully aware of the linguistic form of the problem, Anselm just missed the point I am making. We can express the word 'inexpressible,' he said, but not that which is inexpressible. We can conceive the word 'inconceivable,' he said but we cannot conceive of that which is inconceivable. The truth of the matter, however, is that we can say nothing at all of that which is truly inexpressible, not even that it is inexpressible, and of that which is truly inconceivable we can have no thought at all, not even that it is inconceivable. Language, by its very rule-governed nature, does collapse at some point, and at that point, the tongue is dumb and the mind blank. As we

---

[47] Ibid. 281.
[48] Ibid. 282.

approach that limit, language goes more and more haltingly, falling finally into nonsense or silence.[49]

Following the methodology placed forward in *The Edges of Language*, van Buren is here showing that the word *conceiving* points us not only toward the limitations of our language, but also toward the limitations of our humanity, that is, to the epistemological finitude of human beings.

At the edges of language, then, the word *conceiving* literally 'breaks down.' In Anselm's formula, X, the conceiving which is conceived is a special kind of conceiving, one which is very different that the conceiving which occurs toward the 'center' of language. In other words, van Buren writes, this new use of *conceiving* "indicates *logically*, not descriptively, the last limit of thought."[50] Here, van Buren believes that Anselm has stumbled upon the edges of language, though van Buren does not believe that Anselm was aware of this discovery in his *Proslogium*.[51]

One should remember, van Buren writes, that Anselm's *Proslogium* was written to be a "meditation;" and, as such, is ultimately a *religious*, rather than a strictly philosophical writing. Van Buren writes that

> [t]here is...something genuinely religious about X. The phrase, [X], with its exclusion of all qualification, in its implication of utter limit, captures something characteristic of most major religious traditions.... Anselm's genius as a religious man was to know and to show (even if he failed to describe it properly) that religion consists...in going to the limit of language, to the edge of nonsense.... For where religion is found, there will be found a caring, a concern, a longing, which finds linguistic form in stumbling, stuttering attempts to say the most that could possibly be said...and then to feel that the words are inadequate. In this sense, there is no religion without 'God,' without some such phrase as X, without standing and pushing out at the very limit of language and thought.

---

[49] Ibid. 284.
[50] Ibid. 284, emph. add.
[51] Ibid. 282. Van Buren does, however, believe that some of Anselm's critics, particularly Gaunilo, were on to this anomaly of language in the *Proslogium*, though he admits that almost all critics and philosophical commentators ignore Anselm's *Proslogium* outside of chapters 2-3 (286).

God, then, as van Buren maintained in *The Edges of Language*, is a "border maker;" which, in Anselm's case, means that *God "is that than which nothing more can be said."*[52] Still, one should not mistake Anselm's *Proslogium* as a philosophical text; to the contrary, it is an explicitly religious text whose 'argument for the existence of God' is an argument convincing primarily to the already-converted—the 'ontological argument' is a "home-field" argument. The perceived "issue between Anselm and the Fool," then, "needs to be redefined," because the difference between the believer and unbeliever is in fact a matter of linguistic "life-style."[53] One who speaks of *God* at the edges of language "will live differently" and "will speak differently" than the Fool.

Mystical language, such as that of Anselm's in the *Proslogium*, according to van Buren, is the language of being awestruck. "To be awestruck," he writes, "implies that there is something of which one stands in awe, and one ought to be able to say what that is." While one 'ought to be able to say what that is,' one is usually "rendered almost speechless" in the face of mystical or genuine religious experience, thus the mystics' "paradoxical and self-contradictory utterances [give] way to silence." When reading mystical writings, van Buren writes, one should remember that "religious mystics declare that they are in awe of the presence of God, not the idea or thought of God," since God cannot be the *object* of religion, if the language is truly at the edges of language. It is quite common, he believes, that "in the Christian tradition, as in any other," the 'object' of mysticism is often the *history* of God—"the strange, awesome history—of a people escaped from slavery into communal identity," culminating in the history of Jesus Christ. Any view of language which depends strictly on *God* as an object of awe, van Buren reminds, "depends upon too limited a view of language." He explains further that such language "forgets or fails to notice another part of our language-in-use: speaking at its edge, in which the word 'God' marks the point at which the religious man has come up against the final limit of what he can say about the object of his concern."[54]

The Implied Cage

At the edge of language, doing and *meditating upon* a radical theology in this dissertation we enter, borrowing Nietzsche's words, the "horizon of

---

[52] Ibid. 285-286.
[53] Ibid. 287, 288. Cf. Clark Williamson, "Paul M. Van Buren," *A New Handbook of Christian Theologians*, ed. Donald Musser and Joseph Price (Nashville: Abingdon, 1996), 492.
[54] Ibid. 134-135.

the infinite." This phrase is the title of the penultimate aphorism before his initial declaration of God's death in *The Gay Science*:

> *In the horizon of the infinite.*— We have left the land and have embarked. We have burned our bridges behind us—indeed, we have gone farther and destroyed the land behind us. Now, little ship, look out! Beside you is the ocean: to be sure, it does not always roar, and at times it lies spread out like silk and gold and reveries of graciousness. But hours will come when you will realize that it is infinite and that there is nothing more awesome than infinity. Oh, the poor bird that felt free and now strikes the walls of this cage! Woe, when you feel homesick for the land as if it has offered more *freedom*—and there is no longer any "land."[55]

This work, this journey, is a voyage away from the *safety* of Christianity into a post-Christianity. In its heresy is an expressed need for community, even if that community is composed of my small community of readers. It painfully acknowledges the implied cage surrounding its author, and that, like the thinkers being considered—Tillich, Altizer, and Daly—that my blaspheming is a *Christian* post-Christianity.

That is to say, in this voyage we embark for a new Christian atheism, an atheism genuinely *homesick* for Christianity. We may discover that in constructing new "lands" on which to stand, we Pirates (as Daly calls herself) are only walking the plank. We journey onward, speaking and invoking the words of Qoheleth, seeking wisdom, madness, and folly:

> *I perceived that this is also a chasing after the wind.*
>
> ECCLESIASTES 1:17

---

[55] Nietzsche, *Gay Science*, trans. Walter Kaufmann (New York: Vintage, 1974), §124 (p. 180-181).

PART ONE

PAUL TILLICH AND THE DIALECTIC OF THE SACRED

[E]ven a god would disappear if he were not being-itself.

PAUL TILLICH
ST 1.164

Has Tillich collapsed theology into ontology? Has he transformed the sacred into the secular? Is Tillich's theonomy ultimately Nietzsche's eternal recurrence?

THOMAS J.J. ALTIZER*

Barthianism is dead! Tillichianism is dead!

KENNETH HAMILTON†

PROFESSOR: Dr. Tillich, are you not a dangerous man?

DR. TILLICH: Yes.

UC 188

---

* Thomas Altizer, "A Theonomy in Our Time?" *Christian Scholar* 46.4 (1963), 358.
† Kenneth Hamilton, *God is Dead* (Grand Rapids, MI: Eerdmans, 1966), 78.

24

Chapter 1

Paul Tillich's Post-Christian Theology

Paul Tillich's systematic theology—and his philosophy of religion—is an immense, multi-faceted system that was not always consistent and progressed over Tillich's lifetime. This chapter will attempt to offer a comprehensive glimpse at Tillich's philosophy[1] of God for the purpose of considering the "problem" of transcendence and immanence in his system, and then lead in to a discussion of Thomas Altzier and Mary Daly. More specifically, by unraveling several of Tillich's pervasive themes in the foreground of his theology, a distinctive radical theology will emerge.

One of the most enduring questions about Tillich's ideas is what Tillich really believed about *God*. One of the primary problems with God-language for Tillich is precisely God-language itself: that "God" is always inadequate, that one must transcend above "God" to the "God-above-God," and furthermore, only ontological language can express God in a non-symbolic way. To confuse the public even more—and one should recall that Tillich was a *public theologian*—Tillich's affinity for atheism led some to conclude that Tillich was in fact an atheist. Tillich apparently liked this idea so much that, in his more radical moments, he admitted himself to be an atheist—we will explore Tillich's atheistic claim. This implicit radicalism, the implicit *atheism* of Tillich, we will see, points us toward a philosophical disposition that is ontologically *prior* to his basic ontological understanding of God, that is, *life itself*. This radical reading of Tillich requires us to Voyage through Tillich's corpus within the context of radical theology, a way of doing theology for which Tillich is one of our primary beginning points.

The "Radical Tillich"

Paul Tillich's theological and philosophical writings have always had a radical religious tone to them, from his earliest published writings to his

---

[1] Throughout this discussion it may seem that I am using the words *philosophy* and *theology* interchangeably. The differences are not arbitrary. As we will see, the distinctions between the two are subtle but quite important within Tillich's works. A *philosophy* of God, for example, addresses the philosophical questions that arise from both the philosophical notion of "God" and the theological assumptions that might be made by doctrine, traditions, or scripture.

final lecture. It was this final lecture—"The Significance of the History of Religions for the Systematic Theologian," delivered the night before his death—that was perhaps his most revealingly radical writing. It is almost surprising that Tillich had gained so much prominence as a public theological figure, given how radical his earlier writings were. Theologian Richard Grigg suggests that Tillich's unique theological language had become so prevalent among Protestant clergy trained in main-line seminaries in the 1950s and 1960s that a fertile ground for radical Christian thinking emerged within the churches that has been lost ever since.[2]

Tillich's theology was occasionally criticized for being too churchly to be a genuinely *radical* Christian theology, since a radical Christian theology would be situated in culture, rather than the church, and to be called "radical" in the 1960s would be *post-Christian*. Carl Braaten argued, shortly after Tillich's death, to the contrary, suggesting that Tillich was, in fact, "a *radical* theologian," but one "who searched into the depths of the *tradition* to find positive answers to the questions of modern man."[3] For some, the younger Tillich (indicative especially in his political writing, such as *The Socialist Decision*) was the radical Tillich, though some emerging radical thinkers felt that Tillich's later theology failed because it was, as Leslie Dewart wrote, "insufficiently radical."[4] Even though Tillich "reportedly" told Thomas Altizer that "der real Tillich is der Radical Tillich," the 'early' Altizer (in a 1963 book review) also felt that Tillich had missed the opportunity to have "become a new Luther," had he extended "his principle of justification by doubt to a theological affirmation of the death of God."[5] As it happens, we will see, that while Tillich's 'later' work—the three *Systematic Theology* volumes—do reflect a 'churchly' or more conservative Tillich, the final lecture points toward new directions.

Tillich's writings show a profound respect for Friedrich Nietzsche that was well ahead of the times for an American audience, who had not

---

[2] Richard Grigg, *Gods after God* (Albany, NY: SUNY UP, 2006), 143.
[3] Carl Braaten, "Paul Tillich and the Classical Christian Tradition," in *Perspectives on 19th and 20th Century Protestant Theology* by Paul Tillich, ed. Carl Braaten (New York: Harper, 1967), xxxiii.
[4] Kenan Osborne, *New Being* (The Hague: Martinus Nijoff, 1969), 39; Dewart (1966) 39. Cf. Jean Richard, "The Roots of Tillich's Eschatology in his Religious-Socialist Philosophy of History," *New Creation or Eternal Now*, ed. Gert Hummel (Berlin: Walter de Gruyter, 1991): 26-43.
[5] Grigg (2006), 142; Durwood Foster, "Tillich and the Personal God," *Bulletin of the North American Paul Tillich* Society 33.2 (2007), 23; Thomas Altizer, "A Theonomy in our Time?" (1963), 362.

yet entirely recovered Nietzsche from NAZI revisionist philosophy. For Tillich, Nietzsche was, along with Karl Marx, one of "[t]he greatest anti-Christians in recent history," who showed his "Christian roots with every word" (*IRR* 32). As an "atheist," Nietzsche points toward the 'problem' of God—"the poor idea of God"—better than "many faithful Christians" could (*SF* 42). To speak of the "death of God," in a literal sense, however, "would be absurd" (*PPT* 201). Instead, Tillich suggests that Nietzsche's declaration places an ultimacy upon the immanence of "life," rather than upon the God of tradition (207). In this sense, the death of God "is felt both as a loss and as a liberation" (*CB* 142).

Beyond this, according to Tillich, Nietzsche's attack on the Christian God, that is, the "death of God," was an attack upon what he called "theological theism." Theological theism is defined by Tillich as the type of God which is based upon theological arguments, "dependent on the religious substance which it conceptualizes" (*CB* 184). Such thinking leads to an acknowledgement that most religious conceptions of God are easily argued away, often with the exact same arguments used to argue for God's existence. As such, Tillich suggests the idea of the "God above God or Gods" to separate Gods which *can be killed*—and *should be*—against a *higher* conception of God that is not demonic or idolatrous (*CB* 15). The God-above-God is not a being among other beings, not a thing among other things; in fact, as we will see later, Tillich's God-above-God is the ontological *foundation* of beings and things.[6] This onto-epistemological shift "is the deepest root of atheism," Tillich wrote, "[i]t is an atheism which is justified as the reaction against theological theism and its disturbing implications" (*CB* 185).

Christian Atheism

In this sense of atheism—that is, a denial of theological theism—Tillich is an atheist, or perhaps more clearly, a *Christian* atheist. Although some of Tillich's works smugly pass off atheism as little more than a *different kind* of theological theism, that is, a *theological atheism* (see, for example, *SF* 47), atheism is a philosophical *tool* for Tillich in some of his later writings. Regarding the theological theism implicit in arguments for the existence of God, Tillich writes:

> To such a concept and to such attempts atheism is the right religious and theological reply. This is well known to the most

---

[6] Grigg (2006), 143. Cf. *ST* 1.245.

intensive piety of all times. The atheistic terminology of mysticism is striking. It leads beyond God to the Unconditioned, transcending any fixation of the divine as an object. But we have the same feeling of the inadequacy of all limiting names for God in a non-mystical religion. *Genuine religion without an element of atheism cannot be imagined.* It is not by chance that not only Socrates, but also the Jews and the early Christians were persecuted as atheists. For those who adhered to the powers, they were atheists. (*TC* 25—emph. add.)

The term "atheism" is being used in a few different (though related) ways in this famous passage from Tillich's *Theology of Culture*. First, Tillich refers to the atheistic language of the Christian mystical tradition—such as Pseudo-Dionysus and Meister Eckhart—who offered a *via negativa* toward God in their writings. When, for example, Eckhart prays "that God rid me of God," this is an atheism that "is a correct response to the 'objectively' existing God of literalistic thought" (*OTB* 65).[7] At the same time, any theological thinking that resists literalistic thinking about God is, as an atheism, connected to this tradition; and, as emphasized above, "genuine religion without an element of atheism cannot be imagined." For Tillich, if Christianity is to be genuine, or authentic, one must reject literalistic thinking, but also epistemologically acknowledge that doubt is essential to faith, which is a primary argument throughout Tillich's thought. Finally, the "atheism" of Socrates or the early Christians is one defined by power relationships; that those with power define their own literalistic conceptions of deity as absolute, and all others are then atheistic. This is a more political definition, though it is expressed theologically—by *theological theisms.*

Tillich writes in the first volume of his *Systematic Theology* that atheism is "anti-Christian on Christian terms" (*ST* 1.27). If the term 'Christian' refers to a literalistic religion, then the atheist who rejects this Christianity is, as it happens, doing so for Christian reasons. "Nietzsche," Tillich wrote, "acknowledged this when he said he had the blood of his greatest enemies—the priests—within himself." This points to "the paradox of Christian humanism," namely, that anti-Christian thinking is,

---

[7] Dorothy Emmet, "The Ground of Being," *Journal of Theological Studies*, ns 15.2 (1964), 281; Wessel Stoker, "The Paradox of Complementarity in Tillich's Doctrine of God," *The Theological Paradox: Interdisciplinary Reflections on the Centre of Paul Tillich's Thought/ Das Theologische Paradox*, ed. Gert Hummel (Berlin: Walter de Gruyter, 1995), 107. Cf. *HCT* 92.

"within the Western world, the substance of what is Christian" (*IRR* 32). To this end, *anti-Christian or Christian atheist thinking is necessary for an authentic expression of Christian faith*. Christianity only stays relevant to the current spiritual situation by virtue of its ability to have "continuous self-negation." Without this *semper negativa*, Tillich writes, "Christianity is not true Christianity," because a non-perpetually-negating Christianity would be *irrelevant* (*IRR* 52).

Perhaps Tillich's most courageous theological move along these lines was his famous declaration that "God does not exist" in the first volume of his *Systematic Theology*. Although Tillich denied 'God' to affirm God as *being-itself* "beyond essence and existence," one must *deny* God to affirm a *kind* of Godhead. Just as he writes, "to argue that God exists is to deny him," the only way to arrive to a genuine sense of divinity is to deny 'God' (*ST* 1.205). Tillich's claim that "God does not exist" is to be understood, Edgar Towne observes, both "literally *and* symbolically": it is to say that God is not a being, but being-itself, which has no being beyond being the *power of* and *fountain of* being. Towne observes: "[t]his is the epitome of postmodern irony!"[8]

Although this direction of thinking, which is central in Tillich's thought, is *radical*, a question can be raised whether Tillich was in fact *post-Christian*. Conservative scholars have long accused Tillich as not being a "true" Christian, including a pervasive internet rumor, or "e-rumor" (that evangelicals circulate by e-mail still today), about Tillich being ridiculed by Baptist clergy over simple theological questions posed to Tillich at a University of Chicago alumni event.[9] To begin with ontology or atheism for a Christian theology has been further criticized as an inappropriate methodology for a *Christian* theology; that is, *methodologically* speaking, Tillich's thinking is post-Christian by virtue of its philosophical beginnings.[10] Tillich's friend, theologian Nels Ferré, wrote, almost

---

[8] Edgar Towne, "Tillich's Postmodern View of the Actuality of God," *The North American Paul Tillich Society Newsletter* 29.3 (2003), 26.
[9] The e-rumor text is well documented on the internet, and is listed in its entirety—and investigated to be a false rumor—on the internet at "Theologian Paul Tillich Upstaged by a Simple Preacher—Fiction!" Online, TruthOrFiction.com, accessed online on 16. December 2007.
[10] Georgia Harkness, *Beliefs that Count*, ed. Henry Bullock (Nashville: Graded, 1961), 18-19; Frederick Sontag, "Ontological Possibility and the Nature of God," *Journal of Religion* 36.4 (1956), 240; Guyton Hammond, *A Comparison of the Thought of Paul Tillich and Eric Fromm* (Nashville: Vanderbilt UP, 1965), 75, citing Nels Ferré, *The Christian Understanding of God* (New York: Harper, 1957), 29.

flippantly, that Tillich was not *really* a Christian by any traditionally-accepted definitions of the term; and furthermore, Tillich did not believe in *any* conception of God.[11] While Ferré's is a minority view—and one based upon largely unexplained personal experience—Tillich's use of atheism as a theological and philosophical *utility* for religious thinking certainly points toward a "post-Christian" theological move by Tillich.[12]

Religion of the Concrete Spirit

Tillich *did*, however, make an explicit post-Christian shift in his *final* lecture, delivered at the University of Chicago on the night before his death. "The Significance of the History of Religions for the Systematic Theologian," given on October 12, 1965, was the final lecture offered from a two-year seminar at Chicago's Divinity School with famed historian of religions Mircea Eliade.[13] After opening with a brief critique of the then-emerging "death of God theology"—generally, that Nietzsche was important, but we can move on from Nietzsche—Tillich declared that in liberal Christian theology we have come to the *best*, "the highest and last point" of "revealed religion," but the contemporary religious situation suggests a "post-Christian" era that is searching for something new (*FR* 86).

As such, Tillich proposes a new "Religion of the Concrete Spirit" (*FR* 87). The Religion of the Concrete Spirit comes about by identifying the "inner aim" of the discipline of the history of religions. The new religion cannot be identified "with any actual religion, not even Christianity as a religion" (88). He explains:

> The universal religious basis is the experience of the Holy within the finite. Universality in everything finite and particular, or in this and that finite, the Holy appears in a special way. I could call this the sacramental basis of all religions—the Holy here and now which can be seen, heard, dealt with, in spite of its mysterious character. We still have remnants of this in higher religions, in their sacraments, and I believe that without it, a religious group would become an association of moral clubs, as much of Protestantism is, because it has lost the sacramental basis.

---

[11] Nels Ferré, "Tillich and the Nature of Transcendence," *Paul Tillich* by Nells Ferré, Charles Hartshorne, John Dillenberger, James Livingston, and Joseph Haroutunian (Nashville: Abingdon, 1966), 18.
[12] Richard Grigg, *Symbol and Empowerment* (Macon, GA: Mercer UP, 1985), xv.
[13] Jerald Brauer, "Editor's Preface," *The Future of Religions* by Paul Tillich (New York: Harper, 1966), 7.

(FR 86-87)

The foundation of the Religion of the Concrete Spirit is the experience of the divine in the plane of immanence of the present; the *apocalyptic* procession of the holy and the not-yet-holy into sacramental transubstantiation in the present.[14] Liberal Christianity has turned its back on the sacramental power of Christianity itself, Tillich argued, largely out of fear of the idolatrous (that is, "demonic") temptations of sacramentality; and, as such, liberal Christianity has been reduced to little more than voluntary associations with religious principles.

The Religion of the Concrete Spirit, as a post-Christian religious shift, requires not only an anti-Christian atheism which rejects Christian theological theism, but this anti-Christian atheism must mature beyond a localized rejection of Christianity into a rejection of religion itself. This Religion of the Concrete Spirit is "a fight of God against religion within religion" (*FR* 88). As a religious form of atheism—"within religion"—the Religion of the Concrete Spirit, Tillich concludes in his final lecture, "is my hope for the future of theology" (91).

Tillich's final post-Christian move is an atheism that retreats away from the *tribalism* of theological atheism and resists the "destruction" of "true humanity" implicit in theological theism (*FR* 69). To resist theological theism, Tillich wrote long before his final lecture in *The Protestant Era*, "even if it leads to atheistic consequences, is more religious" than theological theism, "because it is more aware of the unconditional character of the divine" (*PE* 82).[15] Such an atheism is, again, a *religious* atheism; and inasmuch as this atheism is derived from Christian or anti-Christian traditions, it likely remains a *Christian* atheism.

Ontological Argument and Ontological Thinking

Paul van Buren observed, taking clues from Tillich, that St. Anselm's "ontological argument" in the *Proslogium* is really about language than about God. This interpretation is central to the rest of Tillich's thought because the ontological argument not only points toward a theological anthropology (as was the case for van Buren), it points to a new realization *about* God. But the ontological argument for Tillich does not constitute a

---

[14] Cf. *FR* 87.
[15] Du Loi Choi, Transcendence and Immanence in Paul Tillich's Theology and Chutisi's Neo-Confucian Philosophy, Ph.D. diss., Drew University, Madison, NJ (2000), 5.

good argument *for* God; Tillich contended throughout his writing that "[t]here are no valid arguments for the 'existence' of God" and that such arguments are "half-blasphemous" and lead to theological theism (*CB* 181, *TC* 25). And while Anselm was unsuccessful in proving the existence of God, according to Tillich, the God-question implicit in the ontological argument is its *truth*—even if the *answer* offered, that God 'exists,' is "untrue" (*HCT* 161, *ST* 1.205).

That said, Tillich had a great respect for Anselm's *Proslogium*. He describes Anselm's text as "creative" and "courageous" in his yearning for something more "than just an argument" for the existence of God (*HCT* 170, 162). That is to say, "he wanted a direct argument which does not need the world in order to find God," rather, Anselm "wanted to find God in thought itself." The *Proslogium* is indicative of what Tillich called "theonomous thinking": it is thinking that is implicitly "certain of God" (*HCT* 162).

Before moving forward, we should review Anselm's "ontological argument." The "tradition" surrounding Anselm's *Proslogium* generally focuses on the form and content, the *logic* and *argument* in Anselm's text. The argument which is traditionally *derived* from Anselm follows in this way in the form of modal logic.

1. If that which nothing greater can be conceived (X) exists then it has necessary existence.

2. Either X has necessary existence or it does not.

3. If X does not have necessary existence, then it necessarily does not.

4. Either X has necessary existence or it does not (2, 3).

5. If X necessarily does not have necessary existence, then X necessarily does not exist (entrailed by 1).

6. Either X has necessary existence or it does not (4, 5).

7. It is not the case that X necessarily does not exist.

8. Therefore, X has necessary existence (6, 7).

9. If X has necessary existence, X necessarily exists.

10. X exists (8, 9).

Written as a logical syllogism, the ontological argument is an argument for the existence of God; the tenth proposition, the conclusion, is that X—God—exists. To review, premise 2 is the law of the excluded middle; premise 3 is Becker's Postulate, that is, that all modal properties are deemed to be necessary. 9 is taken by the form of the syllogism to be self-evident.[16] A well-known symbolic logic account is offered by philosopher Alvin Plantinga, where p = $(\exists x)$ Px, where P is "perfection":

1. p → □p

2. ~ □ ~ p

3. □p → p

4. □p v ~ (□p)

5. ~ □p → □ ~ (□p)

6. □p v □ ~ (□p)

7. □ ~ (□p) → □ ~ p

8. □p v □ ~ p

9. □p

10. p[17]

To explain: 1 indicates that perfection cannot exist contingently or accidentally; perfection must be necessary (p → □p). 2 states that there is not necessarily not-perfection, or *perfection is not impossible*. Perfection then *is* possible, which could also be expressed as ◊p. Premise 3 states that actuality follows from necessity, □p → p: if *necessarily* p, then *actually* p. 4 is the law of the excluded middle (premise 2 in the first modal syllogism, above). 5 is Becker's Postulate: if not necessarily p, then necessarily not necessarily p. Premise 6 follows from 4 and 5 by rule of substitution. 7 disputes the necessity of the second part of premise 6; 8 follows from 6 and 7 by substitution. Premises 8 and 9—□p, or *necessarily p*, therefore *p*—is a

---

[16] Syllogism adapted from "The Ontological Argument: The Modal Ontological Argument," online, philosophyofreligion.info.
[17] Cf. Alvin Platinga, ed., *The Ontological Argument* (Garden City, NY: Doubleday, 1965); *ibid.* "Aquinas on Anselm," *God and the Good* (Grand Rapids, MI: Eerdmans, 1975), 126ff.

disjunctive syllogism via premises 1, 2 and 8.[18] Just as the modal syllogism before, if X necessarily has existence, then X must *necessarily* exist.

Tillich rejects such logical postulations imposed on Anselm's text, even though he would admit that these syllogisms are present in the *Proslogium*. Tillich himself summarizes Anselm in the following way in his *History of Christian Thought*:

> (1) Even the fool—the fool of Psalm 53, who says in his heart, "there is no God"—understands the meaning of the term God. He understands that the highest, the unconditioned, is conceived in the term "God."
>
> (2) If he understands the meaning of God as something unconditioned, then this is an idea which exists in the human mind.
>
> (3) But there is a higher form of being, that is, being not only in the human mind, but being in the real world outside of the human mind.
>
> (4) Since being both within and outside the human mind is higher than being merely in the intellect, it must be attributed to the unconditional. (*HCT* 163)

In the first volume of the *Systematic Theology*, however, he further notes:

> The Anselmian statement that God is a necessary thought and that therefore this idea must have objective as well as subjective reality is valued in so far as thinking, by its very nature, implies an unconditional element which transcends subjectivity and objectivity, that is, a point of identifying which makes the idea of truth possible. (*ST* 1.207)[19]

For Tillich, Anselm's "argument" for the existence of God is easily refuted, but the most bothersome assumption is the non-impossibility of not-perfection, symbolically expressed as $\sim \Box \sim p$ or $\Diamond p$. Specifically, the

---

[18] Cf. W. Pittenger, "Paul Tillich as a Theologian," *Anglican Theological Review* 43.3 (1961), 274. Special thanks to Karmen MacKendirck for guidance through the symbolic logic.

[19] Tillich continues: "However, the statement is not valid if this unconditional element is understood as a highest being called God. The existence of such a highest being is not implied in the idea of truth" (*ST* 1.207). Even though the highest being would be, non-symbolically speaking, *Deus est esse ipsum*, Tillich does, elsewhere give *truth* and *God* congruence, but on symbolic levels (*TC* 15) (Cf. William Rowe, *Religious Symbols and God* [Chicago: U Chicago P, 1968], 90).

problem is that ◊p is ambiguous for Tillich by the notion of ◊p "in the mind": "It means actually being thought, being intended, being an object of man's intentionality. But 'in' is metaphorical and should not be taken literally" (*HCT* 163). At the same time, the necessity of ◊p is the key component of Tillich's interpretation of the ontological argument, to borrow Augustine's appropriation of Plato (explained by William Rowe): "'x is φ' is true only if (*a*) there is φ-ness, and (*b*) x participates in φ-ness. Point *b* entails that it is through φ-ness that x has φ." If we raise the question of "whether there is any φ-ness," we might conclude that "if we know that x is φ, we can know that there is φ-ness." If you "[s]ubstitute *truth* for φ" in this framework, "[t]he argument now is that anything being true or having truth presupposes truth-itself."[20]

While Tillich suggests that "although it often has been expressed in this form," Anselm's "ontological argument for the existence of God....is neither an argument, nor does it deal with the existence of God"; the argument does, however, address "the rational description of the relation of our mind to Being as such." He continues: "Our mind implies *principia per se nota* which have immediate evidence whenever they are noticed: the transendentalia, esse, *verum, bonum*. They constitute the Absolute in which the difference between knowing and known is not actual" (*TC* 15). In other words, the existence of God is implicit in human thinking. Instead of criticizing Anselm as *assuming* the existence of God before *proving* it in the ontological argument, God, as "*the presupposition of the question of God,*" Tillich writes, is not the "object" or "basis" of the question (13). God, transcending "the split between subject and object," Rowe writes of Tillich, posits God as "the point of identity which unites" subject and object.[21] As neither subject nor object, God is the implicit *power* undergirding and maintaining adherence between the two.

Therefore, *Deus est esse-ipsum*: God is being-itself. "[T]he certainty of God," Tillich writes, "is identical with the certainty of Being itself,"

---

[20] Rowe (1968) 90. From Augustine's *Soliloquies* (I.27, quoted by Rowe [1968] 90):
    R. First then let us see this, whether, as Truth and true are two words, you hold that by these words two things are signified, or one thing.
    A. Two things, I hold. For, as Chastity is one thing, and that which is chaste, another, and many things in this manner; so I believe that Truth is one thing, and that which, being declared, is true, is another....it is not from that which is chaste that Chastity arises, but that which is chaste from Chastity. So also, if anything is true, it is assuredly from Truth that it is true.

Augustine also equated *truth* with *God*, as in *Confessions* 10.24.

[21] Rowe (1968), 91.

again: "God is the presupposition of the question of God" (*TC* 15-16). Recalling Schleiermacher, Tillich further explains that "*[m]an is immediately aware* of something unconditioned which is the prius of the separation and interaction of subject and object, theoretically as well as practically" speaking (22). Furthermore:

> The *prius* of subject and object cannot become an object to which man as a subject is theoretically and practically related. God is no object for us as subjects. He is always that which precedes this decision. But, on the other hand, we speak about him and we act upon him, and we cannot avoid it, because everything which becomes real to us enters the subject-object correlation. (25)

God is "implicit" and "implied" in theological thinking.[22] To equate and assume as *prior* thinking itself with Godhead is, as it happens, reminiscent of Hegel, for whom "human thinking requires the reality of God."[23]

This is, as it happens, a new kind of ontological argument *inspired* by Anselm in Tillich. William Rowe explains Tillich's meaning of his new ontological argument:

> To think what is true presupposes Truth (being-itself). However, being-itself, for Tillich, is the presupposition of thought. Because he holds this, Tillich argues that the ontological argument validly infers the reality of God (being-itself), not because of some particular feature of the thought that God exists but because thinking by its very nature presupposes being-itself. Hence, Tillich wants to construe the argument as not really an argument at all but as an analysis of what is presupposed in human thought.[24]

Following this, John Russell suggests the following simple syllogism as a "literal proposition" of Tillich's ontological argument:

---

[22] John Russell, "Tillich's Implicit Ontological Argument," *Asian Journal of Theology* 22 (1988), 485, 488.

[23] Russell, 491. Rowe (1968): "To think what is true presupposes Truth (being-itself). Hence, being-itself, for Tillich, is the presupposition of thought. Because he holds this, Tillich argues that the ontological argument validly infers the reality of God (being-itself), not because of some peculiar feature of the thought that God exists but because thinking by its very nature presupposes being-itself. Hence, Tillich wants to construe the argument as not really an argument at all but an analysis of what is presupposed in human thought" (91-92).

[24] Rowe (1968), 91-92.

1. If the reality of being-itself is implicit in human thought, then God is real.
2. The reality of being-itself is implicit in human thought.
3. God is real.[25]

While put in this way, the argument is quite simple and even resembles the Cartesian *cogito*. The syllogism commits the same fallacy of affirming the consequent that Descartes did, creating an '*If A, then B; B, therefore A*' construction.[26] In other words, it is quite likely that premise 3, the reality of God, might not directly flow from premise 2; yet, if God is being-itself, then 3 does follow from 1 and 2. Russell emphatically criticizes Tillich:

> How can Tillich identify thinking and being-itself, if thinking presupposes being-itself? His positive reconstruction of the ontological argument *requires that thinking* presupposes an unconditional "ground" **other than itself**. Noetic events represent species of thinking that, in Tillich's mind, concern the separation and interaction of subject and object. Tillich singles out God, or being-itself, as the *prius* of this condition. Can that which is ontologically **prior** to thinking also be equated with thinking? The identity of thinking and God implies ontological **coincidence**, rather than priority. Finally, how can Tillich identify thinking

---

[25] Russell, 486. William Wainwright forwards an alternative to Russell's syllogistic appropriation of Tillich's ontological argument as follows:
1. If something is true, there is such a thing as truth itself.
2. Something is true (e.g., there are true propositions).
3. Therefore, Truth itself is real (1, 2).
4. Truth itself is either the same as, or a manifestation of being itself.
5. Therefore, Being itself is real (3, 4).

Then, "[c]omparing this argument we have a similar one which proceeds from the recognition of value to an avowal of the reality of being itself, viz.":
6. If something is good, there is such as thing as goodness itself.
7. Something is good.
8. Therefore, goodness itself is real (6, 7).
9. Goodness itself is either the same as, or a manifestation of, being itself.
10. Therefore, being itself is real (8, 9).

According to Wainwright, the first and sixth premises—the originating premises for the syllogisms—are Platonic assumptions regarding the *necessity* of being-itself. (William Wainwright, "Paul Tillich and Arguments for the Existence of God," *Journal of the American Academy of Religion* 39 [1971], 171-172.)

[26] Cf. Charles Hartshorne, "Tillich and The Other Great Tradition," *Anglican Theological Review* 43.3 (1961), 246.

with being-itself, when being-itself constitutes the necessary "ground" of [a true] ontological foundation of thinking?

Tillich, according to Russell, affirms the consequent in his ontological argument by requiring the consequent to be an ontologically-prior requirement for the proposition. For Russell, Tillich's ontological connection of being-itself and thinking is too vague and fails to be specific about just *how* they are connected.[27] In Tillich's defense, Rowe offers a Tillichian answer: "The reason Anselm is right is that *thinking*, by its very nature entails that being-itself *is*. Being-itself, for Tillich, is the unconditional element which transcends subjectivity and objectivity and what makes truth possible." That is to say, "being-itself is the presupposition of thought."[28] In Tillich's words: "God is the presupposition of the question of God" (*TC* 13). To *think* otherwise, for Tillich, would be to "make the world the data and God the conclusion"—this is *theological theism*. God would then be "derived from the world," not *implicit* in it.[29]

This ontological shift is, as it happens, Platonic.[30] Epistemologically speaking, Tillich writes in his treatise on ethics, *Love, Power, and Justice*, that "[w]e are all nominalists by birth," and that "as nominalists we are inclined to dissolve our world into things"; however, "this inclination is an historical accident and not an essential necessity" (*LPJ* 18).[31] Nominalistic philosophy and thinking is "non-participatory," but rather an autonomous act of "grasping and controlling things." Beyond this, nominalistic thinking can express itself as indicative of a power of heteronomous epistemic control, which resists the freedom of thought in the individual (*ST* 1.177). Being is *necessary* for thinking. Thought "cannot go behind" being, "but thought can imagine the negation of everything that *is*, and it can describe the nature and structure of being which gives

---

[27] Russell, 491-492.
[28] Rowe (1968), 89.
[29] Carl Armbruster, *The Vision of Paul Tillich* (New York: Sheed and Ward, 1967), 135.
[30] Cf. Nicholas Patricca, *God and the Question of Being*, Ph.D. diss., U. of Chicago (1972), 170-171; Rowe (1968), 90; Kai Nielsen, "Is God So Powerful That He Doesn't Even Have to Exist?" *Religious Experience and Truth*, ed. Sidney Hook (New York: New York UP, 1961), 270; Caputo, *Weakness of God* (2006), 37.
[31] Tillich goes even further to say that not only is ontological thinking ontologically prior to nominalistic thinking, but it is, as this quote from *LPJ* implies, also *historically* prior to all other kinds of philosophical thinking as well (*LPJ* 19). Cf. Raymond Sabin, *Tillich's Concept of God*, B.D. thesis, Meadville Lombard Theological School (Chicago, IL, 1944), 61-63.

everything that is the power of resisting nonbeing" (1.163).³² Nominalism is little more than a philosophical *game* that can be *thought* or invented, and human thinking has the ability to be self-reflective about itself and its nature (this point will become important later, since Altizer will suggest that *thinking-itself* is ontologically prior to *being-itself*). As such, in our situation, Tillich suggests, we must *transcend over* and *against* nominalism into *ontological* thinking, and to think against nominalism happens initially as a result of rebellion against theological theism or the existential shock of the experience of non-being.³³

Esse-ipsum and the Inadequacy of Language

"The certainty" of deity which comes from arguments for the existence of God, Tillich stated in the 1962 Ingersoll Lecture at Harvard Divinity School, is dependent upon "objective objects" and reflect the parameters of the arguments themselves. Such thinking—again, theological theism— leads to placing God as a being among other beings. If God is a genuine reality, Tillich said, "it is implied in immediate existential experiences and cannot be undermined by theoretical criticisms."³⁴ The God of theological theism "does not exist," but one should move to the "God above God" (*ST* 1.205, *HCT* 92). It is the "God above God who is the real ground of everything that is, who is above any special name we can give to even the highest being" (*HCT* 92).

Because theological language must point toward the *edge* of language; ontological language, according to Tillich, must be agreed upon for describing the unconditional. Tillich suggests "being-in-so-far-as-it-is-being," or *esse ipsum*, or being-itself as a nonsymbolic statement to equate with the divine, god-above-god (*LPJ* 18, *UC* 46, *ST* 1.238). "[A]fter this has been said," Tillich remarks, "nothing else can be said about God which is not symbolic" (*ST* 1.238). Rowe explains that being-itself, for Tillich, revolves around two foundational assertions: (1) while "everything is

---

³² Cf. Wainwright 174. Rowe (1968): Tillich "asserts but does not give an argument for the claim that ontology, when properly understood, shows that the reality of being-itself is presupposed by thought" (92).
³³ Barry Baker, *The Mystical Theology of Paul Tillich*, M.Th. thesis, University of Trinity College (Toronto School of Theology, 1970), 147. Cf. *HCT* 143-144, *PPT* 194; Sontag 235-236; Nicholas Patricca, *God and the Question of Being*, Ph.D. diss., U. of Chicago (1972), 151-153; Ian Thompson, *Being and Meaning* (Edinburgh: Edinburgh UP, 1981), 57ff; Robert Carter, "The Nothingness Beyond God," *Eastern Buddhist* ns 18.1 (1985), 120-121, 124-125, 126ff; George Kelsey, "Being and Power," handwritten notes, George Kelsey archive, p. 2.
³⁴ Tillich, "Symbols of Eternal Life," (1962), 3.

subject to the limitations...being-itself is beyond all limitations," and (2) "every being participates in being-itself."[35] *Esse-ipsum* transcends beyond beings, and is not a being among other beings, yet all beings *participate* in *esse-ipsum*.[36] "There is a basic polarity of all life which can be called individualization and participation," Tillich writes, "[e]verythihng stands under this polarity." Within this polarity, "the more individualized a being is, the more it is able to participate," so that in humans "we have complete individualization and universal participation" in *esse-ipsum*.[37] The fact that we can perceive objects as having religious symbolism or sacredness points to the reality that *everything* participates in *esse-ipsum*. We can think of ourselves as having religious experience and also separate from the divine because we participate in the divine as individuals and universally as being—that is, *having* being.[38]

Anything other than God is "being itself" is symbolic and secondary to the ontological reality reflected by the statement *Deus est esse ipsum*.[39] Even to describe God as "living" is symbolic.[40] Tillich explains further in *Love, Power, and Justice*:

> God is the basic and universal symbol for what concerns us ultimately. As being-itself He is ultimate reality, the really real, the ground and abyss of everything that is real.... He is the subject of all the symbolic statements in which I express my ultimate concern. Everything we say about being-itself, the ground and

---

[35] William Rowe, "The Meaning of 'God' in Tillich's Theology," *Journal of Religion* 42.4 (1962), 282, citing *ST* 1.237.
[36] Rowe (1962), 283.
[37] Tillich, "Symbols of Eternal Life" (1962), 4.
[38] Rowe (1962), 281. Rowe: "But if being-itself can account for the aspect of ultimacy by virtue of being beyond all limitations, how is Tillich able to accommodate the aspect of concreteness in the idea of God? For if being-itself is free from all limitations, it cannot be concrete. Tillich's solution here is astounding. He appeals to the second assertion about being-itself. The argument here is that, by virtue that every being participates in being-itself, every being has the potential to express the concrete element in the idea of God. That is, Tillich is arguing that the relationship of participation between being-itself and every being makes it possible for a particular being to become a focal point through which God is disclosed.... When any being becomes such a focal point—a sacred object or a religious symbol—Tillich views that being as an expression of the tendency toward concreteness in the idea of God. Hence Tillich thinks he can account for the concrete element in religious experience and religious discourse about God by means of the presence and disclosure of the divine in the concrete, made possible by the fact that concrete beings *participate* in being-itself (God)" (283).
[39] Cf. Kee Chung Ryu, *Naharjuna's Emptiness and Paul Tillich's God*, Ph.D. diss., Drew U. (1984), 107.
[40] Dong Cheol Yoon, *The Protestant Principle*, Ph.D. diss., Drew U. (1998), 148.

> abyss of being, must be symbolic. It is taken out of the material of our finite reality and applied to that which transcends the finite infinitely....: it cannot be used in its literal sense. To say anything about God in the literal sense of the words used means to say something false about Him. The symbolic in relation to God is not less than the literal, but it is the only true way of speaking about God. (*LPJ* 109)

The word *God* is always symbolic for our ultimate concern, and points toward *esse-ipsum*. Nothing about God can be understood literally. "Symbolic language is valid in the sense that it is the only possible language for expressing the experience of man's participation in the eternal," Tillich admits, noting that symbols "are authentic when they are born out of a genuine participation" and "express the experience correctly and graphically."[41] There is nothing wrong with using symbolic language, Tillich writes, so long as symbolic language remains symbolic.

Tillich's writing on the nature of symbols points to the inadequacy of language for discourse about religion. "Religious symbols need no justification if their meaning is understood," Tillich claims, "[f]or their meaning is that they are the language of religion and the only way in which religion can express itself directly." Symbols can be expressed in philosophy, theology, and artistically "indirectly and reflectively," but when symbols express themselves directly they become "myths."[42] He further explains:

> Religious symbols mediate ultimate reality through things, persons, events which because of their mediating functions receive the quality of "holy." In the experience of holy places, times, books, words, images, and acts, symbols of the holy reveal something of the "Holy-Itself" and produce the experience of holiness in persons and groups. No philosophical concept can do the same thing, and theological concepts are merely conceptualizations of religious symbols.

Esse-ipsum is reflected through symbols; even though it is ontologically prior to the symbols before they are divinized as symbols. Symbols explain

---

[41] Tillich, "Symbols of Eternal Life" (1962), 4.
[42] Paul Tillich, "The Meaning and Justification of Religious Symbols," *Religious Experience and Truth*, ed. Sidney Hook (New York: New York UP, 1961), 3.

the means by which we experience the "holy." But symbols are not always positive.

> Symbols have the same creative and destructive effect on social groups. Symbols are the main power of integrating them: a king, an event, a document in the political realm of representative symbolism, an epic work, architectural symbols, a holy figure, a holy book, a holy rite in religion. But there also are disintegrating possibilities as in some political symbols such as the führer and the swastika, or in religious symbols such as the Moloch type of gods, human sacrifices, doctrinal symbols producing split consciousness, etc. This characteristic of symbols shows their tremendous power of creation and destruction. By no means are they harmless semantic expressions.[43]

Clearly, for Tillich, symbols can be extraordinarily rich elements of religious thought and practice, but they also are the *demonic* element of religion. "The demonic," Tillich said in a series of lectures, "is the elevation of something relative and ambiguous...to absoluteness" (*MSA* 123-133). By taking symbols literally, or by assigning the absolute to them, they become dangerous and demonic.[44] To speak of "God" is always symbolic; and this is acceptable to Tillich, so long as the symbol of "God" is not elevated to the ultimate.[45]

Nothing literal or positive can be genuinely said about *esse-ipsum*, beyond *Deus est esse-ipsum*, and even that statement qualifies *Deus* as the God-above-God.[46] While one could raise the question of whether *esse-ipsum* is itself not symbolic, Tillich's ontic affirmation of *esse-ipsum* is not coincidental; it is part of a larger systematic treatment of language for

---

[43] Ibid. 5-6.
[44] Cf. Baker, 116; cf. Paul Tillich, "The Religious Symbol," *Religious Experience and Truth*, ed. Sidney Hook (New York: New York UP, 1961), 301, 314-315. As an example of Tillich working a symbol, he writes on the idea of the Kingdom of God: it "implies universal fulfillment, a new heaven and a new earth, but not in terms of a receding of the universe into its Ground, but in a reunion of all separated and heterogeneous elements of being in the unity and clarity of the divine life. More than this cannot be said. God will be 'all in all,' as Paul expresses it. In this ecstatic symbol of fulfillment the contrast of the types [of symbols] is lessened but not completely obliterated" (Tillich, "Symbols of the Eternal Life" [1962], 9). For a terrific explanation and exploration of Tillich's 'demonology,' see Raymond Sabin, *Tillich's Concept of God*, B.D. thesis, Meadville Lombard Theological School (1944), 36-39. Cf. Harold Zietlow, *The Living God*, Ph.D. diss., U. Chicago (1961), 60.
[45] John Thatamanil, *The Immanent Divine* (Minneapolis: Fortress, 2006), 108; cf. William Alston, "Being-Itself and Talk About God," *Center Journal* 3.3 (1984), 23.
[46] Rowe (1962), 284.

Tillich.⁴⁷ Robert Scharlemann observes that there are *five* varieties of theological language in Tillich's theology:

1. Religious symbols, such as the word *God*.

2. Concepts "that can only be used symbolically because literally" they are "self-contradictory, like 'omnipresence.'"

3. Concepts "that can be used as a concept and as symbol." *Spirit* has "the polarities of the structure of being in their unity" as a *concept* and refers "to a quality of the depth of the structure" as a *symbol*.

4. "Concept[s] that can be used literally" for the purposes of having "a category of finite being and thinking…but is misleading if used as a symbol." These are usually not first used as a symbol and are often theological or philosophical concepts.

5. Terms that can *only* be religious symbols and nothing else, such as *eternity*, which "expresses the relation of the depth of having no time."⁴⁸

But where does *esse-ipsum* fit into these imposed "types" of language? Nicholas Patricca suggests that as the "ground," "structure" or "fountain of being"—to use Tillich's terms—*esse-ipsum* is *both* concept and symbol (category 3, above).⁴⁹ Robert Corrington suggests that *esse-ipsum* transcends such categories, that it can take the form of all of these, but is not exclusively one. Rather, language that takes the form of these categories is both rooted in and implies *esse-ipsum* as ontologically prior to thought.⁵⁰ While this line of thought may be, as Thomas Altizer suggests (redundantly), a rhetorical and *tautological* "tautology," it is nonetheless "a meaningful tautology," one "which veils the unbelievably daring project of

---

⁴⁷ Ibid. 279; Sabin, 72.
⁴⁸ Robert Scharlemann, *Religion and Reflection*, ed. Erdmann Sturm (Münster: LIT, 2004), 26-27.
⁴⁹ Patricca, 169; cf. 173; cf. Tillich, *ST* 1.238-239.
⁵⁰ Robert Corrington, "Being and Faith: *Sein und Zeit* and Luther," *Anglican Theological Review* 70 (1988) 30. Elsewhere Corrington suggests (by implication) elsewhere that while Tillich maintained that *Deus est esse ipsum* is the *only* non-symbolic ontological affirmation we are able to make, Tillich's naming of "Christ" as "New Being" is so central—at least in Tillich's Christological writings, such as the *Systematic Theology*—that this too is a non-symbolic ontological affirmation as well (Robert Corrington, "The Christhood of Things," *Drew Gateway* 52.1 [1981], 41).

an attempt to know the sacred Reality through the language created by man's profane existence in existing being."⁵¹

While *esse-ipsum* is necessary to human thought, for Tillich the naming of "God"—no matter how it is used—is always problematic for the theologian. Even though language of the *via negativa* is a historical and helpful theological tradition, "in the present situation," he wrote in response to Catholic critics, theologians are nearly *embarrassed* to speak of God. Even "well informed" individuals find it difficult to "speak of God."⁵² This "situation" is a reality in which Tillich lived. Ronald Stone wrote that while Tillich was a chaplain in the First World War, he was "[o]ccasionaly unable to preach" because of the mental devastation that the war caused for him personally, and in sermons he sometimes claimed "that God himself was preaching the message in the slaughter." After the Battle of Tahure (Battle of the Hills), Tillich gathered himself together to confess in a sermon, on 2 Corinthians 4:17-18, of "his inability to speak of things human to his listeners."⁵³

Although Tillich was regularly criticized later in his career that his theological language is "contradictory," "obscure," "ambiguous and diffuse," "confusing," "gratuitous," and even a "gerrymandering" of language itself, one particularly anecdotal story is telling.⁵⁴ While Tillich was a professor at Union Theological Seminary in New York City, he was invited to give a paper to the prestigious New York Philosophy Club. After the Tillich delivered the paper, on the ontological understanding of the "ground of being," the esteemed philosophers in the audience took turns responding. Finally, when G. E. Moore (the analytic, "ethical non-naturalist" philosopher famous for, ironically enough, the idea of "Moore's paradox," a logical contradiction in language) spoke, he replied to Tillich: "I am sorry to say that there is not a single sentence that Professor Tillich has uttered that I was able to understand—not a single sentence!"⁵⁵ Tillich

---

⁵¹ Altizer, "A Theonomy in Our Time?" (1963), 360.
⁵² Paul Tillich, "An Afterward: Appreciation and Reply," *Paul Tillich in Catholic Thought*, ed. Thomas O'Meara and Celestin Weisser (Dubuque: Priory, 1964), 308; cf. Baker, 116.
⁵³ Ronald Stone, *Paul Tillich's Radical Social Thought* (Atlanta: John Knox, 1980), 33.
⁵⁴ O. Thomas, "Tillich's *Systematic Theology*," *Bulletin of the North American Paul Tillich Society* 31.2 (2005), 5; ibid., "Being and Some Theologians," *Harvard Theological Review* 70.1/2 (1977), 147; Robert Ross, "God and Singular Existence," *International Journal for Philosophy of* Religion 8.2 (1977), 141; Nielsen (1961), 279, 270; cf. Aaron Mackler, "Symbols, Reality, and God," *Judaism* 40 (1991): 290-300.
⁵⁵ Robert Coburn, "God, Revelation, and Religious Truth," *Faith and Philosophy* 13.1 (1996), 3.

was cognizant of this; however, the difficulty of his own language is that it is both *indicative* and a *consequent* of the inadequacy of language.[56] "[F]or the sake of provocation," Tillich proposed, in *On the Boundary*, "a thirty-year moratorium" on theological language (*OTB* 65).

Deus est esse ipsum is an example of what Tillich calls "theonomous" thinking—thinking which is neither autonomous nor heteronomous (*HCT* 162). He writes:

> The limits of the ontological argument are obvious. But nothing is more important for philosophy or theology than the truth it contains, the acknowledgement of the unconditional element in the structure of reason and reality. The idea of theonomous culture, and with it the possibility of a philosophy of religion, is dependent on this insight. A philosophy of religion which does not begin with something unconditioned never reaches God. (*ST* 1.208)

This kind of philosophy of religion requires the "courage" to "affirm the power of being," Tillich suggests, "whether we know it or not" (*CB* 181). This Anselmic courage transgresses against nominalism; it points us toward the edge of language and toward courageous reflection where traditional constructions of *theological theism* are theonomously transcended.[57]

Tillich's ontological language is *both* theological *and* philosophical, and Tillich's new *thinking* redefines the ideas of "theological" and "philosophical" languages. While the boundaries of these ideas are blurred, a new *thinking* emerges. To enter into a "Religion of the Concrete Spirit" requires, in Gabriel Vahanian's words, a "new religious paradigm."[58]

The Religion of the Concrete Spirit, as a shift away from Christianity, is a shift also away from our own groundedness in *esse-ipsum*; it is both indicative and a consequence of *self-transcendence*.[59] It requires both self-affirmation and self-negation (*IRR* 52). The form and dynamics of Tillich's theology of culture, when both taken together and acknowledging the ontologically prior *esse-ipsum*, leads to a rejection of nominalism that constructs the world around oneself as symbols and not-

---

[56] Cf. Robert Ross, "A Form of Ontological Argument," *Harvard Theological Review* 70.1/2 (1977), 116; cf. Ferré (1966), 15.
[57] Cf. Wayne Mahan, *Tillich's System* (San Antonio: Trinity UP, 1974), 117-118.
[58] Cf. Gabriel Vahanian, *Tillich and the New Religious Paradigm* (Aurora, CO: Davies, 2004).
[59] Ryu, 159.

yet symbols which invite one toward greater self-reflection and awareness (*HCT* 164).[60] When asked, "what do you mean by theonomy?" Tillich roundaboutly answered:

> Anselm's way of philosophizing, or Augustine's way or…—how I hesitate to say it—"Hegel's".… This theonomous way means acknowledging the mystery of being, but not believing that this mystery is an authoritarian transcendent element which is imposed upon us and against us, which breaks our reason to pieces, which is the *depth* of all reason. Reason and mystery belong together, like substance and form. (*HCT* 160, emph. add.)

Theonomous thinking engages the *depth* of both reason and being, of philosophy (the "structure of being"), theology (the *meaning* of being), humanism, existentialism, and religious experience (*ST* 1.238-239).[61] Such thinking "reveal[s] the depth dimensions of a culture," namely, *our own individual constructions of the world.*[62] It is an "all-of-the-above" reflection, but is "interdependent" upon, as discussed before, the rejection of theological theism and a kind of atheism.[63] A theological Christian theism which claims to have all of the answers of the universe is not theonomous but autonomous, and when contributing to social stagnation, it is heteronomous. If *esse-ipsum* is "the ground of both dynamics and form," John Thatamanil writes, "then it will not do to conceive of God solely in static terms."[64] God, as *esse-ipsum*, is experienced by us through self-reflection and through its participation in religious symbols. But to do so requires *transcendence*.

---

[60] The political aspect of this is explored in Tillich's *The Socialist Decision*.
[61] Patricca, 173; Paul Tillich, et al, *To Live as Men* (Santa Barbara, CA: Center for the Study of Democratic Institutions, 1965), 13; Grigg (1985), 12, 62. Cf. Dewart (1966), 41; George McLean, "Paul Tillich's Existential Philosophy of Protestantism," *Paul Tillich in Catholic Thought*, ed. Thomas O'Meara and Celestin Weisser (Dubuque: Priory, 1964), 53.
[62] Jeffrey Robbins, *In Search of a Non-Dogmatic Theology* (Aurora, CO: Davies, 2003), xvii.
[63] Laurel Schneider, "From New Being to Meta-Being," *Soundings* 75:2/3 (1992), 422.
[64] Thatamanil (2006), 108. Cf. Langdon Gilkey, *Blue Twilight* (Minneapolis: Fortress, 2001), 101.

CHAPTER 2

A PANTHEON OF THEISMS IN TILLICH

Gerrymandering Language

For Tillich, *Deus est esse ipsum*, and nothing else may be ontologically stated without being symbolic. Yet, for the religious practitioner, who—to use Tillich's language—at least in theory *lives* in a world of religious symbols, what is to be said or believed about God?[1] Tillich's system of thought does leave the Christian with the notion that God is the answer to the 'big questions.'[2] The problem is that *esse-ipsum* as the *prius* or *ultima substantia* of theonomous thinking is not what most Christians have in mind when they refer to *God*.[3] To go even further, Martin Gardner observed in his satirical novel, *The Flight of Peter Fromm*, that *esse-ipsum*, as an idea, was *designed* by Tillich to be "safe from all conceivable attack," a *safety* at the price of a Christianity "so thin and bloodless that no ordinary man, woman or child can find it interesting."[4] This perceived safety is indicative of a "gerrymandering of language," some critics argue, so that *esse-ipsum* by default becomes, as Owen Thomas charged, "unavoidable."[5]

Langdon Gilkey draws a distinction between the clause *Deus est esse ipsum* and "God is being-itself" in Tillich. The earlier clause, the Latin version of the second clause, is classified as an ontological statement which is unapproachable; and, as discussed before, Tillich admits that "God is being-itself" is a *religious* statement, allowing being-itself (*esse-ipsum*) to be equated with the Christian symbolic language for God.[6] Radical theologian Robert Scharlemann asks:

---

[1] Cf. Robert Scharlemann, "Critical and Religious Consciousness," *Kairos and Logos*, new ed., ed. John Carey (Macon, GA: Mercer UP, 1978), 78.
[2] Sabin, 70.
[3] Randall Otto, "The Doctrine of God in the Theology of Paul Tillich," *Westminster Theological Journal* 52 (1980), 306.
[4] Gardner, 187.
[5] O. Thomas (1977), 159; cf. Ross, "A Form of Ontological Argument" (1977), 134.
[6] Langdon Gilkey, *Gilkey on Tillich* (New York: Crossroad, 1990), 103.

If God is being-itself, is being-itself God? This thematic question concerning the "is" between "God" and "being-itself" is not explicitly discussed by Tillich. But the question is pertinent to Tillich's correlation of God and being. If we can say "God *is* being" but not "Being is God," what can we say of being-itself in relation to God? Can we say, "Being *defines* God"? Is there a *deificare* in being-itself just as there is the *esse* in God? In other words, is *being* which identifies God as God, also the eternal activity of God? Is being that which God *does*? If it is, then the word *being* not only names what or who God is but also names the activity of God as God. This is to say, in other words, that what is *named* by the three words "God is Being" is one and the same referent. That would be the integration, if not the formulation, of statements such as "Deus est" and "Deus est esse ipsum."[7]

The question of God's *operáre*—the nature of God's *activity*—is inherently related to the grammatical puzzle of *Deus est esse-ipsum*. If the subject and predicate nominative cannot be interchanged, as if they were appositives of one another, if *est* is no longer a special kind of intransitivity which links equivocal terms, *est* might be thought of as *transitive*. God *perpetuates* being. Gilkey argues that *Deus est esse ipsum* is too oversimplified to be adequate for Tillich's complex system; it reduces *Deus* to a language game.[8] Yet Sharlemann's observation reveals some of the problems with the ways in which Tillich *describes* "God." Let us observe a few examples.

The God-above-God [9]

I have already mentioned this concept earlier, which indicates that if there is any God, it must be beyond any understanding of "God" which can be

---

[7] Sharlemann (2004), 7-8. He continues: "Does the oder of the three words 'God is being-itself' (*Deus est esse ipsum*) require an inversion in order to be complete—so that the thought of *being* as the deity is implicit in the thought of God as being? If such an inversion is adopted, it becomes one manner of expressing the universal presence of God. 'God is being itself' and 'Being defines God' (Deus esse ipsum; esse deificat Deum). The sense of such an inversion would be to assert that God, as God, can never *not* be and also that Being, *as being*, names the activity which identifies God as God. Tillich does not use such an inversion...but perhaps such an inversion, however esoteric, is implicit in the way in which he develops the relation between theology and ontology. The inversion of "God is being-itself" would not, strictly speaking, be "Being-itself is God" but something on the oder of "Being defines God (esse deificat Deum)." Each of the three terms serves, linguistically, as the subject, the object, and the unity of the two" (8).
[8] Gilkey (1990), 58ff.
[9] *BR* 82; *CB* 15, 182, 186-190.

conceived. The juxtaposition of the "above" language is that the more "above" the God-above-God is, the more *transcendent*, the more participatory—and perhaps even *immanent*—the God-above-God has the potential to be.[10] Charles Winquist observed that within Tillich's thought the more *ultimate* the God-above-God is, the more *intimate* it can be conceived to be.[11] The language of the God-above-God also indicates Tillich's strong indication of the divine as "unconditioned" and "unconditional." The use of the term *unconditioned* is for Tillich a linguistic ontic device to indicate the use of ontological language over other kinds of religious language. It indicates that the "concept of God" always differs from, and is epistemically preceded by, *esse-ipsum*.[12]

Ultimate Concern [13]

Because God is *the* ontological answer to *the* ontological question, God is "what concerns us ultimately."[14] The question of personal ultimate concern, however, is an existential question regarding for what or whom one lives life. If what concerns someone ultimately is anything but *the* ontological answer—God—one has replaced *the* answer with another being or symbol. The absolutizing of the non-ontological answer to *the* theological question then is *demonic*, since it "is that which has the power to threaten or save [one's] being."[15] Russell McCutcheon, however, has criticized the term *ultimate concern* as a "widely repeated yet still empty claim" that reduces religion to a "personal value judgment."[16] Martin Marty writes, in Tillich's defense, that "Tillich's notion of ultimate concern allows us to consider 'religious' any belief systems that take up the meaning and purpose of human existence," so that the "intermingling of religion" with all aspects of life, when "understood as ultimate concern...is therefore inescapable."[17] Tillich would agree that one's ultimate concern is not only

---

[10] Choi, 68.
[11] Charles Winquist, *The Surface of the Deep* (Aurora, CO: Davies, 2003), 232.
[12] Sabin, 32, cf. 70 n. 4.
[13] *CB* 47, 82; *FR* 87; *SS* 158-160, 166-167; *DF* 1ff.; *ST* 1.10, 12-14, 21, 24-25, 28, 36, 42, 50, 53, 110-11, 115, 118, 120-121, 124, 127, 131, 146, 148, 156, 211, 214-216, 218, 220-223, 230, 273; *ST* 2.9, 14, 26, 30, 87, 116; *ST* 3.102, 125, 130, 154, 223, 283, 287, 289, 293, 349, 422.
[14] Bernard Loomer, "Tillich's Theology of Correlation," *Journal of Religion* 35 (1956), 152.
[15] Ryu, 105.
[16] Russell McCutcheon, *Critics Not Caretakers* (Albany, NY: SUNY UP, 2001), 207, 4.
[17] Martin Marty and Jonathan Moore, *Politics, Religion, and the Public Good* (San Francisco: Jossey, 2000), 11.

a personal value judgment, but it is *the* only value judgment that has ultimate meaning to the individual's existential location and condition.

The Ground and Structure of Being [18]

When our being is theonomous we are grounded in being; the *ground of being* represents all other beings' participation in *esse-ipsum* (*FR* 87).[19] As the ground of existence, *esse-ipsum* "is beyond essence and existence."[20] Beyond this, though, Tillich writes: "God as being-itself is the ground of the ontological structure of being without being subject to this structure himself. He *is* the structure; that is, he has the power of determining the structure of everything that has being" (*ST* 1.238). God is not only the *ground* of being, but the *structure* of the same being of which he is the *ground*, since God cannot be subject to the structure of being (cf. *ST* 1.238-239, 2.9). And further, God has *power* over the same structure that is equivocated with God. And to push it even more: as the structure of being, God is the *end* of philosophy, as well as that which gives the structure meaning. God is the ontological question, the ontological answer, and the *prius* of ontology itself.[21] Just as "God-above-God" signifies *transcendence* it does so by virtue of a juxtaposition of *immanence*.[22]

The Abyss and Depth of Being [23]

Similarly, Tillich's notion of the *abyss of being* is used nearly interchangeably in his writings. The most obvious example is in *Biblical Religion and the Search for Ultimate Reality*, where Tillich writes of the lack of the ontological use of *is* in the Bible:

> Most people, including the biblical writers, take the word in its popular sense: something "is" if it can be found in the whole of potential experience. That which can be encountered within the whole of reality is real. Even the more sophisticated discussions

---

[18] *ST* 1.20-23, 26, 168-169, 205; *ST* 2.7, 9, 10, 87, 126, 161, 167, 174; *ST* 3.99, 142, 190, 283-285, 290, 293-294.
[19] Choi, 5. Cf. Mark K. Taylor, *Paul Tillich* (London: Liturgical, 1987), 22-24.
[20] Ryu, 116.
[21] Randall Otto, 306.
[22] Thatamanil (2006), 139.
[23] *ST* 1.79, 110, 113, 119, 156, 158-159, 164, 174, 216, 226; *SF* 52ff. Cf. Sigridur Gudmarsdotti, *Abyss of God*, Ph.D. diss., Drew U. (2007), 208. [This important dissertation was later published as *Tillich and the Abyss* (New York: Palgrave Macmillan, 2016). I wrote a review of this book for the AAR's Reading Religion (online, 2018); my review is directly connected to this dissertation.]

> about the existence or nonexistence of God often have this popular tinge. But, if God can be found within the whole of reality, then the whole of reality is the basic and dominant concept. God, then, is subject to the structure of reality.... The God who *is* a being is transcended by the God who is *Being* itself, the ground and abyss of every being. (*BR 82*)

Although the use of "abyss" seems equivocal here, he elsewhere uses the notion of *abyss* to point to, in my own terminology, the *ground-grounding-ground of being*; a concept rooted in Jacob Boheme's notion of *ungurd*; Schelling's *first potency*; *meonic freedom*; Rudolph Otto's *mysterium tremendum* and *fascinosium*; and Oskar Pfister's *ideal-realismus*.[24] For Boheme, for example, the abysmal notion of God is a term to remind us we cannot say "that God's Essence is a distinct thing, possessing a particular place or abode" that God is not a being among other beings, but "the abyss of nature and of creation is God himself."[25] Kee Chung Ryu suggests that the terms *ground* and *abyss* provide "a safeguard for the inscrutable mystery of God."[26] *The depth of being* (*SF 57*) has a similar meaning for Tillich, again juxtaposing the image of the God-beyond-God.

The Power of Being [27]

Theonomous thinking leads to the accepting the implication of *esse-ipsum*, and we then recognize the power of being within ourselves.[28] Referring to the language of *The Courage to Be*, Donald Dreisbach explains the power of being:

> This is the discovery of the "God above God," the power of being which appears in the midst of despairing doubt about one's power to create meaning and about the reality of the god above mysticism or of theism. It is an awareness of one's own being and vitality, of one's ability to seek and even establish meaning, but, because the context of this awareness is radical doubt about one's own power, this being or vitality is something of a gift and surprise. This God

---

[24] Ryu 118; John Irwin, *Psychoanalysis in Christian Thought*, Ph.D. diss., Drew U. (1974), 239; Ferré (1966), 11. Cf. Irwin, 261; Ryu, 118, 120, 128 n. 84; Herberg, "The Resurgence of Theology in America" (1974), 6.
[25] Jacob Boheme, in Ferré (1966), 11.
[26] Ryu, 120-121.
[27] *CTB* 88-89, 159-160, 172-173; *PE* 163; *ST* 1.137, 2.6, 8; *ST* 2.10, 11, 12, 20, 125; *TC* 25-26.
[28] Gilkey (1990), 102.

above God of whom we become aware is the power of being-itself, present neither symbolically nor as an object of conceptual thought.[29]

The power of being is the religious experience of *esse-ipsum* that is not a call to adherence to doctrine or literalisms, but rather a call to *becoming*, to *self-transcend*.[30] In the human person, the power of being gains its existential power because of the looming reality of death, of non-being.[31] The power of being presupposes all other descriptions of God, without human thinking there is no *prius* of theonomous thinking.[32] "Even a God would disappear," Tillich wrote, "if he were not being-itself" (*ST* 1.164).

At bottom for Tillich, God is *mystery*.[33] "God can reveal Himself," he once preached in a sermon, "only by remaining veiled" (*SF* 89). The experiences of non-being and of the *absence* of God in human life are also a mystery.[34] The language and concepts are not always consistent because they are dialectical, and that for Tillich an absurd life should reflect an absurd theological conception of the divine. A significant problem remains of how does "God" remain the *prius* of thought and *esse-ipsum* simultaneously, not to mention being at the same time the structure, ground, abyss, and power *of being*?[35] Furthermore, does such a understanding of *esse-ipsum* have any meaning left?

Is it still Christian? Durwood Foster describes Tillich's conception of God to be an "annulment" or "*aufhebung*" of the Christian notion of a personal God into a 'grand concept' of *esse-ipsum*, and, as such, the Christian

---

[29] Donald Dreisbach, *Symbols & Salvation* (Lanham, MD: UP America, 1993). Cf. *CB* 176-190.
[30] George Tavard, "The Protestant Principle and the Theological System of Paul Tillich," *Paul Tillich in Catholic Thought*, eds. Thomas O'Meara and Celestin Wisser (Dubuque: Priory, 1964), 86.
[31] Hammond (1965), 98. Cf. Sabin 63; Ross (1977), 134; Herberg, "The Resurgence of Theology in America" (1974), 6; Randall Otto, 306; Patricca, iii; Winquist (2003), 134; Joseph Fitzer, "Paul J. Tillich on Natural Theology," *God in Contemporary Thought*, ed. Sebastian Matczak (New York: Learned, 1977), 645; Philip Mueller, *The Centrality and Significance of the Concept of Ecstasy in the Thought of Paul Tillich*, Ph.D. diss., Fordham U. (1972), 62.
[32] Carl Vaught, "Confronting Paul Tillich," *Bulletin of the North American Paul Tillich Society* 31.5 (2005), 8.
[33] John Thatamanil, "Against the Mystical as Exceptional," *Bulletin of the North American Paul Tillich Society* 30.4 (2004), 28.
[34] Ryu, 121; Gudmarsdotti, 208.
[35] O. Thomas (1977), 146-147.

God "disappears as a *distinct divine hypostasis*."[36] Guy Hammond charges that the intellectual move of *Deus est esse-ipsum* is ultimately—and "unfortunately"—post-Christian, and is the "result" of Tillich moving too far away from, and even subverting, the language of the Bible.[37] For all of these reasons, Tillich scholar Owen Thomas declared Tillich's notion of being-itself "contradictory and obscure," and ultimately a "big failure."[38]

Models of Divinity

Randall Otto suggests that Tillich "has been described as a theist, a deist, a pantheist, a panentheist, a metaphysician, a mystic, an atheist, and a humanist."[39] Though Tillich would, as discussed earlier, call himself an atheist, he had to break and redefine the term *atheism* to describe himself in that way. The same could be said of the term *theism*: in some aspects, Tillich is a theist, and in others he is not. The negative theology and Christian mystical tradition, mentioned earlier, is highly influential on Tillich's work as well. Tillich also has some knowledge and theological use for the "occult" mystical tradition (*RS* 166ff.). Tillich described himself as a thinker who wished to combine humanism and Protestant theology in a co-authored, rarely cited text called *To Live as Men*.[40] Between the dialectic of atheism and theism, a case could be made that Tillich was a dualist, pantheist, a panentheist, an ecstatic naturalist.[41] The meaning of *transcendence* and *immanence* will arise from this discussion.

Dualism

Tillich's Platonic intellectual move of *esse-ipsum* creates a dualism.[42] Rowe summarized Tillich's statements about God in the following way:

1. God transcends the world. (*ST* 1.237)

2. Every finite thing participates in the world. (*ST* 1.237)

3. God cannot have a beginning and an end. (*ST* 1.189)

---

[36] D. Foster, 23.
[37] Guy Hammond, "Tillich on the Personal God," *Journal of Religion* 44.4 (1964), 289.
[38] O. Thomas (2005), 5. Cf. Ross (1977), 134.
[39] Randall Otto, 303.
[40] Tillich, *To Live as Men* (1965), 13.
[41] D. Foster, 23.
[42] Arthur Lovejoy, *The Great Chain of Being* (Cambridge, MA: Harvard UP, 1936), 315ff.

4. Non-being is literally nothing except in relation to God. (*ST* 1.189)

5. God precedes non-being in ontological validity. (*ST* 1.189)

6. God is his own beginning and end, the initial power of everything that is. (*ST* 1.189)

How is it, then, Rowe asks, "that to say, 'There *is* a God' is to be held as having no meaning, if 'every finite being depends on God for its existence?'" Rowe concludes that Tillich may really have *two* Gods in his system.[43] Just as Plato had Socrates forward the notion of the good beyond all, "exceeding in dignity of power," in *The Republic* Glaucon responds to Socrates, recognizing the dualistic nature of the "good," swearing, "Apollo, what a demonic excess!"[44] The excess here is that there is (1) a "God" of which the faithful *might* speak, which is the ground, power, fountain, structure, and abyss of being; and (2) *esse-ipsum* as a separate entity.[45]

Following this, *Esse-ipsum* is the "excess," as Glaucon put it, it is the God-above-God, but Tillich takes seriously the second "God" of the God-above-God. Even though this "-God" is easily lowered to a being among other beings, it is still a God that is genuinely worshiped that points toward the "God-above-." I include the second hyphen in the phrase "God-above-" (*esse-ipsum*) to indicate that to speak of *esse-ipsum* as "God" requires the acknowledgement of symbolic language and the lower "-God" (cf. *WR* 70-72).[46] "God-above-" needs "-God": the two terms are "nominally deduced dialectically" from each other.[47] Tillich would have resisted this interpretation of himself, though the post-Christian move made in the last lecture—"The Significance of the History of Religions for the Systematic Theologian"—seems to silently acknowledge this problem and drop *both* the "-God" and the "God-above-" for a post-Christian move to *Geist* or *Spirit*.[48] Owen Thomas criticizes Tillich for his dualism, writing, "[a]s one

---

[43] Rowe (1968), 82-83.

[44] Plato, *The Republic*, trans. Alan Bloom, 2nd ed. (New York: Basic, 1991), Book VI, 509b (p. 189).

[45] Rowe (1968) claims that a similar intellectual move happens with Plotinus' concept of the *One*, Spinoza's *substance*, and Kant's *thing-in-itself* (48). Cf. Patricca, 170; Sabin, 130.

[46] Cf. Nels Ferré, "Three Critical Issues in Tillich's Philosophical Theology," *Scottish Journal of Theology* 10 (1957), 230.

[47] Lovejoy, 82.

[48] Zietlow, 8.

standing in the Neo-Platonist tradition," Tillich should have known better.[49]

Deism

Although a minority view of Tillich, process theologians John Cobb and David Griffin have criticized Tillich for being a deist—namely, that God does not in the present have a participatory relationship with the world. Cobb writes that Tillich's God "'being-itself' and not 'a being' interacting with others involves a denial that God is a causal influence on the world, even though much of Tillich's language *illegitimately* gives the impression that creative influence is exerted by God."[50] By the phrase "denial of causal influence" they are claiming that God is no longer perpetuating being in the world in the present. But the 'hard' transcendence implied by conceptions of *deism* is not what Cobb and Griffin are discussing here. They explain further that Tillich "held that participation and individuality are polar, so that the more we participate with others in community the more we can become individuals, and the more we become individuals, the more richly we participate in community." Solipsistic understandings of human existence are then "illusory."[51]

While Tillich would deny any sense of deism about his understanding of God, Cobb and Griffin's point is that the *existential meaning* of Tillich's God for human life has little to do with any *actual* sense of *esse-ipsum* as the perpetuating force of being; rather, it is a *perceived* interpretation that has meaning for theonomous thinking and living.[52] This question regarding the relationship of *gesture* and *reality* will be returned to later.

Panentheism

The most common interpretation of Tillich's understanding of God is that he is a pan*en*theist. Tillich's most popular writings suggest this fairly clearly; in the final pages of the third volume of his *Systematic Theology* he describes divinity as an "eschatological pan-en-theism" (*ST* 3.420-421). In a 1948 sermon Tillich preached:

---

[49] O. Thomas (2005), 5, critiquing *ST* 1.236.
[50] John Cobb and David Griffin, *Process Theology* (Philadelphia: Westminster, 1976) 51, emph. add.
[51] Ibid. 82.
[52] Grigg (2006), 16.

> When the earth grows old and wears out, when natures and culture die, the Eternal changes the garments of His infinite being. He is the foundation on which all foundations are laid; and this foundation cannot be shaken. There is something immovable, unchangeable, unshakable, eternal, which becomes manifest in our passing and in the crumbling of our world. On the boundaries of the finite the infinite becomes visible; in the light of the Eternal the transitoriness of the temporal appears. (*SF* 9)

Tillich here recognizes the God-above-God, or *esse-ipsum*—"He"—as beyond everything conceivable. It is not only *that which nothing greater can be conceived*, but beyond *conception*: beyond "the totality of beings"; beyond the death of nature (*ST* 1.205). Tillich's panentheism appears, at first, to be a transcendence which spatially and temporally *includes* and *transcends* immanence:

> As the power of being, God transcends every being and also the totality of beings—the world. Being-itself is beyond finitude and infinity; otherwise it would be conditioned by something other than in itself and the real power of being would be beyond both it and that which conditioned it. Being-itself infinitely transcends every finite being.... On the other hand, everything finite participates in being-itself and in its infinity. Otherwise it would not have the power of being. (*ST* 1.237)

Being-itself is beyond finitude and infinity, transcending the totality of the world. This view was also maintained in Tillich's final lecture—"The Significance of the History of Religions for the Systematic Theologian"— though the terminology that he employed was a bit different (*FR* 87).[53]

Tillich's panentheism, however, is not a simple transcendence which includes immanence, but a complex one that is *contingent upon* immanence:

---

[53] Tillich: "Then there is...a critical moment against the demonization of the sacramental, making it into an object which can be handled. This element is embodied in various critical ways. The first of these critical movements is mystical. This mystical moment means that one is not satisfied with any of the concrete expressions of the Ultimate, of the Holy. One goes beyond them. Man goes to the one beyond any manifoldness. The Holy as the Ultimate lies beyond any of its embodiments. The embodiments are justified. They are accepted but as secondary. One must go beyond them in order to reach the highest, the Ultimate itself. The particular is denied for the Ultimate one. The Concrete is denied" (*FR* 87).

> The so-called ontological points to the ontological structure of finitude. It shows that an awareness of the infinite is included in man's awareness of finitude. Man knows that he is finite, that he is excluded from an infinity which nevertheless belongs to him. He is aware of his potential infinity while being aware of his actual finitude....
>
> The ontological argument in its various forms gives a description of the way in which potential infinity is present in actual finitude. As far as the description goes, that is, as far as it is analysis and not argument, it is valid. The presence within finitude of an element which transcends it is experience both theoretically and practically. (*ST* 1.206)

Potential infinity is present in actual finitude. In this sense, panentheism is a metaphor for the dialectic of the *perception* of human finitude and the *potential* for self-transcendence in the immanence of the present. Panentheism for Tillich is less an actual description of God than another symbol which describes the existential condition.[54]

Pantheism

Another minority view of Tillich is that he is a pantheist separate from an *ecstatic naturalism*. A pantheist view of Tillich is a misreading of his work. The similarity of *esse-ipsum* to Baruch Spinoza's notion of *substance*, for example—along with Tillich's affinity for Spinoza—is often reduced by some in the same way Friedrich Schleiermacher criticized Spinoza and his pantheistic "Spinozism."[55] One reason for this position is because of Tillich's consistent rejection of what he calls, as early as 1939, "exclusive monotheism," that is, "God as the Lord of time controlling the universal history of mankind, acting in history and through history" (*PE* 27). Playing on the assumption that what is not a *classical theism* must be a *pantheism*, some critics made the assumption that Tillich *must* be a pantheist, since he was definitely not a classical theist.[56] A close reading of Tillich, however, does suggest a *kind* of pantheism at work (*ST* 1.233), partially because there is a sense of recognizing that if "God" exists outside

---

[54] Piet Schonenberg, "From Transcendence to Immanence: Part II," *Transcendence and Immanence*, ed. Joseph Armenti (Villanova, PA: Villanova UP, 1976), 2.274. Cf. Bowman Clarke, "God and the Symbolic in Tillich," *Anglican Theological Review* 43.3 (1961): 302-311.
[55] T. O'Connor, 423.
[56] Kenelem Foster, "Paul Tillich and St. Thomas," *Paul Tillich in Catholic Thought*, eds. Thomas O'Meara and Celestin Weisser (Dubuque: Priory, 1964), 100.

of nature—if there is a spatial or temporal transcendence—that transcendence is related to the reality of the parameters of nature itself.[57] This leads to the next model of divinity.

Ecstatic Naturalism

The term "ecstatic naturalism" can mean a number of different things, but I use the term in the way in which Tillichian interpreters have, namely, that it is a kind of pantheism which allows for transcendence. Robert Corrington defines it "as that moment within naturalism when it recognizes its self-transcending character" characterized by a "transition from preformal potencies to the realms of signification in the world."[58] Tillich himself alludes to this idea only somewhat directly once, in a book review in *The Journal of Religion*, calling it "neo-naturalism," but adds that "I do not think that the question of the name is very important."[59] In the *Systematic Theology*, a new kind of naturalism comes from a recognition of the inadequacy and misuse of the term *pantheism*: that divinity should never be equated with nature. Further, God "is not the totality of natural objects," either, but instead "the creative power and unity of nature, the absolute substance which is present in everything" (*ST* 1.233). *Pantheism* in this sense, Tillich claims "is as necessary for a Christian doctrine of God as the mystical element of the divine presence" (1.234).

Tillich's sense of "panentheism" is a different kind of panentheism than the popular usage of the term; to use the term in any other way is a "myth" or "absurdity" (*ST* 2.6). As an *ecstatic naturalism*, the primary idea is the power of being. "Being itself," Tillich wrote, "is a power of Being but not the most powerful being; it is neither *ens realissimum* nor *ens singularissimum*": *a* power of being, not *the* power of being (*TC* 25-26). *Esse-ipsum*, as *the* power of being, "is the power in every thing that has power, be it a universal or an individual, a thing or an experience" (26). The power of being is the power of self-transcendence for humans or the potential power of things or experiences to transition from the not-yet-holy to

---

[57] Ferré (1966), 11. Cf. Zietlow, 11; Allen Killen, "Tillich, The Trinity, and Honest to God," *Bulletin of the Evangelical Theological Society* 7.1 (1962), 23.
[58] Robert Corrington, *Ecstatic Naturalism* (Bloomington, IN: Indiana UP, 1994), 18. Further: "The concept of *jouissance*...points in the direction of a self-realized ecstatic naturalism with its recognition that the production of a sign requires a release of energy and power in the direction of an alienated duress that yet contains internal traces of its lost origin" (19).
[59] Paul Tillich, Rev. of H. Weinman, *The Growth of Religion, Journal of Religion* 20 (1940), 71-72. Cf. *ST* 1.234.

becoming religious symbols.[60] An ecstatic naturalism, as Nels Ferré has interpreted Tillich, denies "a world beyond this world" and points toward the possibility for the experience of the holy *transcending* into the *immanence* of this world; there is limit to nature.[61]

Tillich's ecstatic naturalism is also closely related to Tillich's idea of the *depth* of being. The depth of being, Thomas Altizer describes (in a very early lecture) as "the ultimate ground of the being which we now are."[62] Jacob Taubes describes the depth of being as indicative of what he calls "Dionysiac theology," that is, "an 'ecstatic naturalism' that interprets all supernaturalistic symbols in immanent terms."[63] Ideas or terms which suggest *transcendence* dialectically relate, clash, and *theonomize* with immanent terms.[64] In the process of theonomy, at the *edge* of language—approaching the *prius* of thinking—symbolic religious language implodes, self-subverts, dies and resurrects. *Transcendence* and *immanence* have, as much as they can, taken on new meanings for Tillich, and he has in turn re-rooted the terminology into that which is 'unconditional' as symbolic language. The ideas have come into new meanings.

Transcendence and Immanence

Transcendence and immanence, as concepts, have taken on new meanings in Tillich's thought that are not particularly intelligible outside of his system. He does, however, discuss the ideas at the end of the first volume of his *Systematic Theology*, while discussing naturalistic versus supernaturalistic conceptions of divinity.[65] He writes:

> The question whether the relation between God and the world should be expressed in terms of immanence or transcendence is usually answered by an "as well as." Such an answer, although it is correct, does not solve any problem. Immanence and transcendence are spatial symbols. God is not *in* or *above* the world or both. The question is what does this mean in nonspatial terms?

---

[60] Irwin, 252.
[61] Ferré (1957), 231-232; ibid. (1966), 11; cf. T. O'Connor, 419.
[62] Thomas Altizer, "Nietzsche's Understanding of Christianity and Its Influence Upon Contemporary Theology," lecture notes in the Altizer archive, Syracuse U. (c. 1958/1960), 10. Altizer here is discussing Jacob Taubes.
[63] Jacob Taubes, "On the Nature of the Theological Method," *Journal of Religion* 34.1 (1954), 21.
[64] Altizer, "Nietzsche's Understanding of Christianity" (1958/1960) 10; Herberg, "Paul Tillich: Being Itself," lecture notes in the Herberg Archive (1974?), 5.
[65] Cf. Ferré (1957), 231.

> Certainly, God is neither in another nor in the same space as the world. He is the creative ground of the spatial structure of the world, but he is not bound to the structure, positively or negatively.

These words appear to be less panentheistic and suggestive of an ecstatic naturalism: while God is the structure of being, God is not bound to it. Prepositional relationships are not helpful when discussing that which is not a being among other beings: *esse-ipsum*. Tillich continues:

> The spatial symbol points to a qualitative relation: God is immanent in the world as its permanent creative ground and is transcendent to the world through freedom. Both infinite divinity and finite human freedom make the world transcendent to God and God transcendent to the world.

Divine immanence is the fixed perpetuating creative force; God is present "through freedom," through the latent possibility inherently in finitude. Further, with my emphasis:

> The religious interest in the divine transcendence is not satisfied where one rightly asserts the infinite transcendence of the infinite over the finite. *This transcendence does not contradict but rather confirms the coincidence of the opposites.* The infinite is present in everything finite, in the stone as well as in the genius. Transcendence demanded by religious experience is the freedom-to-freedom relationship which is actual in every personal encounter. Certainly, the holy is the "quite other." But the otherness is not really conceived as otherness if it remains in the aesthetic-cognitive realm and is not experienced as the otherness of the divine "Thou," whose freedom may conflict with my freedom.

"The meaning of the spatial symbols for divine transcendence," Tillich concludes, "is the possible conflict and the possible reconciliation of infinite and finite freedom" (*ST* 1.263). In a 1944 unpublished preliminary outline for the first volume of the *Systematic Theology*, Tillich further explains that when transcendence and immanence are directly contradictory, the contradiction is on the level of symbolic language.[66] The traditional

---

[66] Paul Tillich, "Systematic Theology, First Part: Preliminary Draft for the Private Use of My Students," unpub. manuscript (c. 1944), 7.

understandings of transcendence and immanence are only helpful to a point for Tillich, and the terms' inadequacies point for the need for better terminology and concepts.

To speak of transcendence or immanence in Tillich requires us to qualify the terms because of their Tillichian meanings. While there is what I would call *radical* immanence and *radical* transcendence in Tillich's system, the term *self-transcendence* is more commonly accepted by Tillich scholars. Beyond this, radical immanence and radical (self-)transcendence are not equally important concepts withiin a hierarchy of ideas, but they are interdependent and interrelated.[67] In the end, it is my opinion that a radical immanence is the most important over-arching concept in a Tillichian worldview.

Radical Transcendence and Self-Transcendence

If there is a God for Tillich, *Deus est esse ipsum*; and if one can state *Deus est esse ipsum* with religious faith and with literal meaning, then there is a radical transcendence in Tillich's theology. To connect a religious sense of "God" to ontological concepts, such as "the ground of being" would seem to "protect transcendence."[68] To connect religious God-language to *esse-ipsum* in this way implies a panentheism, a mystery in which we finite beings participate, but an "ineliminable mystery" (to use John Thatamanil's term) nonetheless.[69] Tillich's "God" in this sense is so big as this Inelimanable Mystery that all language that attempts to describe it is inadequate, if not poisonous, and the Inelimanable Mystery, while inelimanable, is Ultimately Unknown.[70]

Yet this panentheistic view, of God having a radically transcendent transcendence requires not only literalistic (if not simplistic) religious belief in God's existence, but also a simplistic interpretation of Tillich's understanding of transcendence. Lewis Ford writes that while, for Tillich, "[t]ranscendence requires radical otherness," this radical otherness cannot be obscured by Tillich's qualified *sense* of transcendence, namely, that "this transcendent power of being is called upon to provide the power of being

---

[67] This position is a minority one; the opposite is explicitly stated, for example, in Patricca ii or Stoker 107-108. Cf. Grigg (1985), 14, 16.
[68] Baker, 120.
[69] Thatamanil (2004), 28; cf. Martin Gallagher, "Paul Tillich, The Mystical Overcoming of Theism, and the Space for the Secular," *Bulletin of the North American Paul Tillich Society* 31.2 (2005), 11.
[70] Jonathan Kvanig, "Divine Transcendence," *Religious Studies* 20 (1984), 377.

appropriate to finite beings."[71] After all, as quoted before, for Tillich, the otherness of God "is not really conceived as otherness if it remains in the aesthetic-cognitive realm and is not experienced as the otherness of the divine 'Thou'" (*ST* 1.263). *If it remains in the aesthetic-cognitive realm*: if it is not taken in any literal sense as a religious belief.

Instead of a *radical* immanence, *self-transcendence* is a more appropriate description of Tillich's positive use of transcendence. In the concept of self-transcendence is a convergence of nearly all of Tillich's other primary concepts: the power of being, theology of culture, "the relations between meaning, courage, and the power of death (nonbeing)" all collapse in, as Robert Corrington puts it, "his analysis of the human process."[72] Since the concept of self-transcendence is so prevalent in his thought, it is discussed by Tillich throughout his body of work at various places. In *Theology of Culture*, he discusses self-transcendence as a consequence of theonomous thinking. As such, by thinking theonomously, "man discovers *himself* when he discovers God; he discovers something that is identical with himself although it transcends him infinitely, but from which he never has been and never can be separated." Like a "stranger" meets "God," Tillich writes, "[t]he meeting is accidental" (*TC* 10). In *My Search for Absolutes*, self-transcendence is "the cognitive encounter" of the realization of *Deus est esse ipsum* (*MSA* 127).

Elsewhere, Tillich describes self-transcendence as the theonomous moment for an individual, where she transcends herself in a kind of religious experience. It is, as Tillich quotes Søren Kierkegaard, "being grasped by an infinite interest and an infinite passion," that is, "a self-transcendence toward the ultimately sublime or…*holy*" (*SS* 159). The power of being, as the power of existential courage theonomously arising out of our depths, gives us the power to experience transcendence as a means of experiencing our selves' own finitude. William Stevens summarizes Tillich's concept of self-transcendence that while any sense of a "transcendent Being" can "only be spoken in broken analogy [and] not

---

[71] Lewis Ford, "Tillich's Tergiversations Toward the Power of Being," *Scottish Journal of Theology* 28.4 (1975), 340.
[72] R. Corrington (1994), 173.

ideological narrative" for Tillich it "provides the hope and goal of the reconstructed self."[73]

Participation of the finite in the infinite is a primary topic in the *Systematic Theology* volumes. Self-transcendence is participation in the infinite implicit of all that has being: *Deus est esse ipsum* (*ST* 1.190, 191). "Being-itself is not infinity; it is that which lies beyond the polarity of finitude and infinite drive of the finite beyond itself," Tillich writes, "[b]ut being-itself cannot be identified with infinity, that is, with the negation of finitude. It precedes the finite, and it proceeds the infinite negation of the finite" (1.190). *Esse-ipsum* remains beyond infinity; through self-transcendence we participate in infinity. This participation is, as it happens, a negation of our finitude, even though we remain grounded in infinity. This *ecstasy* is the same ecstasy implied in a Tillichian sense of ecstatic naturalism: as we are part of nature, we participate in infinity. As such, we *necessarily have the potentiality* for self-transcendence (2.5).[74]

This possibility for self-transcendence through theonomous thinking is, as a philosophical anthropology, what makes us *human*.[75] Tillich explains in a long passage from his second *Systematic Theology* volume:

> The term "self-transcendent" has two elements: "transcending" and "self." God as the ground of being infinitely transcends that of which he is the ground. He stands *against* the world, in so far as the world stands against him, and he stands *for* the world, thereby causing it to stand for him. This mutual freedom from each other and for each other is the only meaningful sense in which the "supra" in "supranaturalism" can be used. Only in this sense can we speak of "transcendent" with respect to the relation of God and the world. To call God transcendent in this sense does not mean that

---

[73] William Stevens, "Paul Tillich and the Postmodern Self," *Encountering Transcendence*, ed. Lieven Boeve, Hans Geybels, and Stijn Van den Bossche (Leuven: Peeters, 2005), 92. Cf. Anthony Padovano, *The Estranged God* (New York: Sheed and Ward, 1966), 239.
[74] According to Zietlow, Tillich's sense of "ecstatic self-transcendence" has its origins in Schelling's understanding of nature (Zietlow, 353, 56). Cf. Slavoj Žižek, "The Abyss of Freedom," *The Abyss of Freedom/Ages of the World* by Slavoj Žižek and F. W. J. Schelling (Ann Arbor, MI: Michigan UP, 1997), 6-7; F. W. J. Schelling, *Ages of the World*, in *The Abyss of Freedom/Ages of the World* by Slavoj Žižek and F. W. J. Schelling (Ann Arbor, MI: Michigan UP, 1997), 171ff., 181-182.
[75] Thatamanil (2006), 139; Jari Ristiiemi, *Experiential Dialectics* (Stockholm: Almqvist and Wiksell, 1987), 57, 66. Cf. Ryu, 174.

> one musty establish a "superworld" of divine objects. It does mean that, within itself, the finite world points beyond itself. In other words, it is self-transcendent. (*ST* 2.7)

Transcendence here is speaking of divinity in a religious sense, but there is no coincidence that Tillich has termed it *self*-transcendence. He explains further:

> Now the need for the syllable "self" in "self-transcendent" has also become understandable: the one reality which we encounter is experienced in different dimensions which point to one another. The finitude of the finite points to the infinity of the infinite. It goes beyond itself in order to return to itself in a new dimension. This is what "self-transcendence" means. In terms of immediate experience it is the encounter with the holy, and encounter which has ecstatic character. The term "ecstatic" in the phrase "ecstatic idea of God" points to the experience of the holy as transcending ordinary experience without removing it. Ecstasy as a state of mind is the exact correlate to self-transcendence as the state of reality. Such an understanding of the idea of God is neither naturalistic nor supranaturalistic. It underlies the whole of the present theological system. (*ST* 2.7-8)

Thinking theonomously to the point of self-transcendence is a congruent expression of an ecstatic state of mind. Finally, he continues:

> The self-transcendent idea of God replaces the spatial imagery— at least for theological thought—by the concept of finite freedom. The divine transcendence is identical with the freedom of the created to turn away from the essential unity with the creative ground of its being. Such freedom presupposes two qualities of the created: first, that it is substantially independent of the divine ground; second, that it remains in substantial unity with it. Without the latter unity, the creature would be without the power of being. It is the quality of finite freedom within the created which makes pantheism impossible and not for the notion of a highest being alongside the world, whether his relation to the world is described in deistic or theistic terms. (2.8)

Pantheism is impossible because there *is* transcendence within a world with ecstatic self-transcendence. If spatial transcendence is required for any traditional definition of Christianity, then Tillich here is being post-

Christian. For Tillich, no legitimate understanding of God is as a totality of "the household of reality," Richard Grigg writes, but instead "our pragmatic construct of the depth is the idea of the actual *unity of the possibilities of self-transcendence*, a whole greater than the sum of its parts."[76] Our religious experience, if it is genuine, is the experience of the power of being that comes with a realization of the necessity of our own possibility for transcendence. Through theonomous thinking (as Anselm put it, ~ □ ~ p) it is the '*acknowledgement of the necessity* of *Deus est esse-ipsum*' (or ◊p), that leads us to self-transcendence.[77]

As a *theonomous event*, self-transcendence arises out of our own personal "depth of darkness" implicit by our finitude (*SF* 50). Courage is the power of being that leads to self-transcendence. As the power over non-being and "the anxiety of fate and death," the courage to be transgresses against our self-negation (*CB* 158). To the contrary, self-transcendence is essential for *self-integration*, or the process of maturing the self. The transcendence remains *embodied*.[78] Tillich writes that

> self-transcendence remains within the limits of finite life. One finite situation is transcended by another; but finite life is not transcendence. Therefore, it seems appropriate to reserve the term "self-transcendence" for that function of life in which this does occur—in which life drives beyond itself as finite life. It is *self-transcendence* because life is not transcended by something that is not life. Life, by its nature as life, is both *in* itself and *above* itself, and this situation is manifest in the function of self-transcendence. (*ST* 3.31)

Self-transcendence occurs *within* the human reality of *life itself*, of *vita-ipsum*. It occurs when "life drives beyond itself as finite life." *In* and *above* itself, *within* the necessity and pervasiveness of life, self-transcendence is possible; when we speak of this life, we speak of *vita-ipsum*.[79]

---

[76] Richard Grigg, "Remaking Tillich as a Pragmatist," *Bulletin of the North American Paul Tillich Society* 30.2 (2004), 39, emph. add. Cf. George McLean, "Symbol and Analogy," *Paul Tillich in Catholic Thought*, ed. Thomas O'Meara and Celestin Weisser (Dubuque: Priory, 1964), 145.

[77] Patricca, 179-181; Sabin 62-63; Wainwright, 174.

[78] A. Reimer, "Prayer as *Unio Mystica*," *Das Gebet als Grundakt des Glaubens*, eds. Werner Schüßler and A. Reimer (Münster: LIT, 2004), 110, 129, 134.

[79] An opposing interpretation of Tillich's concept of self-transcendence, one that is extremely helpful to mine is Guy Hammond's. For Hammond, self-transcendence is more of a descriptive term to forward Tillich's depth psychology and not one which points to a

Radical Immanence

Through the idea of self-transcendence, Tillich has interpreted religious experience into the necessity and possibility of life itself, of *vita-ipsum*. Even though the notion of transcendence of Tillich is clearly not a *traditional* understanding of a "God's" spatial or temporal relationship to the "world," self-transcendence does indicate spatial or temporal relationality in a "qualitative" sense.[80] The ecology within which transcendence is possible is *vita-ipsum*, where time and space are perpetuating relational concepts. In this way, one may speak of a *radical immanence* which is *vita-ipsum*: it is the spiritual situation which is present, here-and-now, *the eternal now*.[81]

In a classic sermon, "The Eternal Now," on Revelation 21:6, Tillich preached that "[t]he mystery is that we *have* a present," explaining: "But there is no 'present' if we think of the never-ending flux of time. The riddle of the present is the deepest of all the riddles of time." (*EN* 130). Further:

> Again, there is no answer except from that which comprises all time and lies beyond it—the eternal. Whenever we say "now" or "today," we stop the flux of time for us. We accept the present and we do not care that it is gone in the moment that we accept it. We live in it and it is renewed for us in every new "present." This is possible because every moment of time reaches into the eternal. It is the eternal that stops the flux of time for us. It is the eternal "now" which provides for us a temporal "now." But sometimes it breaks powerfully into our consciousness and gives us the certainty of the eternal, of a dimension of time which cuts into time and gives us our time. (130-131)

"People who are never aware of this dimension," Tillich adds, "lose the possibility of resting in the present." To live in the present is to have the "courage to accept 'presence' because it has lost the dimension of the eternal"(131). In other words, to *authentically* live in the present is to accept the temporal paradox of time and trust in the possibility of an existence (*or* existing) absolutely *within* and *beyond* time.

---

radical immanence. See Guy Hammond, *The Power of Self-Transcendence* (St. Louis: Bethany, 1966), esp. 37, 65, 144, 146; and ibid. (1964), 290-291. Cf. Hammond (1965), 138; *ST* 1.190-1; Will Herberg archive, folio 169: "Paul Tillich and Contemporary Theology" (1974), 2; Ryu, 177.
[80] Ryu, 178; Victor Taylor, "Theography," *Secular Theology*, ed. Clayton Crockett (London: Routledge, 2001): 189-197. Cf. Sabin, 69; Padovano, 237.
[81] Choi, 5. Cf. Osborne, 18.

Tillich's immanence of the eternal now is an interpretation of one of Nietzsche's most perplexing philosophical concepts, the eternal return of the same. For Nietzsche, the eternal return is declared by Zarathustra as surely as it is declared ambiguously: the idea is contrary, systematic, fragmented, and symphonic at once. To be sure, the concept of the eternal recurrence of the same is an inherently *simple* idea, which Nietzsche traces from Heraclitus and the Stoics, though other nineteenth century thinkers, such as Novalis and Friedrich Schlegel, have also tried to resurrect the idea.[82] The eternal return, as Nietzsche describes it, is "the unconditional and infinitely repeated circular course of things," denies the *linear* understanding of time or history that is commonly accepted in the Western world and advocates for a *circular* view of history.[83]

To be brief, the eternal return of the same suggests that all that has happened infinitely recurs, along with all that is to be in the future. All is cyclically occurring, eternally recurring. Everything that happens will infinitely happen, just as everything that has passed will infinitely repeat. The future is eternally happening; it is all the *same*. The eternal return of the same can be interpreted from a kind of Kantian ethical perspective, that one should live every moment *as if* one were to eternally live each moment, but the eternal return has much more literally to say about humanity than morality. Nietzsche writes in *The Gay Science*:

> *The greatest weight.* – What if some day or night a demon were to steal after you into your loneliest loneliness and say to you; "This life as you now live it and have lived it, you will have to love once more and innumerable times more; and there will be nothing new in it, but every pain and every joy and every thought and sigh and everything unutterably small or great in your life will have to

---

[82] Kaufmann (1974), 321. Cf. Sabin, 61.

[83] Nietzsche, *Ecce Homo* 3 (p. 273-274). Further: "I have the right to understand myself as the first *tragic philosopher*—that is, the most extreme opposite and antipode of a pessimistic philosopher. Before me this transposition of the Dionysian into a philosophical pathos did not exist: *tragic wisdom* was lacking; I have looked in vain for signs of it even among the *great* Greeks in philosophy, those of the two centuries *before* Socrates. I retained some doubt in the case of *Heraclitus*, in whose proximity I feel altogether warmer and better than anywhere else. The affirmation of passing away *and destroying*, which is the decisive feature of a Dionysian philosophy; saying Yes to opposition and war; *becoming*, along with a radical repudiation of the very concept of *being*—all this is clearly more closely related to me than anything else thought to date. The doctrine of the "eternal recurrence," that is, of the unconditional and infinitely repeated circular course of all things—this doctrine of Zarathustra *might* in the end have been taught already by Heraclitus. At least the Stoa has traces of it, and the Stoics inherited almost all of their principal notions from Heraclitus."

return to you, all in the same succession and sequence—even this spider and this moonlight between the trees, and even this moment and I myself. The eternal hourglass of existence is turned upside down again and again, and you with it, speck of dust!"

Would you not throw yourself down and gnash your teeth and curse the demon who spoke thus? Or have you once experienced a tremendous moment when you would have answered him: "You are a god and never have I heard anything more divine?" If this thought gained possession of you, it would change you as you are or perhaps crush you. The question in each and every thing, "Do you desire this once more and innumerable times more?" would lie upon your actions as the greatest weight. Or how well disposed would you have to become to yourself and to life *to crave nothing more fervently* than this ultimate eternal confirmation and seal?[84]

While the eternal return is a kind of apocalyptic ethics for Nietzsche, it is more of a philosophical anthropology. As such, the eternal return points to the polarizations and ambiguities of the human condition: it points to human frailness, brokenness, terror, and tragedy as much as it suggests the possibility for the will to power, hope, and genuine "gospel" of humanity. The presence of the demon that Nietzsche describes demands one of two responses—it either crushes or changes the individual, or it causes enormous angst or tremendous joy for the possibility of *becoming* eternally joyful. The eternal return is the "eternal confirmation and seal" of humanity's perplexing condition—one may wear it as an affirmative confirmation of faith in oneself or a seal of one's own fallenness and negative fate.

For Tillich, the death of the Ptolemaic universe—the *death of God*—is the signification for a radical immanence of life (*SS* 186). In fact, according to Ronald Stone, it was the *experience* of the death of "the God of king and fatherland" for Tillich that led him to accept Nietzsche's Dionysian "elements," that is, to seek a theology which is "seeking life in affirmative actions beyond bourgeois morality" as something not only to be *believed* and *preached*, but "lived."[85] Jacob Taubes explains that within the Dionysian *vita-ipsum*,

---

[84] Nietzsche, *Gay Science*, 241 (p. 273-274). Cf. Kaufmann (1974), 322-323.
[85] Stone, 36. Cf. ibid. 34, 35.

> The ecstasy does not lead to a "beyond," in a supernaturalistic sense, but signifies an "intensity" of the immanent. In the last analysis, it is the idea of a Dionysiac theology that secretly impels all philosophical theology, and in the convergence and union of the bacchantic dance and mystery of the cross, I see the mythical original of the dialectical method.

Self-transcendence (ecstasy) suggests the *intensity* of *vita-ipsum*. And, as Tillich said, the ontological assumption of *Deus est esse ipsum*, in Taubes' words, "impels all thought." "Nietzsche's last utterances point in the same direction," Taubes explains:

> At the end of his *Ecce Homo*, Dionysus stands symbolically against the Crucified. In the letters and fragments, however, written in a last clarity of mind before he entered into the night of madness, the veil is lifted from Nietzsche's ultimate concern: Dionysus and the Crucified, merged into one symbol.... Hence, Tillich's ontological interpretation of theology, which is his most original contribution, adds a chapter to the history of Dionysiac theology in the Christian frame of reference.
>
> ....
>
> Tillich's Dionysiac theo-*logy* challenges the ecstatic Dionysiacs like Ludwig Klages, [Arnold] Keyserling, and other disciples of the pagan cult, who descend into the night and worship earth, race, blood, [and] flesh as sacred powers, abhorring reason as the enemy of the soul. The spirit pulses through the Dionysiac elements in Tillich's theology, which tries to reconcile the powers of the deep that are sacred and the powers of light that are divine. The spirit does not live in enmity with life, but even the abyss of being is illuminated by a logos.[86]

For Taubes, Tillich is a genuine continuation of Nietzsche's Dionysian resurrection, a reconciliation of "the powers of the deep that are sacred and the powers of light that are divine." Thomas Altizer would later write of Taubes' interpretation of Tillich that as a Dionysiac theology, "all supernaturalistic symbols" are now expressed in "immanent terms,"

---

[86] Taubes (1954), 21-22.

following Nietzsche, whose "Dionysian program" was to make "immanent of the transcendent."[87]

Tillich concludes his "Eternal Now" sermon, having done the *philosophy*, that is, asked the big questions, to end with the *theology*, the big answer. "There is *one* power that surpasses the all-consuming power of time—the eternal." Tillich continues, on Christ, "He Who was and is and is to come, the beginning and the end," concluding: "He gives us forgiveness for what has passed. He gives us courage for what is to come. He gives us rest in His eternal Presence" (*EN* 132). But, Altizer observes, this Christ which "produces an existential intensity which deepens man's participation in being, his existence in the immediate moment" is a Christ of *immanence*, and is not the Christ of transcendent Christianity. Instead, in Tillich there is a radical reversal of Christ so that, given Taubes' Dionysian observations, "it is not Christ but Dionysus who triumphs in Tillich's ontological eschatology."[88]

Vita-ipsum, as the existential milieu of individualization, participation, self-integration, and self-transcendence, *is the perpetuating eschatological eruption of the present as the lived content of the eternal now.*[89] "Although everything remains the same," from moment to moment in the eternal now, Charles Winquist writes, "everything is changed." Through the metaphor of the New Being, or Christ, "the discursive complex" within which "the finite, transcendent, and temporal remain…has been radically transformed." Winquist writes further that Tillich's eschatological language of the Eternal Now is a "theological assertion of the identity of God with being-itself when it bears witness to the *otherness* of God."[90] All sense of the traditional understanding of *transcendence*—divinity as 'other'—collapses "into vacuousness" in the Eternal Now; the fullness of the immanence of the present, *vita-ipsum*, is implicit of the *esse-ipsum* which is the *prius* of thought.[91] As this immanence is an "eschatological figuration," it is, Winquist observes, "*metonymical.*"[92]

---

[87] Altizer, "Nietzsche's Understanding" (1958/1960), 10.
[88] Ibid. Cf. Stevens, 89.
[89] Paul Bischoff, "*Participation:* Ecclesial Praxis with a Crucified God for the World," *Journal for Christian Theological Research* 8 (2003), 26.
[90] Charles Winquist, "Eschatology in the Thought of Paul Tillich," *New Creation or Eternal Now*, ed. Gert Hummel (Berlin: Walter de Gruyter, 1991), 201, 202.
[91] Carter, 122.
[92] Winquist (1991), 201, emph. add.

The Holy and the Not-Yet-Holy

In an early review of Tillich's third volume of the *Systematic Theology*, Thomas Altizer asked: "Has Tillich collapsed theology into ontology? Has he transformed the sacred into the secular? Is Tillich's theonomy ultimately Nietzsche's eternal recurrence?" and "[A]re we to assume that biblical faith has evolved to a theonomous form, that the sacred has become united with the secular?" Altizer concludes that "[n]eedless to say, Tillich never focuses on such questions." All of these divergent ideas and concepts—theology and philosophy, Christ and Dionysus, theism and atheism, sacred and secular—all seem to collapse together into Tillich's notion of theonomy.[93]

Although the tension between the sacred and secular is pervasive throughout Tillich's theology, he only discusses the ideas in a few places and develops them briefly.[94] Nonetheless, Tillich's fondness for Rudolph Otto's shift to the abstraction of "the holy," or *"Das Heilige,"* as the "numinous" indicates Tillich's passion for developing an ontological language as a non-religious alternative to "God."[95] Because of the absolute prevalence of *esse-ipsum*, the "holy" is inescapable so long as human thinking is experiencing and interpreting the world. "Never consider the secular realm Godless just because it does not speak of God," Tillich wrote: "To speak of a realm of divine creation and providence as Godless *is* Godless. It denies God's power over the world. It would force God to confine Godself to religion and the church" (*IRR* 62-63). Furthermore, it is demonic to think of the "secular" as independent from the "sacred," in fact, to draw such a division is not only Godless and demonic, but is indicative of "the basic evil in humanity's predicament" (51). Theonomous thinking resists thinking that opposes the sacred and the secular as a process of "de-demonizing" religious thought (*FR* 89). In fact, Tillich described his theology of culture as a means of escaping a false, religious construction of the secular (*PE* 57).

There are two different usages of the terminology of "sacred" and "secular" in Tillich's thought; the first is in a historical understanding of secularization and assumptive origins about the holiness or evil of 'space.'[96]

---

[93] Altizer, "A Theonomy in Our Time?" (1963), 358, 359, 362.
[94] Vahanian (2004), 5.
[95] Rudolf Otto, *The Idea of the Holy*, trans. John Harvey (London: Oxford UP, 1923), 5ff; Terrance Thomas, "Paul Tillich and Mircea Eliade and Their Use of Paradox," *The Theological Paradox*, ed. Gert Hummel (Berlin: Walter de Gruyter, 1995), 247ff.
[96] Vahanian (2004), 36.

To think through the secular—without spatially constructing it as an oppositional sphere or realm against the sacred—is to "use the secular as a critical tool against" religion itself (*FR* 82). Tillich explains in a lecture recorded in the collection *My Search for Absolutes* that

> The immediate consequence of the Thirty Years' War was the most powerful development of secularization in all history, beginning with the secular state that took control in order to save Europe from complete self-destruction. At the same time, a secularized philosophy and the relativizing tendency that went with scientific progress undercut the struggling churches' claims to absoluteness. Secularism in this sense can be considered a judgment by the true Absolute of demonic claims to absoluteness made by particular religions and by groups within a particular religion. (*MSA* 133)

The secularization of Europe had positive and negative effects—the most negative being the resistance of religions against secularism, which led to further demonization of religions. The secularizing force also led to the creation of quasi-religions, religious expressions not rooted in the ultimate. He explains further:

> [T]he relation of religion to the secular world, to secularism, must be changed from both sides, from the secular as well as from the religious side. Religion must affirm the right of all functions of the human spirit—the arts and sciences, the law and social relations and the state beyond them—to be independent of religious control or interference. At the same time, the secular world must affirm the right of religion to turn toward the Ultimate-itself in its language and in all its expressions of the experience of the holy. (141)

Between any constructed sense of the "sacred" and "secular" there must exist a balance. Constructed boundaries of the two are not genuine religious expressions but are rather "man's reaction against being without a structure of meaning." Authentic religion "acknowledge[s] this struggle" and resists "arrogant dogmatism" (142).

The second use of Tillich's understanding of "sacred" and "secular" is related to ecstatic self-transcendence. In Tillich's final lecture, "The Significance of the History of Religions for the Systematic Theologian," he states that '[t]he sacred does not lie beside the secular, but it is its depths."

Any sense of the sacred must be understood as "the creative ground and at the same time a critical judgment of the secular....a judgment which must use the secular as a tool of one's own religious reflection" (*FR* 82). The sacred is *in* the secular (82-83). He expounds later in the lecture:

> You know the meaning of the term, profane, "to be before the doors of the sanctuary" and the meaning of the secular, "belonging to the world." In both cases somebody leaves the ecstatic, mysterious fear of the Holy for the world of ordinary rational structures. It would be easy to fight against this, to keep the people in the sanctuary if the secular had not been given critical function by itself. And this makes the problem so serious. The secular is the rational and the rational must judge the irrationality of the Holy. It must judge its demonization. (89)

To render the secular is to be critical of religion when it should be critical and is a form of self-discovery that leads to *self-transcendence*. To resist the power of the sacred within the sacred is to accept the profanity of the world, which Tillich calls "'resisting self-transcendence,' that is, remaining before the door of the temple, standing outside of the holy": rejecting *esse-ipsum* as the *prius* of thought (*ST* 3.87).[97] From an acceptance that "[e]verything secular is potentially sacred" (*ST* 1.217), Tillich writes, "a profound dialectic appears": "The secular which is right in fighting against the demonization of the Holy, becomes empty and becomes victim of ... [the] 'quasi-religious,' which implies "an oppressiveness like the demonic elements of the religious." In *theonomy*—"the Religion of the Concrete Spirit"—the sacred and secular *fragment*, as "eschatological fulfillment" (*FR* 90).

This apocalyptic sense of the secular, as the not-yet-holy, yet with the holy residing within it, suggests an historical understanding of the ontology of the world. It is, as a dialectical understanding of the sacred, a *diachrony* of the sacred.[98] Tillich's understanding of "eschatology" is "looking at that which is not yet and will come" (*RPT* 17). The sacred seeks out the not-yet-holy and could be described as having "a passion for the profane."[99] At the same time, an incarnational theology must render such thinking of secular to sacred dialectically with a procession from sacred to secular, as well. Taking queue from the liturgical expression *saecula*

---

[97] Ross, "A Form of Ontological Argument" (1977), 134.
[98] Ibid. 84.
[99] Ibid. 3.

saeculorum ("world without end") Gabriel Vahanian interprets Tillich's diachronic eschatology as designating "the eternal as it breaks into time, a *kairos*, a worlding of the Word become flesh."[100] "The secular is not merely secular," Vahanian explains: "Nothing is secular that is not at the same time symmetrical with something religious. And just that is the paramount reason why traditional [Christianity] must address its own irrelevance."[101]

For Tillich, when the holy theonomously breaks through the secular, holy objects (as symbols) become "mediums" for the holy (*ST* 1.216). This epiphany of the holy is a "breaking" of the present order, a "disruption," and a "transformation" (*OB* 72). The content of *vita-ipsum* mediates the sacred and profane. To think otherwise, for Tillich, would be to accept the demonic powers implicit in religious belief by absolutizing that which is not absolute, which Tillich refers to being a rejection of sacramental power. Beyond this, to think contrary to Tillich is to reject hopefulness for the not-yet-holy, to not have what he calls "the element of 'ought to be'" (*FR* 87). To be sure, there is also a hopefulness for the not-yet-secular, as well, since, in some cases for Tillich, Vahanian writes, "nothing is more religious than the secular and more secular than the religious." "It bears repeating," he observes, "they belong together" even if they are not polar opposites.[102] The diachrony of the sacred and the secular for Tillich is indicative of the power of transcendence's ability to not simply change the world, but to change *our* worlds.[103]

Following Vahanian's reading of Tillich, this latter understanding of the ideas of the *sacred* and the *secular* is a reinvention of traditional terminology, just as, I have shown, Tillich has done to so many other theological terms. (Some of the clumsiness of Tillich's development of these terms, Vahanian mentions, was a result of a cultural difference between Germans and Americans regarding the language of "sacred" and

---

[100] Gabriel Vahanian, "Theology and the Secular," *Secular Theology*, ed. Clayton Crockett (London: Routledge, 2001), 13, 23 n. 1. Cf. Georgia Harkness, *The Recovery of Religion* (New York: Henry Holt, 1936), 69-70; Catherine Keller, *Face of the Deep* (London: Routledge, 2003), 74.

[101] Vahanian (2001), 1. Vahanian explains further: "To wit Israel: instead of merely remembering the past, listens to that God that would be no God should God make room for the world and hold there be no world here and now, should there not be once and for all the world as ephemeral and contingent as it is secular, i.e. a pro-vision of the new heaven and the new earth, of the newness of the world—its worldhood."

[102] Vahanian (2001), 11, 13; cf. ibid. (1961), 65ff.; ibid., *Wait Without Idols* (New York: Braziller, 1964), 235.

[103] Weil Eggen, Rev. of *Paul Tillich and the New Religious Paradigm* by Gabriel Vahanian, *Exchange* 34.1 (2005), 81.

"secular.") Although the sacred operates dialectically, the sacred is not in a polar-binary dialectic with the secular; rather, the sacred operates *within* the secular.[104] By shifting the notions of sacred and secular to the holy and the not-yet-holy (and the not-yet-secular), Vahanian argues that transcendence has now become an immanence as the immanence of *vita-ipsum*.[105] Clayton Crockett writes that in Vahanian's reading of Tillich, "the *saeculum*," as *vita-ipsum*, "implies that we live in a world of immanence which functions as the location of human and divine meaning and value."[106]

Metonymical Immanence

Should we take this immanence as an actual, philosophical metaphysics? Does Tillich *really* believe that there is a diachronical ontology pervasive throughout the world? I suggest that Tillich's thought leads us into a state of theonomous thinking where we can accept the metonymy implicit in Tillich's theology. Beyond this, this metonymy points us toward an understanding that all theology is metonymical; and, as such, all hermeneutics is metonymical. By *metonymy*, I refer to the rhetorical move of replacing one idea or concept for another which is related (such as an attribute), but not necessarily a literal identification. Clearly, much of Tillich's innovation and genius is in his ability to reinterpret traditional Christian theological concepts that would seem to be post-Christian, rather than Christian ideas; the post-Christian theological language is then used and morphed within a systematized Christian theology. The term *metonymy* comes from the Latin *meonymia* and the Greek *metonumia*, 'name change.' In psychology, metonymy is a manifestation of schizophrenic behavior when appropriate words are substituted for inappropriate words.

Tillich's metonymic theological behavior points toward theology as a *kind* of madness. By "madness" I refer to the madness of which Plato writes in the *Phaedrus* that connects language, memory, and ontology.[107] Beyond this, those whose madness is connected to their high abilities with language are said by Plato (speaking through the voice of Socrates) to be

---

[104] Vahanian (2001) 23 n. 1, 13; Clayton Crockett, "Introduction," *Secular Theology*, ed. Clayton Crocket (London: Routledge, 2001), 1. Cf. Eggen, 81.
[105] Vahanian (1964), 233.
[106] Crockett, "Introduction" (2001), 1.
[107] Plato, *Phaedrus*, 249D (p. 37). For Plato, the philosopher, the one enlightened with theonomous thinking is unable to "rise up" to the Forms through earthly, banal beauty; and in turn, his or her behavior is branded with "the charge that he has gone mad" (249E). Cf. Stoker, 108; Lovejoy, 11, 315, 317; A. Thatcher, *The Ontology of Paul Tillich* (Oxford: Oxford UP, 1978), 86.

"the ones who tell the future," which is to say, "weaving insanity into prophecy."[108] The madness of Tillich's theology is that for all of his voluminous writing and preaching, there is little outright commitment to the Christian *faith* despite an obsession with an *engagement* with the Christian faith's ideas, symbols, and traditions. For example, Tillich writes while discussing the sacred and the secular:

> Let me say something in a well known, popular form. The reformers were right when they said that every day is the Lord's Day and, therefore, they devalued the sacredness of the seventh day. *But in order to say this, there must have been a Lord's Day, and that not only once upon a time but continuously* in counter-balance against the overwhelming weight of the secular. (*FR* 82-83, emph. add)

The third sentence above, I believe, is revealing. Tillich does not say "in order to say *this*," as a statement to which Tillich agrees, "there must have been a Lord's Day, and not only once upon a time but continuously in counter-balance against the overwhelming weight of the secular." He escapes making a *literal* commitment to a "Lord's Day," but also avoids an *actual* one. Instead, "in order to say this," Tillich qualifies, "*that* not only once upon a time but continuously."

Even when engaging a basic theological concept of Christian faith and practice, the ideas and commitment to a Christian interpretation of history—that is, a historical aspect of ontology—is abstracted. In another text, Tillich uses the same example of the Lord's Day to make the same argument about the sacred and the secular to explicitly point toward an anthropology (*IRR* 51). The point about the Lord's Day is not history, it is not really about the sacred and the secular, nor is it at bottom a theological anthropology. Rather, *Tillich is offering a system of metaphors and symbols as a madness we may choose to live within*. He is offering, as he writes in *The Recovery of the Prophetic Tradition in the Reformation*, a "positive description of man" (*RPT* 17). In another essay, where Tillich discusses the spiritual practice of devotion to the crucifixion, he speaks of it as a *devotion to a*

---

[108] Plato, *Phaedrus*, 244C (p. 25). These individuals, by virtue of their madness, are epistemologically *above* other humans' ability for knowledge, even in its greatness (what Plato calls "*oionoïstic*" or "*oionistic*"); and their madness is both godly and demonstrates the reality of humans' past lives (244D-245C). Further: "Similarly, the clear-headed study of the future, which uses birds and other signs, was originally called *oionoïstic*, since it uses reasoning to bring intelligence and learning into human thought, but now modern speakers call it *oionistic*, in both name and achievement, madness from a god is finer than self-control of human origin, according to the testimony of the ancient language givers" (244C-244D).

devotion—though a powerful, meaningful devotion—which is symbolic of something else, which is "*a* symbolic expression for an experience of what concerns us ultimately."[109]

Again, it is a theological anthropology *in which we may choose to live.* Even Tillich admits very quickly in the second volume of the *Systematic Theology* that "Being as such...does not designate anything real," and then to speak of the existence of God as within the realm of *possibility* (*ST* 2.11). The whole of Tillich's thought, beginning with the ontological assumption of *Deus est esse ipsum* and the necessity of being-itself ($\Diamond p$), then, must be regarded, as a whole, as an unlikely reality. Yet it is the reality in which Tillich advocates and chooses to live. "The ground of the discussion" for Tillich, then, has shifted to "meaning."[110] It is in this aspect of Tillich which Tillich emerges as an existentialist: we are forced to live within a plane of immanence, *vita-ipsum*, and our fundamental realities consequently flow from the meaning which we ascribe to our realities. As Charles Winquist observes: "An ultimate concern is an existential concern. It has a place. Life is not elsewhere or nowhere."[111]

"To think like Tillich," Robert Scharlemann writes, requires a "second naiveté."[112] This naiveté is clearly beyond any literal or critical assumption about religion, but seems to choose and accept the likely falsehood or madness of religious thinking against the odds of doubt because choosing to be-in-the-world in this manner, for Tillich, is a genuine life worth living. When we have control of our reality through choice, we are in control of our selves, our own immanences; and we choose positive religious experience against the negative.[113] Following the continuing theme that doubt is required for faith ("[t]he courage to be is rooted in the God who appears when God has disappeared in the anxiety of doubt"), the disconnection between theological gesture and reality, as an expression of doubt, is the way in which religious madness might be tolerable or authentic for Tillich (*CB* 190). Winquist writes that the reason

---

[109] Tillich, "The Religious Symbol" (1961), 301.
[110] Julia Mitchell, "The Theist-Atheist Controversy," *Religious Humanism* 17 (1983), 169. Cf. *WR* 70-72.
[111] Charles Winquist, "Untimely History," *Truth and History*, ed. Gert Hummel (Berlin: Walter de Gruyter, 1998), 70.
[112] Scharlemann (1978), 78.
[113] Charles Winquist, "Heterology and Ontology in the Thought of Paul Tillich," *God and Being: The Problem of Ontology in the Philosophical Theology of Paul Tillich/ Gott und Sein* (Berlin: Walter de Gruyter, 1989), 70; Robert Scharlemann, *Reflection and Doubt in the Thought of Paul Tillich* (New Haven, CT: Yale UP, 1969), 15n.

why "foundational categories of Tillich's theology are neither purely epistemological or purely ontological," nor anthropological, philosophical, or Biblical, is because they are "boundary concepts" on the *edge of language* that provide "a double-edged quality of a frame." As a frame the boundary concepts "introduce an ambiguity" in the "functioning" of *vita-ipsum*. Outside of any religious value of the idea of *esse-ipsum*, "without any reference beyond itself," it "doesn't mean anything."[114]

Nels Ferré, who was close to Tillich, wrote shortly after Tillich's death, as mentioned earlier, that to think of many traditional theological concepts to have any literal or traditional meaning is "nonsense," and further, there is no literal sense of transcendence in Tillich. "The key to Tillich's view of the transcendent," referring to transcendence as *God*, Ferré wrote, "is that there is no transcendent realm, *only transcendent meaning*."[115] To critics of Tillich, who claim that *esse-ipsum* is not a God worthy of worship, a proper response is that *esse-ipsum* has no meaning if one places meaning in the worship of beings.[116] Other typical responses to Tillich, such as Bishop Fulton Sheen's public remarks in *Cosmopolitan* regarding Tillich's understanding of doubt—"Go to confession first, and then we'll discuss your doubts"—also miss the *point* of Tillich on numerous levels.[117] Such "hard readings" of Tillich are misreadings of Tillich, even if they are fairly typical of responses to Tillich from both church and academic circles.[118]

The immanence of life, *vita-ipsum*, made meaningful by a positive vision led Tillich as a theologian to engage the "homiletical situation" and preach what was Good News to him.[119] A central assumption of this situation is that while we all live and experience *vita-ipsum*, it is "divinely ordinary." "It is good news," Winquist writes, "that life can be lived meaningfully under the conditions of finite existence and that there is meaning in meaninglessness and despair."[120] Theology provides us for the possibility of a "New Reality;" that is, the means by which we may divinize

---

[114] Winquist (2003), 137, 138.
[115] Ferré (1966), 7, 10, emph. add.
[116] Ross, "God and Singular Experience" (1977), 133.
[117] Quoted in T. F. James, "The Agony of Religious Doubt," *Cosmopolitan* (Dec. 1959), 90.
[118] Winquist (2003), 215.
[119] Hyung Suk Na, *Paul Tillich's Theology of Preaching*, Ph.D. diss., Drew U. (1996), 75ff. Cf. *An Experiment Communicating the Numinous Through Preaching*, D.Min. diss., Drew U. (1979).
[120] Charles Winquist, "Theology Beside Itself," *The Theological Paradox*, ed. Gert Hummel (Berlin: Walter de Gruyter, 1995), 19.

the banal and make meaning and value out of the plane of immanence implicit within *vitae-ipsum*.[121] To say yes to meaningfulness requires courage, and even moreso to recognize that the yes-saying is an intentional construction of reality. The acknowledging that "[t]he world does not have to be more than it is meaningful" is the *courage to be*: "it is lived and thought in the ironic necessity of saying yes to divine ordinariness."

To do this, Winquist further interprets from Tillich, one requires a radically theonomous, "new thinking" that Scharlemann describes as an 'indescribably strange' kind of thinking.[122] Clayton Crockett describes this thinking as committing the death of God. He explains that by this he does not mean either "the traditional notion of God dying kenotically on the cross, nor the expiration of deity in the modern world." Instead, since all theology becomes symbolic, or systems of symbols, theology becomes freed from "cosmological discourse." As such, Tillich, by *thinking the death of God* has *deconstructed* theology.[123] With the death of God, the deconstruction of theology, the self is also "opened" and "de-centered" through "the processes of reflective self-transcendence and transformation" to resist "totalization, closure, stagnation," and other "inhibitions" of "self-transcendence."[124]

Tillich, following the form of the rest of his theological thinking, even uses the symbol of the Kingdom of God to describe this state of *vita-ipsum*. Taking Jesus' riddle of the Kingdom of God in Luke 17:20-21, Tillich writes:

> The Kingdom of God is…independent from every form, even the churchly and confessional. It breaks into the world of relativity in every period and every place, whatever the unconditioned is experienced through any relative form. Because it is independent from every form, however, it is mediated through the destiny-bearing mass which is never and nowhere a *massa perditionis*, but

---

[121] Na, 356.
[122] Winquist (1995), 19, 13; Scharlemann (1978), 78. Cf. John Dourley, "The Problem with Essentialism," *Paul Tillich's Theological Legacy*, ed. Frederick Parrella (Berlin: Walter de Gruyter, 1995), 133.
[123] Crockett, "Contact Epistemology for the Sites of Theology" (2001), 206.
[124] James DiCenso, "Anxiety, Risk and Transformation," *Secular Theology*, ed. Clayton Crockett (London: Routledge, 2001), 56. Cf. ibid. 52.

always and everywhere a *massa sancta* through the paradox of the unconditional.[125]

In the immanence of *vita-ipsum*, Tillich's theology offers an escape from *massa perditionis* and exposes other destructive options that claim to be holy. This experience of choosing *massa sancta* over *perditionis* is the "Gestalt of grace," a "reality" into which we are "drawn" (*PE* 211). The *faith* implicit in *vita-ipsum* choosing *sancta* is a healing act of the self to live "courageously" with tensions, to choose a dialectical system of theology over the stagnancy of the literal, and "to discover finally...ultimate unity in the depths of our own souls and in the depth of the divine life" (*BR* 85).[126] Faith informed by the death of God is the transition, Tillich writes, from a theological assumption of "thou shalt" to "I will" (*PPT* 201-202) and involves a risk (*TC* 27).

The Dialectic of Theism and Atheism

As such, we are, at our most basic authentic state, living the immanence of *vita-ipsum*. The question of whether there is a God or not is not an intelligible question for Tillich; rather, the *kind* of God in which one chooses to believe is an existentially important choice, and our theological choices reflect the brokenness, vagueness, or ambiguities about our selves. Through self-transcendence we become more self-aware and self-assertive; and through self-transcendence the immanence of life, *vita-ipsum*, becomes more clear.

Vita-ipsum may be understood as reflective of Tillich's correlative dialectical method.[127] "Life itself is dialectical," Tillich writes in the second volume of the *Systematic Theology*, and if life is "applied symbolically to the divine life, God as living God must be described as dialectical statements" (*ST* 2.90). The dialectic of theism and atheism runs throughout Tillich's thought. From *Deus est esse ipsum* to the declaration that "God does not exist" and from the assumption that "to argue that God exists is to deny him" to the implicit piety of the denial of God, the meaning of Tillich's ideas are often subtle and obscure outside of the entire context of his project (*ST*

---

[125] Tillich, quoted from "Masse und Geist," in A. Reimer, "The Kingdom of God in the Thought of Emmanuel Hirsch and Paul Tillich," *New Creation or Eternal Now*, ed. Gert Hummel (Berlin: Walter de Gruyter, 1991), 49.
[126] Padovano 238. Cf. ibid. 237; Reimer, (1991), 47, 50; *PE* 163; Stevens, 85; Albert Winn, "Holy Spirit and the Christian Life," *Interpretation* 33 (1979), 55; George Kelsey, George Kelsey archive, Drew University, Box 34, Fl. 2.
[127] Hammond (1964), 290.

1.205, *EN* 98). The negation of "God" and "theological theism" into an atheism is an implicit step along Tillich's intellectual journey toward an acceptance of the immanence of *vita-ipsum* (*PPT* 207, *CB* 185, *BR* 83).

The dialectic of the sacred, that is, the acknowledgement of the non-theistic nature of the immanence of *vita-ipsum*, is the dialectic of atheism and theism. This dialectic is not a bifurcated polar binary; rather, theism dialectically comes about only within the context of atheism. Beyond this, it only grows, deepens, changes, and matures dialectically against and because of atheism, which holds the possibility of the negation of all theism. Atheism is contingent upon theism—not in the popular sense of *atheism* as a simple rejection—because *some* theism, even if it is *atheistic* (in the popular sense), must arise from the atheism of *vita-ipsum*. We must ascribe meaning to life, even if it is descriptively meaningless. To *choose* a positive theology, an actually life-rendering belief, is what Tillich calls "absolute faith" (*CB* 185). "Absolute faith" he explains, "and its consequences, the courage that takes the radical doubt, the doubt about God, into itself, transcends the idea of God" (182).

Through the identification of theology as a *gesture* through which meaning and value are placed upon reality, Winquist writes, "Tillich gives credibility to theological thinking."[128] Theology within the *vita-ipsum* does not attempt to be something it is not and does not aim to transform finitude into an absolute. Rather, it is believable because it is unbelievable, fantastic because it is fantastical. Theology drives us toward life rather than death and appreciating the life offered to us in the immanent, even and especially if there is hope for more while remaining rooted in immanence. It is a radical immanence because self-transcendence is a theological construction contingent upon its immanence. The *possibility* of theology makes the immanence of *vita-ipsum* radical.

---

[128] Winquist (2003), 230-1. He continues: "He gives credibility to a theology that is situated in a history and in the world. He gives credibility to thinking in the think specificity of symbolic life. He gives credibility to a theology of the religion of the concrete spirit." Cf. Zietlow, 19.

Part Two

Thomas Altizer and the Gospel of Christian Atheism

So far as I am concerned, I don't know who I am going to miss more, God or Paul Tillich!

Rev. David Clyburn
Letter to Thomas Altizer
11. November 1965

If God is God, his death is also his supreme strangeness.

Jean-Luc Nancy
The Inoperative Community

[T]he voice of honest indignation is/ the voice of God...

William Blake
"The Marriage of Heaven and Hell"
Pl. 12, Ln. 9-10

For only that which has actuality begun can actually die, and if God has truly and actually died then God Himself is inevitably the consequence of a truly actual genesis or beginning.

Thomas J. J. Altizer
LDG 133

Introduction to Part Two

Thomas J. J. Altzier may be one of the most unlikely figures to rise to prominence in the history of Christian theology in the second half of the twentieth century. Altizer's academic background was not in theology but in the history of religions; Altizer never taught regularly in a theological school; most of his career was spent working in an English department for a public university (SUNY at Stony Brook); and Altizer was never ordained.

As it happens, Altizer was not ordained by the Episcopal Church because he did not pass the church's required psychological exams. He writes on an experience shortly before his denial of ordination:

> Shortly before this examination, I was in a turbulent condition. While crossing the Midway [Plaisance, at the University of Chicago] I would experience violent tremors in the ground, and I was visited by a deep depression, one that had occurred again and again throughout my life, but now with particular intensity. During this period I had perhaps the most ultimate experience of my life, and one that I believe profoundly affected my vocation as a theologian, and even my theological work itself. This occurred late at night, when I was in my room. I suddenly awoke and became truly possessed, and experienced an epiphany of Satan which I have never been able fully to deny, an experience in which I could actually feel Satan consuming me, absorbing me into his very being, as though this was the deepest possible initiation and boding, and the deepest and yet most horrible union. (*LDG* 4)

Altizer's experience of a *theosis* of Satan is fairly unique to modern academic theology. Altizer bases his theological vocation around an "old-fashioned Methodist conversion experience," except instead of the goodness of God it is the horror of Satan which is experienced and enfleshed. As a "Satanologist," Altizer claims, "Satan and Christ soon became my primary theological motifs, and my deepest theological goal eventually became one of discovering a *coincidentia oppositorum* between them" (*LDG* 4-5). Altizer explained in an interview about this conversion, "it hit me," "I felt it," "'I sensed it" that 'God really is dead': and the effect of this experience has 'never left me.'"[1]

Altizer participated in the Tillich-Eliade seminar at the University of Chicago—in fact, a photo of the participants, including a young pipe-smoking Altizer—is memorialized in the posthumous Tillich collection *The Future of Religions* (*FR* 32[1]) Tillich for Altizer was the enigmatic Christian figure of his day, Altizer claimed in an interview that reading Tillich's *The Protestant Era* "led" him "once again to the Christian faith": it is important to note that this is a fairly common experience among Christian intellectuals in the U.S. during this time.[2] While participating in the Tillich-Eliade seminar, Altizer writes that he "was able to conduct a genuine theological dialogue with Tillich himself." To this end, this experience with Tillich "was the time of a comprehensive theological breakthrough for me" (*LDG* 11). Altizer was present during Tillich's final lecture—"The Significance of the History of Religions for the Systematic Theologian," discussed in the previous section—and had a long, "excited" theological discussion, perhaps Tillich's last, "the very night before Tillich's fatal heart attack."[3] One legacy of this relationship was Altizer's claim that Tillich himself admitted to him that "der real Tillich is der radical Tillich."[4]

Altizer's declaration that "God is Dead" made him one of the most hated men in the United States, and his name was evoked as an example of the untrustworthiness of academic theology in pulpits across the country.[5] Fundamentalist spokesman James Bales very publicly challenged Altizer to a debate—in a 40-foot-long telegram—which Altizer refused.[6] Evangelist Billy Graham denounced Altizer in his single attempt at writing academic theology, and backed out of a televised debate with

---

[1] Eric Meyer, *A Critical Analysis of the Death-of-God Theology of Thomas J.J. Altizer in Its Origins and Developments*, Ph.D. diss. Wilhelms-Universität Münster (1971), 14.
[2] Ibid. 4.
[3] Ibid. 21. The episode of Altizer and Tillich's discussion the night before Tillich's death, immediately after "The Significance of the History of Religions for the Systematic Theologian" lecture, is documented—in contradictory ways—in *Life* magazine's obituary for Tillich ("The Great Radical Theologian was 'Apostle to the Skeptics': Paul Tillich [1886-1965]," *Life* 59.19 [5. Nov. 1965], 40D), which prompted a letter to the editor of *Life* by Chicago's Divinity School patriarch Jerald Brauer (*Life* 59.22 [26 Nov. 1965], 25).
[4] D. Foster, 23
[5] Meyer (1971), 18.
[6] This telegram is archived in Syracuse's Altizer papers, Box 2, folio 18.

Altizer.[7] Altizer's ideas graced the cover of *Time* magazine and he even appeared as a guest on *The Merv Griffen Show*.[8] This situation contributes to Altizer's uniqueness within the landscape of contemporary theology: he was perhaps the final public theologian to survive the 1960s civil rights movement—even his course syllabi and a cookbook written by his Episcopal priest became nationally newsworthy items.[9] In fact, I suggest that Altizer may have rendered hopeless any truly public theology for the future. For this reason, in 1970 John Cobb and Nicholas Gier called Altizer "the boldest evangelical theologian in our time."[10]

Working as a professor in the college at Emory University, Altizer came under public attack by the newly-formed United Methodist Church; Emory is a Methodist-related institution. The Methodists could not defrock him because he was not ordained, nor could they excommunicate him because we was not even a Methodist—Altizer was Episcopal and appeared to be in good standing with the Episcopal Church. Altizer did not teach in Emory's school of theology, but in their college, so Emory could not remove him by virtue of him intellectually poisoning ministerial candidates. Instead, Emory stood by Altizer in what would later become cited as not only a key moment for Emory's transition from a church-related college to a national university but also a defining key battle for academic freedom in American higher education. The situation left Methodists outraged that they had lost doctrinal control of their own university (and with the loss of Vanderbilt's school of theology in a not-so-distant memory) and led the Southeastern Bishops of the United Methodist Church to pass a resolution denouncing Altizer's theology in 1966 (*LDG* 13). The nearly five-page denouncement was, according to the *Christian Advocate*, "signed by 10 active bishops supervising Methodist work by 3

---

[7] Billy Graham, "Is God Dead?" published in *The Godless Christians*, ed. Virginia Ball (Atlanta: Pendulum, 1966), 91-96.

[8] The story ran as "Toward a Hidden God," *Time* (8. April 1966), accessed online 19. June 2008. Another major article in *Time* was "The 'God is Dead' Movement," *Time* (22. Oct. 1965), accessed online 19. June 2008—Altizer himself gave an endorsement of this article in a letter to the editor, *Time* (29. Oct. 1965). Follow-up articles in *Time* were "Is 'God is Dead' Dead?" *Time* (2. May 1969), and the cover story "The New Ministry: Bringing God Back to Life," *Time* (26. Dec. 1969), both accessed online 19. June 2008.

[9] "Literature in the Divinity School," *Time* (22. Dec. 1967), accessed online 19. June 2008; "A Cook for All Seasons," *Time* (4. April 1969); accessed online 19. June 2008.

[10] John Cobb and Nicholas Gier, "Introduction," *The Theology of Altizer*, ed. John Cobb (Philadelphia: Westminster, 1970), 11.

million members in 9 states in the Southeast, and four retired bishops."[11] Few mainline denominations in the 20th century have paid any attention to academic theology; and it is truly unique for a large American denomination to condemn a single theologian's ideas—this is another instance of Altizer's uniqueness within the landscape of contemporary theology.

After the Bishops' pronouncement against Altizer, public interest in Altizer declined and the other young death of God theologians (discussed in the introduction) distanced themselves from Altizer's "death of God" theology movement. Shortly thereafter, Altizer admitted in an interview for a regional magazine: "Today I'm no longer the bad boy of theology. Today I feel like the invisible man."[12] Altizer was immediately dismissed as a "fad."[13] Catholic theologian David Tracy suggests that such attitudes seem "to miss the profound and enduring consequences of that important period" in American theology; that is, the period where a diverse group of young theologians took up Nietzsche's declaration of the death of God in a very serious fashion.[14] To wit, Altizer's theology is in a sense a *return* to *thinking God* as *the* primary activity of theology, while, he writes that "nothing," *especially* in contemporary theology, "is more forbidden today than thinking about God" (*GG* 1). "Rare is the theologian whose theology is always explicitly about God," Tracy writes, naming the "God obsessed thinkers—a Spinoza, a Nietzsche, or in our own period, an Altizer."[15]

This *God-obsession*, is more specifically a "haunting," David Jasper observes, since Altizer "insists upon the central event of the death of God." "It is a dark vision," Jasper writes, from a "priest whom the church could not endure, the prophet doomed to be misunderstood, not the least because his very language itself is an extraordinary achievement" as the language

---

[11] "Southeastern Bishops Condemn Altizer Theology," *Christian Advocate* ns 11.4 (24. Dec. 1966), 3. The actual statement was published as "Statement of the College of Bishops, Southeastern Jurisdiction," *The Mississippi Methodist Advocate* ns 19.17 (2. Feb. 1966) 6.
[12] Betsy Fancher, "Altizer: Two Years after the Death of God," *Atlanta* 7.7 (Nov. 1967), 51.
[13] Weissman, 21-22.
[14] Tracy (1996), 41 n.58. For a more detailed description of Altizer's relevance, particularly in the context of the late 1960s, see Lonnie Kliever and John Hayes *Radical Christianity: The New Theologies in Perspective* (Anderson, SC: Droke, 1968), esp. 266-267. Cf. Theodore Jennings, "Thomas J. J. Altizer," in *A New Handbook of Christian Theologians*, ed. Donald Musser and Joseph Price (Nashville: Abingdon, 1996): 15-21.
[15] David Tracy, *The Analogical Imagination: Christian Theology and the Culture of Pluralism* (New York: Crossroad, 1981) 52.

itself invokes a new theology.[16] This new Christian theology, while remaining Christian, we will see, is in fact post-Christian in the Tillichian (and Nietzschean) sense (*AM* 8). This post-Christian theology is clearly not, as John Cobb observed, a "church theology" because churches had already long abandoned their radical core.[17] Yet Altizer's theology is a *Christian* post-Christian theology.

Mark C. Taylor suggests that "[w]hen the history of twentieth-century American theology is written, one of its major chapters will be devoted to the work of...Altizer."[18] In the contemporary milieu of American theology, however, Altizer seems to be at best misunderstood or overlooked, and at worst, forgotten. This section of the dissertation will attempt to correct this error by placing his theology within the post-Christian trajectory initiated by Tillich in Part One. Ultimately, I will show, Altizer is saying something about *our* language—saying, "God is dead" *in our language*.[19] Clayton Crockett has suggested that it is through the death of God that we can begin to mediate any biblical notion of "God" to "modern secular culture."[20] But for Altizer the death of God is much more than this, it is a way of doing and thinking theology; beyond this, it leads us to transcend any sense of doctrinaire belief to an act of *thinking Godhead* in a secular world where transcendence has *died* and immanence has transfigured human flesh. It is, ultimately, a means by which an individual gives meaning to a world where God is not immediately recognizable in the immanence of the present.

In this section, Part Two, I will consider Altizer's work as a whole, forgoing—as I largely did with Tillich—a practice of drawing distinctions between an "early" and "late" Altizer. Even though Altizer's theological vision has been surprisingly consistent over several decades, as early as 1969 Altizer's critics were already talking about the "early" and "late

---

[16] David Jasper, Rev. of *Living the Death of God* by Thomas Altizer, *Contributions in Religion and Theology* 5.2 (2007), 160.
[17] Cobb (1987), 331.
[18] Mark C. Taylor, "Altizer's Originality," *Journal of the American Academy of Religion* 52.3 (1984), 569-570. Cf. Thomas Altizer, "Absolute Nothingness and Taylor's Imagology," *Journal of Cultural and Religious Theory* 2.2 (2001), online; John Carey, "The Death of God Movement and Twentieth-Century Protestant Theology," *The Death of God Movement and the Holocaust: Radical Theology Encounters the Shoah*, ed. Stephen Haynes and John Roth (Westport, CT: Greenwood, 1999), 89.
[19] Trevor Greenfield, *An Introduction to Radical Theology* (Winchester, UK: O Books, 2006), 86.
[20] Crockett, "Introduction" (2001), 4.

Altizer!"[21] Keeping this in mind, Altizer's language is a language full of ambiguities, contradictions, hardheaded definitions, and terminologies that developed over time that make, as one early critic observed, "a confident evaluation difficult."[22] Altizer's language *betrays* language itself, as his theology betrays theology itself, and, we will see, *thinking* itself (*reputo-ipsum*) as well. This *thinking now occurring* (*reputo ipsum iam evulsum*) is iconoclastic, "idiosyncratic," and subversive: to this end, Altizer writes in *The Genesis of God* that "genuine theological thinking can now only be a transgressive thinking, and perhaps most deeply transgressive as a thinking which is theological thinking" (*GG* 2).[23] It is consistent only within the context of the radical reversal embodied in, for example, William Blake's "The Everlasting Gospel":

> The vision of Christ that thou dost see
> Is my Visions Greatest Enemy
> ....
> Thy Heaven doors are my Hell Gates
> ...
> Both read the Bible day & night
> But thou readst black where I read white[24]

And in Blake's Notebook, Blake explicitly reverses God and the Devil, having previously "worshipd the Devil" and not the true "God of worldly things."[25] Altizer's is a contrary vision; a prophetic calling and provocation that Walter Brugemann called a "pervasive and perverted understanding of the prophets" in an essay ironically titled "The Triumphalist Tendency of Exegetical History."[26] One should recall that for Blake, "[t]he voice of honest indignation/ is the voice of God."[27] Altizer's theological project is one whose *pervasive* and *perverted* heresy could only originate in response to a pervasive and perverted Christianity as a theology of *honest indignation*, one which seeks to unravel Christianity to reveal the enfleshed immanence of that ultimate heretic, Jesus.

---

[21] James Ross, "From World Negation to World Affirmation," *Journal of the American Academy of Religion* 37.4 (1969), 353.
[22] Jay, 34.
[23] Crockett, "Introduction" (2001), 4.
[24] Blake, "The Everlasting Gospel," *The Complete Poems*, ed. Alicia Ostriker (London: Penguin, 1977), ln. 1-2, 8, 13-14 (p. 851).
[25] Blake, "Notebook in Epigrams and Satanic Verses," "To God," p. 629.
[26] Walter Bruegemann, "The Triumphalist Tendency of Exegetical History," *Journal of the American Academy of Religion* 38.4 (1970): 369-370 n. 10.
[27] Blake, "The Marriage of Heaven and Hell," pl. 12, ln. 9-10.

Summary of the Chapters

Chapter 3 will further introduce Altizer's theology, focusing primarily upon his Christology. As a "Christian atheism" Altizer's theology of Christ is a central element. The death of God indicates a radical reversal of transcendence in the incarnation of Christ, and Altizer further applies this radical reversal of Christ to a metaphysics of the Hebrew scriptures. That is to say, the death of God represents the primordial event of creation and begins the historical progression of transcendence into immanence. Altizer calls this progression the "self-embodiment of God."

Chapter 4 continues this discussion of reversal and self-embodiment, focusing upon the nature of Godhead, particularly upon the historical progress of Godhead, identifying primordial transcendence, alien transcendence, and absolute transcendence. If the incarnation and resurrection of Christ is a death of God and a primary reversal of Godhead in history, Godhead shifts to "the Nothing" for Altizer in the present. This Nothing is a complex and difficult concept, operating upon the dialectical logic of G. W. F. Hegel and Mircea Eliade's "coincidentia oppositorum." Godhead is then understood as an abysmal absence often mistaken as an absolute transcendence, as well as the immanent Total Presence out of which Godhead becomes manifest and historically ruptured by individuals. This rupturing is a convergence upon the apocalypse of history and is to participate in what Altizer calls "thinking itself."

Finally, Chapter 5 engages Tillich's theological legacy within Altizer's ideas and numerous critiques of Altizer. Following these discussions we will return to the notion of "thinking itself" as ontologically prior to being. For Altizer, however, immanence is prioritized as the object of thinking; therefore, life itself, *vita-ipsum*, again—as with Tillich—emerges as the primary reality. Life itself, we will see, is the immanence impregnated with possibility. The bizarre nature of Altizer's ideas lends itself into a consideration of the notion of fantasy as ground for theological thinking: what is the role of fantastical thinking for the Christian theologian? What would it mean if Altizer's theology is a *gesture* toward a particularly American, modern, or post-modern situation?

CHAPTER 3

ALTIZER'S CHRISTOLOGICAL PROJECT

The basic premise of Altizer's theological project, as a theology of culture, is that Christianity has become irrelevant to modern humanity. This has happened for two reasons, Altizer believes: first, because the contemporary church has "for the most part dissolved the image of Jesus in the Christian tradition" (*GCA* 55), and second, as Nietzsche prophesied, "the belief in the Christian God has become unbelievable."[1] These two causes are intertwined with each other. Similar to Nietzsche, Altizer believes that Christianity, on the whole, has betrayed Jesus Christ; and in this betrayal Christianity is destined to become irrelevant.[2] Particularly in the twentieth century, Altizer believes, Western humanity has socially, technologically, and philosophically "come of age": the world has arrived to the conclusion that the problems of some of the basic claims of Christianity will be lost in the coming pluralism of encountering other world religions. To Altizer, the resurrected Christ of traditional Christianity seems a bit too much "like the Krishna who appears before Arjuna in the Bhagavad-Gita" as "a monarchic Lord and cosmic Logos" (*GCA* 43).[3] In other words, within the discipline of the history of religions, Altizer is searching for a *uniqueness* to Christ which is undisputedly *Christian*.

Second, to use Nietzsche's words, the belief in the Christian God has become unbelievable, and that God is irrelevant to contemporary

---

[1] Nietzsche, *The Gay Science*, §343 (p. 279).
[2] Altizer, "Nietzsche's Understanding of Christianity and Its Influence Upon Contemporary Theology (1958/1960), 1.
[3] Altizer details further: "What distinguishes the Christian proclamation of Jesus from the devotional or bhakti forms of Hinduism and Buddhism? First, we cannot fail to note that Christianity limits the name of the redeemer to the historical name of Jesus, whereas bhakti religion can either be open to a wide variety of savior gods and goddesses, as in Hinduism, or it can follow the Buddhist way of devotion to a single savior deity (Amitabha or Amida) who is wholly dissociated from the historical founder of the religion (Siddartha Gautama" (*GCA* 56). Altizer concludes in his search for a uniqueness in Christianity (as I will discuss later): "God negates himself as a sovereign Creator in becoming incarnate in Christ: God as creator and Lord undergoes a metamorphosis in Christ, so that he passes into the opposite of his original epiphany" (92). Cf. Herberg archive for an apt critique of Altizer's use of the metaphor of the "world come of age," in folio 186.

humanity.[4] Altizer recalls that if the world participates in some way with the *logos* (John 1:1ff. *via* Proverbs 8:22ff.), God is surely working in amazing ways, not just *through* the Christ, but *by virtue of* the Christ in the present moment and at all times. Following this, Altizer says, Christians have in contemporary times lost their belief in the Christ as Divine Word. This loss of belief happened as a result of a lost connection between the Christ of "archaic language" and any linguistic attempt at creating a credible method of intelligibly speaking of God's activity in the world today. As such, the contemporary Christian is unable to speak of God's present activity without an adherence to the God of the past-tense. (*GCA* 76).

In this sense, I believe that Altizer's theology is a modern apology, similar in form to Paul Tillich before him, to restructure Christianity in a way that is explainable to the public of the time. That is to say, it is a correlative, mediating (Tillichian) theology of culture. "Our situation calls upon us to negate the religious forms of Christianity," Altizer writes, "just as the reform prophets of the Bible called for a new form of faith that negated the pre-exilic forms of Israel's religion" (*RT* 131). Similarly, Altizer understands the culture around him as the sign of the irrelevance of Christianity, as the "atheistic prophets" of Dostoevsky, Nietzsche, and Blake "venerated Jesus" and "were fully persuaded that the Christian tradition has either buried or inverted his message," yet would "invoke either the name of Jesus or the Christian symbol of the Incarnate Word to sanction their most radical proclamation" (*GCA* 20-21). To Altizer, then, cultural, philosophical, literary, and socioeconomic trends in society are rejecting Christianity for very *Christian* reasons—that is to say, society is calling for a "Christian atheism" in this world 'come of age.'

We will see that when it comes to Altizer's Christology, his term, "atheism," as in "Christian atheism," usually means "negation": therefore, a Christian atheism is really a negation of all things *traditionally* Christian.[5] If theology and Christendom resists the atheism, or negation, which

---

[4] Nietzsche, *Gay Science* §343 (p. 279).

[5] It is appropriate to emphatically note that Altizer's rendering of *traditional* Christianity is clearly reductionist and generalizing, and may even be guilty of creating a straw-man argument. In his defense, he is writing against a perceived new, distinctly American fundamentalism or evangelicalism in the late 1960s that would find its political voice in the following decades, perhaps culminating in the election of George W. Bush in 2000 and the terrorist attacks the following year upon the United States on September 11, 2001. Also, regarding the word "atheism," we will see that this terminology works on several complex levels for Altizer, but never in a situation where there is a literal absence of "Godhead."

society demands from theology, Altizer says, Christianity will die into further irrelevance. "Is the situation so desperate," he asks, "that the primary task of the Christian theologian is one of creating a fortress of faith that is unapproachable by the world?" (*TNC* 7) In response, Altizer responds to his own question that the task of the theologian must return to witnessing to the presence of God *in the world*, which requires in the current situation a faith that abandons "all nostalgia for the lost world of Christendom, and seek that Christ who is real here and now for us"—to believe otherwise "is an idle and irresponsible fantasy" which maintains that both the Christian faith and the institution of the Church will ultimately survive without serious reform (*TNC* 11, *RT* 127). To this end, Altizer's theological method is of a *confessional* nature, as he states that theology is a form of autobiography "in the sense that it is an attempt to witness to a reality dawning in humanity at this time." (*AM* 69-70). Altizer describes his motivations behind his theological project: "since the summer of 1955 I had been torn between an interior certainty of the death of God in modern history and experience and a largely mute but nevertheless unshakable conviction of the truth of the Christian faith," initiating a search to find the language to speak of Christ intelligibly in a "post-Christian" age (*TCA* 301-302). Altizer's *task*, then, is to restructure Christian theology in an apologetic way that reconciles the understanding of Christ in "atheist" culture that is always present, forward-moving, and constantly negating itself.

Altizer's Christology seeks to be a solution to his *task* as an apologetic theologian (which is explicitly to "seek the presence of Christ in the world") (*TNC* 301-302, *GCA* 11).[6] To this end, I have discerned two main "poles" of Altizer's Christology.[7] The first is that God has died— *kenotically*—in Christ. Second, the Incarnate Word is a forward-moving process; that following Christ's death, the process of redemption is

---

[6] Altizer also describes his theological task as a public, mystical venture ("Radical Theology and Political Revolution," *Criterion* 7.3 [Spring 1968], 5-10). To Altizer, however, radical theology should have Christology as its central problem. He writes: "The radical theologian has a strange but compelling interest in the figure of Jesus. This must not be confused with the nineteenth-century liberal quest for the historical Jesus. The new theologian has died to the liberal tradition and is in quest of that Jesus who appears in conjunction with the death of God" and adds that "what should be noted in [the] radicals is above all their conviction that the life and energy of Christ is present wherever the world is most active and real" (*RT* xii; *TNC* 14).

[7] Altizer also outlines his theological project using these two main theses as the basis of his system of thought in a debate at the University of Chicago's Rockefeller Chapel, published in *AM* 14-15.

dialectically gradual, so that the presence of Christ as Incarnate Word is an ever-changing, always-negating force in existence. I will now explain these two "poles" in some detail.

The Death of God in Christ

By coining his theology and school of thought "death-of-God theology" or "radical theology," Altizer places emphasis on the importance of the motif—or trope—of the death of God. As mentioned before, Altizer begins his thought as an apology which plays out in his earlier writing as a 'respectful recognition' of those who have recognized the death of God before him: most notably, William Blake, Friedrich Nietzsche, Simone Weil, and Fyodor Dostoevsky. Altizer then employs the motif on a second level as the basis of his Christology; that is, the death of God means that God *kenotically* dies in Christ.

Altizer turns to the Christian scripture to look at the language of the relationship between God the Father and Jesus, just as the ancient Christians did in the early Christological debates. As a result, Altizer concentrates on the use of the Greek word *kenosis* (lexical form) in the letters of Paul, which appears only five times in the New Testament. First, in Philippians 2:7, God is described as *"eauton ekenosen,"* that is, *emptying himself* into Jesus Christ. Other forms of the lexical *kenosis* appear elsewhere in the New Testament: in 1 Corinthians 9:15, meaning to render void or invalid; as a passive form in Romans 4:14 and 1 Corinthians 1:17, meaning to lose justification; and similarly employed in 2 Corinthians 9:3. This use of *kenosis* by Paul in Philippians to Altizer reveals an important characteristic about the relationship between God and Jesus; namely, that relationship is really a motion, that God *empties Godself into* the form of the Christ. The incarnation of Spirit into flesh is a kenotic movement of the Divine, "of Eternity becoming time, or of the sacred becoming profane" (152). God negates Godself—as *invalidating* or *unjustifying*, which the other scriptural uses of *kenosis* suggest—that is, the most extreme limit of self-denial (or even "self-estrangement," as Altizer suggests) of the Divine. This act of self-invalidation, Altizer concludes, as the book of Philippians suggests, is an act of *humbling* before humanity: an act which could only be an act of love (153).

To be sure, in Altizer's kenotic Christology, God, through a self-emptying process of negation, leaves a transcendent (which is to say, *unconditioned* or *unconditional*) form and enters time and space in a human (*conditioned*) form. It is at this point that Altizer's own proclamation of the death of God becomes intelligible. As a process of self-negation, God's kenotic emptying of Godself into a self-estranging embodiment is literally *God dying*, which is to say: the ultimate, final ground of Being as understood by those who spoke of the Godhead in the Hebrew scriptures has died, and has ceased to be. The Good News—or *Gospel*—of this *atheism* is that God, in God's death in Christ, *is* God, but the Godhead has changed Godself as a redemptive means of making possible a "final reconciliation of Himself with the world" (*AM* 8). God has, in essence, become present in the world, in time, and in energy as the Christ (12). To summarize, Altizer says, "to speak of the death of God is to speak of a movement of God Himself from transcendence to imminence, from Spirit to flesh" (11).[8]

As I mentioned earlier, there are two main "poles" to Altizer's Christology: first, the one which we have just discussed, the kenotic movement of God *into* Christ; and secondly, the God who operates in the present time *through* Christ—which I will now explain in detail.

The Incarnation and History

To review: in Altizer's kenotic understanding of Christ, since the relationship between the 'Father' and 'Son' can be described as a process of kenotic motion from God *into* the Christ, *God the Father* cannot exist apart from *God in Christ* as separate persons. If God actually incarnates Godself into the Christ, there is an authentic change and movement when God *becomes* incarnate in the Word: Altizer writes, "to say that 'God is Jesus' is to say that God has become the Incarnate Word, he has abandoned or negated his transcendent form"—and to state otherwise would be to deny a true, real, and consistent understanding of the incarnation in Christ (*GCA* 43-44). When God kenotically becomes incarnate in Christ, Altizer writes, God negates Godself, or "dies," into a negated form, namely, as a human, conditioned by Creation and prone to suffering; and furthermore, Jesus, as an incarnated God, is a suffering God (68). This kenotic movement of God is not an act upon God's behalf for humans out of necessity; but better stated: this act is one of *love*; God becomes flesh in an act of love, and God—as Jesus Christ—suffers for humanity out of love (67).[9] In short, the

---

[8] Further: "If Spirit truly empties itself in entering the world, then its own essential or original Being must be left behind in an empty and lifeless form. Now, Spirit can exist and be real only in a kenotic or incarnate mode that is the very opposite of its original Being" (*GCA* 69).

[9] Altizer elaborates: "It is precisely because the radical Christian seeks a total union with the Word made flesh that he must refuse the God who alone is God and give himself up to a quest for the God who *is* Jesus" (*GCA* 62).

declaration that 'God is Jesus' inherently confesses, according to Altizer, *the death of* God *in* Christ, which, as an act of extreme negation or self-estrangement, is a proclamation that *God is love*.[10]

What of the *incarnation* at the death of Jesus Christ? To Altizer, this question is the same question as "if God died in Christ, how is it possible to speak of the death of God in the modern world?" As an apologist, Altizer's Christology must inevitably pose this question as addressing Christ's relevance to the current situation. "The answer," he says, "is that the coming of Christ did not immediately affect the total transfiguration of all things, that the coming of Christ did not immediately embody redemption for all." In other words, Christ is the movement or embodiment of God's kenotic movement into the world, "as a redemptive act" to a world where "obviously redemption is not complete" (*AM* 13).[11] Since Jesus Christ is a *kenotic* Christ, the Christ is "the embodiment of a forward-moving process" who, at the death of Jesus the Christ, becomes manifest as the Word of God in the world. This 'body of Christ'—this *Logos*—is "an ever changing, ever more comprehensive, ever more universal body," that is to say: "Christ is most truly understood as the source of *all* life and energy whatsoever" (14).[12]

The Self-Embodiment of God

Over the decades, Altizer's kenotic theology has evolved into a full metaphysics of history. Eric Meyer was the first to significantly probe this aspect of Altizer in a 1971 dissertation, where he suggested that there are five primary epochs of Godhead are implicit in Altizer's thought. His scheme of Altizer is as follows:

---

[10] To be sure, Altizer continues, specifying that "a Christian proclamation of the love of God is a proclamation that God has negated himself in becoming flesh, his Word is now the opposite or the intrinsic otherness of his primordial Being, and God himself has ceased to exist in his original mode as a transcendent or disincarnate Spirit: God *is* Jesus" (*GCA* 69). Altizer comments on God as love: "Even when theologians have re-discovered the *agapé* or total self-giving of God, they have confined it to the movement of the Incarnation, and have dualistically isolated God's love from the primordial nature and existence of God himself. So long as God is known in his primordial form as an eternal and unchanging Being, he can never be known in his incarnate form as a self-giving or self-negating being" (67).
[11] Stob, "The Apologetic Stance of Christian Atheism" (1966), 10.
[12] Altizer summarizes that his theology "is attempting to say that…the totality of God Himself is embodied, is made flesh, in Christ in such a way that the original divine reality is itself emptied of its preincarnate power and glory by the process of its becoming incarnate in Christ" (*AM* 13).

1. God as primordial totality;

2. God as the transcendent God who alone is God because he is other than the world and humanity;

3. God as emptying himself into Jesus of Nazareth and his death into the world and humanity;

4. God as the Incarnate Word or the Christ or the Spirit ever more immanent throughout or one with the world and humanity; and

5. God as final totality.

To speak of "Godhead," Meyer notes for Altizer, is to speak of the *totality* of these five movements.[13] In short, Altizer's metaphysics of Godhead is kenotic: the history of God is an apocalyptic movement of God sacrificing Godself in, as Lissa McCullough describes, a "liberating releasement of Omega from Alpha," a "pure and total *exitus*."[14] The perpetuating death of God apocalyptically reflects the kenotic reality of God, Altizer writes, "[f]or only that which has actually begun can actually die, and if God has truly and actually died then God Himself is inevitably the consequence of a truly actual genesis or beginning" (*LDG* 133). The kenotic Christology implicit in Altizer's earlier work, as it happens, through the history of Altizer's writing, developed into a theological method for *thinking* through the death of Godhead.

Altizer interprets traditional Christian thinking and its committal to an immutable deity as a denial of the incarnating, apocalyptic, and kenotic nature of Godhead which is disclosed through Jesus Christ. He writes in *The New Gospel of Christian Atheism* that orthodox Christianity has

> Reversed its original ground, knowing incarnation and crucifixion as culminating in ascension, an ascension to an absolutely primordial heaven, an eternal life that is the very opposite of the eternal death of the crucifixion, and an absolute transcendence that is the very opposite of an apocalyptic immanence and a truly incarnate body or flesh.... [I]f orthodox Christianity has never been able to envision or to know a truly incarnate Godhead, this is

---

[13] Meyer (1971), 457-458.
[14] Lissa McCullough, "Theology as Thinking of Passion Itself," *Thinking Through the Death of God*, ed. Lissa McCullough and Brian Schroeder (Albany, NY: SUNY UP, 2004), 39.

> the very Christianity that knows the absolute transcendence and the absolute immutability of God, an immutability foreclosing all possibility of wither the incarnation or crucifixion of Godhead itself. (*NG*105)

Therefore, traditional Christian theology will resist immanence because it believes that the primordial God remains, eternally, transcendent. For Altizer, the opposite must be true; as the crucifixion enacts the transfiguration of God into "a full and final union between 'flesh' and Spirit or 'darkness' and light," a Christian theology with an immutable God is closed to a "new" and "total totality" in the present (*GN* 100, 115). Just as Altizer's theology is ultimately a transgression against traditional Christian theology, the kenotic progression of Godhead is revealed by Altizer to be "a total transgression, or transgression that truly and absolutely changes a primordial totality" (115).

This kenotic, apocalyptic motion of the Godhead in history is named by Altizer as a "descent into Hell," appropriating the classical Christian doctrine of the harrowing of Hell.[15] The descent into Hell indicates, for Altizer, the forward-and-downward spatial metaphor of transcendence progressing into a total immanence (*DH* 118-120). Traditional Christian teaching, for example, affirm in its creeds that the risen Christ must return to heaven in the doctrine of the ascension of Christ; Altizer repudiates this doctrine, claiming that the ascension is a reflection of traditional Christianity's apprehension of the forward-and-downward movement of Godhead.[16] Instead, the ascension reflects, for traditional Christianity, a *reversal* of forward-and-downward movement by requiring Christ to "withdraw" and return, "carried up into Heaven" (Luke 24:51), to then , as the creed states, "sit at the right hand of God," the primordial "Father" (*DH* 105-106). Altizer explains:

> So it is that resurrection is here known as ascension, and as an ascension which reverses the movement of incarnation and reverses it so that Christ can return to the glory of heaven. Clearly, this movement of glorification is a reversal of the movement of incarnation, of the Word's becoming "flesh," and as such a movement of reversal it nullifies the event of incarnation, or

---

[15] Scriptural foundation for this teaching include Is. 24:21-22; Zech. 9:11; Acts 2:27, 31; 2 Cor. 2:14; Eph. 4:8-10; and 1 Peter 3:19-20, 4:6. Cf. William Finch, *The Descent into Hell*, Ph.D. diss., Drew U. (1940).
[16] Described in the Bible primarily in Mark 16:19; Luke 24:51; John 20:17; and Acts 1:1ff.

transforms it, radically transforms it, into a moment of absolute glory. Then the event of incarnation is an epiphany of absolute glory, and such an epiphany of the Christ who is wholly other than the kenotic Christ of passion and death.

This resistance of the "glory of God" in the world of history is called the "Christian apprehension of the incarnation" (*GA* 116). Further:

> [T]he full reversal of backward into forward and of transcendence into immanence cannot be a total act and actuality apart from a reversal in Godhead itself, a reversal occurring through the absolute opposition and the very center of Godhead, and a reversing itself through the self-negation or self-emptying of the Godhead. Nothing more clearly makes manifest such a reversal in the Godhead than does the decisive correlation between the backward movement of the return and the transcendence of transcendence, and the forward movement of history and the immanence of immanence. (115)

The perpetual kenotic downward-and-forward movement is a *self-annihilation*, "a pure negation of negation, and a negation which can be real or realized only through the final advent of a purely Satanic world and totality" (*HA* 193). The descent into Hell, as a trope and paradigm for theological thinking, moves forward in history without moving "toward closure," as Steven Smith writes, "but can spiral forever."[17] Even though the collapse of transcendence into immanence is a "full reversal," the negating *movements* along the process of this reversal do not work between polar binaries but rather *coincidentia oppositorum*, coincidence of opposites.

The act of creation, for Altizer, is the initial willed act of self-annihilation or self-sacrifice of the primordial Godhead.[18] In the willing of speaking creation, Godhead enacts Godhead's own subjectivity as a self-sacrifice and crucifixion (*GA* 78). The willing of speaking, McCullough writes, for Altizer "is the advent of a negativity that sacrifices primordial plenitude." This "disruption of primordiality...is an absolute disruption, an apocalyptic rupture of the quiescence of God before any act."[19] Meyer

---

[17] Steven Smith, Rev. *The New Gospel of Christian Atheism* by Thomas Altizer, *Journal of the American Academy of Religion* 73.3 (2005), 892-893.
[18] Some of the Augustinian ideas which led to Altizer's later development of this are found in Altizer's master's thesis, *NGT* 37-38.
[19] McCullough, "Theology as the Thinking of Passion Itself" (2004), 35; McCullough here cites *GG* 179.

describes this Kabalistic first willed act as a "real beginning" of the "breakup of the Primordial Totality." "Its fall made possible the entire forward-moving, dialectical process of all existence, energy, life, perception, consciousness and history"; and therefore, "[t]he whole Christian movement of salvation is founded on the fall of the Primordial Totality, the primordial form of Christ or the Spirit or the Divine Process."[20] Ray Hart describes Altizer's intellectual movement away from traditional Christianity as a paradigm shift from *creatio ex nihilo* to *creatio ex nihilo sive Deo ipse*: "God creates from nothing, that is, from God Godself."[21] "Creation shatters the eternal now (*nuc stans*) of God," McCullough writes, "enacting a fall into time, which is the advent of an 'antithesis between is and was' generated by the universal perishing of all things."[22]

Altizer more fully explored these ideas in *The Self-Embodiment of God*, a book that Altizer himself praised later as perhaps his best book and as a "Torah theology" as a highly metaphorical, metonymical text (*LDG* 33).[23] Beginning with a theological phenomenology of speech, Altizer begins with a *via negativa* reminiscent of Paul Tillich's ontology of language, writing that "[w]hen we say God we say the unsayable, and when we name God we name the unnamable, but it is precisely thereby that we speak," and that "[b]y speaking of God we make manifest the ground of speech, and our naming of God makes this reversal manifest or audible" (*SEG* 40, 41). To name a Godhead in the fullness of history is to name an alien transcendence and actual total immanence at once. "In naming God speech simultaneously negates the namelessness of otherness and sanctions otherness in its pronunciation of the divine name," he writes: "Not only does speech sanction a pure or final otherness in speaking of God, thereby it evokes that otherness as call, and embodies it as final call.... Otherness speaks in our speech when we speak of God. Then the namelessness of others is negated and reversed by speech, and reversed by that speech which names final otherness as ultimate call" (41). Just as the

---

[20] Meyer (1971), 434. Altizer on the Kaballah: "History as Apocalypse" (1982), 149, 155; "A Response" (2004), 222.
[21] Hart (2004), 51. Also: "If *indeterminate Godhead* does not equal cosmos, *determinate God* is not and cannot be a 'proper' name. Creation *ab origine*, however *sui generis*, does not close or exhaust the transformation of indeterminate Godhead; *creation continua* is the covenant of epiphantic transformation of the selfsame but redemptive Godhead the apocalypse of salvation for both humanity and God" (50).
[22] McCullough, "Theology as the Thinking of Passion Itself" (2004), 36.
[23] Pretentiously, Altizer adds, "the book belongs within the sacred circle of the Torah"! (*LDG* 33)

primordial Godhead reverse the primordiality of that Godhead's totality, so also do we enact a reversal ourselves when we actually speak.

In the act of speech the primordial Godhead "calls all identity out of itself, and calls it out of itself by calling it into exile from itself, an exile wherein identity ceases to be only itself." Godhead's speaking is, inasmuch as it is self-negation, is self embodiment, "embodied by passing into the otherness of itself," willing an act which is "embodied insofar as it is in exile, an exile free from an unrealized...identity, and therefore an exile from an identity of silence, an exile from the identity of the unsaid" (*SEG* 40). When the debased Godhead then speaks Godhead reveals Godself on the edge of language, at once as a riddle and as the presumed foundation of all act; when "otherness actually speaks, and when it speaks we hear: 'I AM'" (44; Exodus 3:14). In other words, Altizer writes, "'I AM' is heard whenever voice speaks, for it sounds in the voice of speech itself, and its sounding negates every possibility of a self-enclosed identity within the horizon of speech" (46). Godhead speaking is self-transfiguring Godself; it enacts a self-transfiguration to the listener, as well. Mark C. Taylor observes that for Altizer "[t]he death of God is the birth of the Word God" and "vice versa."[24] "The hearer who hears 'I AM' in the voice of call," Altizer argues, "does so only by way of the act of self negation." 'I AM' as such does not transfigure the listener but the act of transfiguration "is truly the hearer's own, and so much so that it is only this act of self-negation which realizes the hearer's self-identity," concluding that "[i]ndeed, self-identity now becomes identical with self-negation (47).

Like Tillich's concept of the power of being which leads to self-transcendence, the act of hearing divine speech reflects the self-negation of Godhead's willed act of speech; and as Godhead enacts divine subjectivity in willed act so also does the listener identify subjectivity in response. Divine, alien transcendence for Altizer is meant to be negated: self-transcendence is for us a self-negation. "Now it is precisely the act of hearing 'I AM,' and hearing the voice of call," Altizer writes, that we "realize" subjectivity that "is manifest and real only insofar as it is not itself....for only thereby can identity pass beyond or transcend itself." Again, self-negation is self-transcendence, but it is an actual self-transcendence, "wherein identity loses and leaves behind all simple identity with itself" (*SEG* 48). As an ultimate self-transcendence, subjectivity is at

---

[24] M. Taylor, "Text as Victim" (1982), 73.

once affirmed and denied: subjectivity is fully realized and negated, crucified and resurrected.[25]

At this point in *The Self-Embodiment of God*, Altizer's language enacts a ritual sacrifice of language itself. Taking on the liturgical rhythm of a Eucharistic *sacerdos secreto* (for example, St Cyrill's invocation of *ignem materiae expertem qui cogitatione comprehendi non potest*) Altizer officiates a Black Mass upon which language itself is dismembered on the high altar (*LDG* 152).[26] Altizer writes:

> Voice speaks. And when it speaks, and as it speaks, it embodies itself. Speech is the embodiment of voice, and that embodiment is the act of voice itself. Therefore speech is also the enactment of voice, the self-enactment of voice, it is that act wherein voice enacts itself. Only voice is act and self-identity at once, and is self-identity in its act of speech, an act which is necessarily individual and unique. Voice is that act, and that act alone, which is ever other than every other act, and is other, and truly other, solely because it is itself. Therefore voice is otherness itself, and is otherness in its own identity, in its own act. This otherness if fully and truly its own, and is its own because voice acts; it speaks. Speech is the self-identity of voice, but as speech, voice is other than itself, and is other than itself precisely because it speaks. (*SEG* 63)

---

[25] Ibid.

[26] St. Cyrill, *Liturgia*, in Eusebe Renaudot, ed., *Liturgiarum Orientalium Collectio* (London: Joannem Leslie Bibliopolam, 1847), 1:38. My translation of the St. Cyrill's 'secret prayer':
> Creator of all things, visible and invisible, you who governs all things providently ruled, for all are yours, Lord, lover of souls: I bid you, O omnipotent Lord; I am cowardly, lacking virtue, and most worthless of all your servants, while I assent toward your holiest of holies (*sancta sanctorum tua*) for the purpose of celebrating this holy mystery. Give me, O Lord, your Holy Spirit, the fire devoid of matter (*ignem materiae expertem*), which is not able to be comprehended in thought (*qui cogitatione comprehendi non potest*), that consumes all hardness, that burns slanderous inventions (*qui duritias omnes consumit*), and slays corporeal members, that holds back the movements of the spirit, that impel plentiful imaginations full of passion and sorrow: And even as it is becoming of priests, make me above all mortal thoughts, and give to me pure words, in order that I may perform this proposed offering (*oblationem propositam*), which is the mystery of all mysteries, in fellowship and communion with your Anointed (*Christi tui*), to whom glory is due with you, due to the Holy Spirit who restores life (*et Spiritui sancto vivificanti*), both of whom are of like nature (*consubstantiali*) at the present, *etc*.

While it is Altizer that re-enacts this *sacerdos secreto*, it is, in my estimation, D. Leahy who fully realizes it in his writing.

"Voice enacts itself only by negating itself," he continues, "and it embodies itself only by embodying the otherness of itself, and otherness which is truly and only its own" (64). He explains further that self-negation is actualized in speech:

> When "I AM" is heard, and is heard as "I AM," it realizes its self-identity, its own identity as "I AM." Therein the voice of "I AM" passes into hearing, and the hearing of the voice of "I AM" becomes the speech of "I AM" itself. This occurs through the simultaneous self-negation of hearing and speech. For hearing negates itself as hearing to realize itself as speech, and speech negates itself as speech to realize itself as hearing. Each movement is not only a movement of self-negation, but also a movement of transcendence. Not only does hearing transcend itself in becoming speech, but so likewise does speech transcend itself in becoming hearing.
>
> Only in hearing does speech realize its self-identity, and only therein does it realize itself as act. Hearing embodies speech, and it enacts it well, and it is precisely thereby that speech truly becomes itself. Accordingly, the repetition of speech in hearing is the act of speech itself. Speech enacts itself in hearing, and it enacts itself to the extent that it is heard. (65)

Hearing is self-transcendence and speech transfigures its transcendence in becoming hearing. Self-transcending speech is liturgical speech, that which is repeated and "enacted in hearing to the extent that it is *heard*." Altizer concludes this discussion:

> The voice of "I AM," the actual identity of "I AM," is the embodiment of "I AM." And the embodiment of "I AM" is the hearing of "I AM," a hearing wherein "I AM" is identical with itself even in its otherness from itself. Embodiment is act, and act is self-negation, the self-negation of an original or undifferentiated identity. Therefore embodiment is empting, and not only emptying but self-empting, the self-emptying of original totality. Identity empties itself in its embodiment, and it is precisely thereby, and only thereby, that identity actualizes or realizes itself. "I AM" actualizes and realizes itself in its voice, but only the hearing or the embodiment of its voice is the self-realization of "I AM" that occurs whenever identity is self-emptied or embodied. But it only fully occurs in pure or total self-emptying, and only therein does the ground of all actual identity fully realize and actualize its own self-

identity. That self-identity is the self-realization of its ground and source, the self-actualization of an original "I AM." (69)

Self-realization, self-actualization, self-negation, self-transcendence, and self-embodiment are all related to a kenotic metaphysics of God. God kenotes, not as "a simple or immediate act" but one that is in process and culminates when actual divine speech is heard (69).

Yet while actual speech moves from the quiescence of primordiality into the kenotic emptying of speech in creation, that speaking moves again into quiescence. Speech itself has been negated; "God" is no longer speaking in the same speech actualized out of creation. This perpetual negation of speech in the kenosis of Godhead in history is ritually enacted and re-enacted—embodied, disembodied, and re-embodied—in the self-embodiment of divine speech. "[T]he descent of speech into silence is ever again renewed and resurrected even now, and resurrected now because it once fully and finally occurred," Altizer proclaims: "Once speech has fully perished as speech, or has finally perished as a speech which is only speech, then speech is resurrected wherever hearing occurs, or wherever hearing is fully actual and real. That hearing is real now, actual now, and is actual whenever actuality is immediately at hand" (*SEG* 95). In response to the negation and dismemberment of speech, a renewed affirmation and re-membering of the naming of "Yahweh as the Creator," known and spoken of as "I AM." "The full presence of "I AM" is the absolute reversal of all other presence and power," Altizer writes in *History as Apocalypse*, "the deconstruction or de-presenceing of presence as such, as the fully actual presence of absolute otherness enacts and brings forth a fully negative identity to everything that exists" (*HA* 55). Even if the ritual repetition of "I AM" "is a silent re-saying, it is a re-saying nonetheless, a re-saying reversing all given identity, and reversing it so that identity or self-identity now becomes the other of itself" (54).[27] To survive in the exile of self-transcendence, then, is only made possible "by way of the silent pronunciation of the Divine Name, a silent pronunciation which nevertheless speaks in the very writing of the text of the Bible, as Bible itself is born in response to the silence of the [exiled] people of Israel"

---

[27] "To know Yahweh as the creator is to know the groundlessness, and the absolute and total groundlessness, of existence as such, and therefore to know and to realize ex-istence as exile, and not only as exile, but as exile which is exiled from itself. Now identity becomes its own other, and realizes itself as the otherness of itself, and otherness which is actualized with the pronunciation of 'I AM'" (*HA* 55).

(55).²⁸ To speak and to listen in this manner, David Jasper observes, is to engage "an apocalyptic language that is yet hardly born, and thus hardly to heard let alone comprehended." The speech "cannot compromise, speaking to our time and yet not of it."²⁹

"Word speaks," Altizer writes in *Total Presence*, "finally or eschatologically, and Word speaks finally because Word irreversibly becomes 'flesh'" (*TP* 2-3). The Word, as Godhead incarnated, Christ, is dialectically manifested and manifesting in the world. Following the event of the crucifixion of Jesus Christ, God dies again though an act of negation or estrangement to become "fully incarnate in every human hand in face," to be totally present in the present age (*GC* 71).³⁰ Because Christ is dialectically embodied in existence, then, the death of God is a continual process that is not confined only to the death of Jesus in a particular time and place, as the redemptive nature of Christ's presence in history is a (Hegelian) "salvation history" which can be understood as a eschatological process of atonement (*GCA* 71-72, 74).³¹ The self-sacrifice of God in Christ on the cross is "the original enactment of the self-reversal of life and power" of the Word of God working *through* humanity as Christ, which is an atoning "universal process, a process present wherever there is life and energy, wherever alienation and repression are abolished by the self-

---

²⁸ "'I am' only wholly enacts its own silence by finally bringing an end to the speech of 'I AM.' Then the voice of silence is the voice of speech only insofar as the self-identity of speech has come to an end. Or, rather, the voice of silence is the voice of speech when the voice of speech has passed into silence. This can occur only by way of an actual end of the voice of speech. An actual end is an actual ending, a real ending of the voice of 'I AM.' That real ending is the silencing of 'I AM,' the self-silencing of 'I AM,' a self-silencing whereby 'I AM' passes into 'I am.' Then 'I am' is voice only insofar as it embodies the silence of the voice of 'I AM.' And that silence is an embodied silence, an enacted silence, a self-enacted silence, a silence which is act because it is enacted, and pure act because it is finally and totally enacted. Now speech is total because it is totally embodied, and it is totally embodied because a speech which is only speech has come to an end, and actually and finally come to an end" (*SEG* 92-93).
²⁹ Jasper (2007), 161.
³⁰ Interestingly, Altizer seems to interpret the death of God again as a liberating message for humanity, like Nietzsche, in this transformation. He writes: "The radical Christian knows that God has truly died in Jesus and that his death has liberated humanity from the oppressive presence of the primordial Being" (*GCA* 71). Continuing: "Speaking in the traditional symbolic language of Christianity, we could say that radical faith transposes the traditional vision of the resurrection into a contemporary vision of the descent into Hell: the crucified Christ does not ascend to a heavenly realm but rather descends ever more fully into darkness and flesh" as "the dead body of God cannot be dissociated from the Christ who has descended into Hell" (120).
³¹ Cf. Thomas Altizer, "Hegel and the Christian God," *Journal of the American Academy of Religion* 59.1 (1991): 71-91; Hegel (1977), §785.

negation of their ultimate source" (113).[32] Christ is kenotically present, "paradoxically," Altizer writes, as Christ's Spirit, whose "implicitly completed self-sacrifice...only becomes realized or historically actualized in self-consciousness while Spirit is in a state of self-alienation and estrangement from itself"—a Spirit who first appears "in its kenotic form as the man, Jesus of Nazareth." (*GCA* 66).[33]

This Spirit, or continual motion of Christ, Altizer believes, has gone unnoticed by traditional Christians today because the Church universal has committed "the original heresy" of identifying the Church as the *Logos*—the 'body of Christ'—thereby conditioning the presence of Christ to an institution, rather than *into* humanity (*RT* 137, *GCA* 132). The ecclesial logos, he says, ultimately refuses the reality of Christ, "who is present in our flesh." (*GCA* 156). Christ, however, "is the totality of the moment before us" who "draws us into the fullness of life and the world" and "is a totally incarnate love" (157). Writing from the 1960s, Altizer says that the contemporary Christian is prepared to reject Christendom's "abstraction of the Word from history" in a time when existentialism has unmistakably manifest itself in popular culture, Christianity has begun its signs of *rigor mortis*, finally "stripped" of her "archaic and otherworldly glaze" (83).[34]

To be sure, the negation that occurs in the crucifixion of Christ is not to be understood as God negating Godself as usual, but instead the crucifixion is *the negation of a negation*, "the reversal and transformation of the fallen or transcendent epiphany of Spirit." In the death of God in Jesus the Christ on the cross, Godhead self-sacrifices *Godselfhood*, kenotically "emptying himself of his primordial sacrality." In the dissolution of this selfhood, "the life and movement of the transcendent realm" is reversed,

---

[32] Continuing: "we know his Word as a Word pointing to an eschatological future, and we must not be dismayed if it is no longer meaningful as a word of the past. Only by shattering all those images of Jesus that are present in our past can we be open to an eschatological end" (*RT* 132).

[33] To clarify: Christ "becomes embodied in [the] process, that movement, that energy, that life that derives from Christ and which the Christian believed is even now in process of renewing and transfiguring all things whatsoever and preparing all things so that they might pass into a final apocalyptic, redemptive end"—I will briefly mention Altizer's understanding of the apocalypse later (*AM* 9).

[34] Kliever and Hayes, 266. "Even the remembrance of the original glory and majesty of God," Altizer writes, "roots the Christian in the past, inducing him to evade the self-emptying and negating of a fully incarnate divine process and to flee from the Christ who is actual and real in our present" (*GCA* 133). Hence, contemporary forms of Christianity are inherently anti-Christian as they literally reject the Word of God in existence.

"transforming transcendence into immanence, thereby abolishing the ground of every alien other" (*GCA* 113). Christ becomes manifest into existence, and the kenotic reality of the Incarnate Word begins in a new form in history (67).[35]

The *process* of God's embodiment in the world through Christ dialectically continues, with time, to negate itself in an "unfolding process," becoming "more deeply incarnate in the body of humanity," losing "every semblance of [God's] former visage, until he appears wherever there is energy and life" (*GCA* 74-75).[36] In this sense, a new humanity is born in the manifestation of God within itself at the crucifixion of Christ; as Christ dialectically negates, estranges, and empties itself in humanity—out of love—until the point of an ultimate end, that is, an apocalypse of complete reconciliation between the kenotic God and creation (72).[37] "In this final

---

[35] Meyer (1971) explains further: "The Word in its transcendent form, God as the transcendent and sovereign Lord and Creator who alone is God, negates and reverses itself in its Incarnation-Crucifixion in Jesus Christ to become fully immanent in the world and man. Jesus of Nazareth is the consequence of God's emptying himself into man; and God himself dies in the Crucifixion of Jesus. This is not just the death of an idea of God; God as the actual ground of transcendence decisively undergoes self-annihilation, with the result that what had been known as transcendence becomes increasingly alien and ever darker as God himself moves into the world and man. The movement of the Incarnation is a continual downward, self-negating movement from Sprit to flesh through kenotic self-annihilation or transformation. The Resurrection (Jesus Christ's total release into the world and man as the energy and life that moves all things forward to their Final End is a culminating point in this movement of Incarnation-Crucifixion; it is not an Ascension of Jesus Christ to a transcendent Lordship that preserves his individual person as such.... All the energy and life of the transcendent form of the Word of God as transcendent dies to itself in Jesus' death, for it empties all of itself into Jesus and, in his death, Jesus empties all of himself into the world and man. The Incarnation cannot be separated from the Crucifixion because Jesus was not decisively Christ (the Incarnation of God in the world and man) until his Crucifixion and death. The Word began to be incarnate in the world and man as soon as God revealed himself, but it was first fully incarnate when God emptied himself fully into Jesus and dies to any separate existence of his own by dying into the world and man with Jesus in his Crucifixion and death" (438-439).

[36] Grigg (2006), 8. Altizer further explains: "By a kenotic negation of its primordial reality, the sacred becomes incarnate in the profane" and "is inseparable from a parallel movement of repetition and renewal.... Consequently, a consistently Christian dialectical understanding of the sacred must finally look forward to the resurrection of the profane in a transfigured and thus finally sacred form" (*RT* 155).

[37] "When the Word becomes flesh," Altizer writes, "it ceases to be active and real in its original epiphany, and its preincarnate form thereby becomes lifeless and immobile, gradually regressing to a formless state of an abstract and empty nothingness," that is, "the Christ who lives upon our horizon no longer appears in his traditional form—indeed, he may never again appear in a form that is in continuity with his previous expressions" (*GCA* 101; *RT* 138). "Inevitably," he concludes, "the radical Christian believes that the end of the world, whose immediate coming was proclaimed by Jesus, is the total transfiguration of the

apocalypse," Altizer says, "God will become all in all precisely because he has died as God to make possible a reconciliation of all things with each other, a totally new life of redemption, joy, and love in Jesus Christ" (*AM* 17). The death of God in Christ, as "an extension of the atoning process of the self-annihilation of God throughout the totality of experience," is a redemptive event which is finally realized in the apocalypse. "Such an apocalyptic and dialectical understanding of the atonement," Altizer proposes, "demands a new conception revealing not simply that God is the author and the agent of atonement but is himself the subject of reconciliation as well" (*AM* 13, *GCA* 112). In affirmation, in Altizer's process theology, God is subject to the same (if not more) negation and change, as is the chaos of existence—again, portraying the Christian God as a God who benevolently actualizes Godself as a sacrifice for and into creation.[38]

The Contemporary Jesus

If the Incarnate Word of God is dialectically moving as a process throughout history, then, it *is* possible to speak of Christ apocalyptically existing in the present; to continue Altizer's intentions of developing a consistent kenotic Christology. The Christ-event is "the consummation of the historical acts and movements of God," that is, the forward-moving process and "kenotic energy" which evolve out of God's sacrifice on behalf of human atonement, self-estranging and self-negating Itself continually in the world (*GCA* 88-89).[39] "Insofar as the body of Christ incorporates and

---

fallen form of the world, the end of a flesh that is isolated from Spirit, and so likewise the end of a Spirit that is isolated in flesh" (*GCA* 47).

[38] Kliever and Hayes summarize: "God moves toward a Final Completion through a continuing succession of self-expressions and self-emptyings which lead to ever fuller self-expressions. ....this phase describes an event in history when God as an otherworldly Being and Power died in Jesus Christ. But this 'death' was the *dialectical* emptying of an otherworldly into a this-worldly expression of God." Concluding, "for yet another dialectical transmutation lies ahead when God's this-worldly self-expression passes over into a Final Completion which will sum up all things in God's eternal self-fulfillment" (265-266).

[39] Altizer elaborates on the forward-motion of God: "Only by a continual process of negating its own past expressions can the Word be a forward-moving process, and only by a process of reversing the totality of history can the Word be an eschatological Word.... It is precisely the forward movement of history that testifies to the presence of the Word. Such a movement is real movement. It is not a perpetual cycle revolving about itself, but a movement opening into the Eschaton of the future, and Eschaton that dawns wherever history negates its past to realize its future. While an eschatological movement of the Word must necessarily negate the past movements of its own expression, it does so not to negate the reality of history itself, but rather to annul a past which forecloses the possibility of a realization of its own future" (*AM* 132-133).

embodies the death of God," Altizer writes, "the death of God in Christ is gradually made manifest throughout the whole body of humanity and the whole body of the cosmos," so that "now every man who lives in the history following the advent of Christ lives the death of God," precisely because we undeniably live under the condition of time (*AM* 15, 16). God, then, is present in all existence as the Word of God, which has historically *kenotically* moved from Jesus the Christ to "the universal body of humanity, thereby undergoing an epiphany in every human hand and face," and continues to move in a "kenotic metamorphosis" in the present (*GCA* 83, 92).[40]

The Jesus Christ which can be spoken of today, then, is an "anonymous Jesus," who approaches humanity in unexpected, humble, and nameless ways (*CJ* 186). More often than not, Altizer says, a contemporary epiphany of God occurs in silence, as a humble activity of the Word's self-negation (*RT* 138). Living in the contemporary world as a Christian and attempting to recognize God's movement is an angst-driven life, Altizer says, because in living the death of God in the present, "no suffering can be foreign to the Christian...for the way of the Christian is to bear with Jesus all the pain of the flesh," in recognition of Christ's kenotic presence in God's Word (*GCA* 23). To understand Christianity otherwise would be to turn to "priestly religion" where there is not a recognition of God's forward movement, but rather observes the sacred events of the past, which is inevitably "backward-moving" (*RT* 131). Such faith focuses its attention on "a disincarnate and primordial form of Spirit....grounded in the sacred authority and power of the past"(*GCA* 133). In other words, traditional Christianity, in Altizer's opinion, denies God's active (kenotic) presence in the present and "isolates...the events of salvation history into a series of unique and once and for all events," implying that God's expressions of atonement have ended in the past (*RT* 131).[41] To be sure, Altizer affirms that "once we truly come to understand the Christian God as an actual and moving dialectical process, we shall finally be purged of the Christian religious belief in the existence of a unique and absolutely autonomous

---

[40] Altizer states that "since the Christian Word is neither timeless nor primordial, it has no existence apart from its movement" (*RT* 138).
[41] Altizer clarifies: "Yet it is no less true that to identify Jesus wholly with a particular and isolated person of the past is to foreclose the possibility of his present life or forward movement. Indeed, we can know Jesus as the ancient Jesus of Nazareth only insofar as we are closed to his contemporary presence" (*GCA* 57).

God," rather than a God actively present and incarnate around us (*GCA* 89).

If God is to be understood as dynamic, kenotic, or self-transfiguring in the present, Altizer believes, no understanding of the Christian Word can become fused with any set of particular images. "An active or forward-moving process," he writes, "must necessarily negate its particular expressions, and progressively transform itself as it becomes incarnate in a continually changing series of historical movements" (*RT* 130). It would be only natural, then, that traditional images of Jesus the Christ appear in negated forms in culture which at first seem to be *estranged* from orthodox Christologies. Searching for examples of this in culture, Altizer does not have to look very far from his own theology and finds two primary "prophets" of this understanding of a negated Christ in the work of William Blake and Friedrich Nietzsche (*RT* xii, *GCA* 56).

William Blake, considered by Altizer to be "the greatest biblical poet of our era," has a strikingly similar Christology present in his poetry.[42] He writes in his long poem *Jerusalem* that God is immanent in the present, as the Word says to the narrator, "I am in you and you in me, mutual in love divine," and continues:

> I am not a God afar off, I am a brother and a friend;
> Within your bosoms I reside, and you reside in me:
> Lo! we are One; forgiving all Evil; Not seeking recompense![43]

Not only is God "not a God afar off," but there is a very intimate connection between humanity and the incarnate, redeeming God. Similarly, Altizer's interpretation of the death of God motif is strikingly similar to Blake's, as the poet writes:

> Wouldest though love one who never died
> For thee or ever die for one who had not died for thee
> And if God dieth not for Man & giveth not himself
> Eternally for Man Man could not exist! for Man is Love:
> As God is Love: every kindness to another is a little Death
> In the Divine Image nor can man exist but by Brotherhood[44]

---

[42] Thomas Altizer, Rev. of *Blake and the Assimilation of Chaos* by Christine Galant, *Journal of the American Academy of Religion* 47.3 (1979), 486.
[43] Blake, "Jerusalem" 4:7, 18-20 (p. 638).
[44] Ibid., "Jerusalem" 96:23-28 (p.842).

Here, Blake proclaims (though, through what seems to be a rhetorical, interrogative statement) in very simple terms the death of God; specifically, that humanity could not exist without the death of God, and that in all acts of love in the world—as Blake reminds the reader, "for Man is Love: /As God is Love"—God is surely present, as "a little Death" (*GCA* 71). Further, Blake also appears to have an undeveloped sense of a God-embodied "Humanity," to which he elaborates, "who is the Only General and Universal Form/To which all Lineaments tend & seek with love & sympathy," and is, as Altizer describes, "Jesus as the expanding or forward-moving process who is becoming 'One Man'; that is to say, in an apocalyptic vision, the Form which is embodied as love (75).[45]

More than a literary relationship between Blake and Altizer is the fact that Altizer believes William Blake to have a true sense of the reversal implicit for a radical Christian theology. In Blake's "Everlasting Gospel," for example, the language of Blake seems to be attempting to enact a radical reversal of Christian orthodoxy; that true Christianity is contrary to, if not the opposite of, orthodoxy.[46] More prominently, though, is the notion of the perpetuating "little Death/ In the Divine" as a "Self Annihilation" and "Eternal Death" in "The Ghost of Abel."[47] This death is an apocalyptic transfiguration, a reversal, as in Blake's "America," Altizer writes, "the red fires of Orc's rebellion melt the heavens and impel the dark descent of…God."[48] More directly, Blake writes of his radical reversal of Christianity is to *blame* Christianity for its own demise: "The Moral Christian is the Cause/ Of the Uneliever & his Laws," and later, "That they may call a [*crime*] shame & Sin / [*The*] Loves temple [*where*] that God dwelleth in/ And hide in secret Hidden Shrine/ The Naked Human form divine." Blake adds: "Blaspheming Love" is "blaspheming thee."[49] As a reversal of traditional Christianity's compulsion toward an "increasing dissolution of the Descent into Hell," Altizer writes, is to affirm the descent into Hell as a reversal not of eternal life but eternal death (*LDG* 68). As "[t]he forward-moving occurrence of advent and perishing," McCullough explains, history must be known "theologically as the passion of God, even

---

[45] Ibid., "Jerusalem" 38:20-21.
[46] Ibid., "The Everlasting Gospel," 17ff.
[47] Ibid., "Jerusalem," 96:27-28 (p. 842); "The Ghost of Abel," pl. 2 (p. 867).
[48] Thomas Altizer, "Mircea Eliade and the Death of God," *Cross Currents* 29 (1979), 266.
[49] Blake, "The Everlasting Gospel," 3, ln. 7-8; 5, ln. 63-68, 72.

as the passion of God enacts itself through this history of advent and perishing."[50]

While the connection of the philosophy of Friedrich Nietzsche to Altizer should be obvious in the centrality of the 'death of God' in both of their work, Altizer points to Nietzsche's Christology as a formative negation of traditional Christologies, which suggests, like Blake's incarnational Christ, the necessity of negation of traditional forms of Christ. Just as Nietzsche declared that "in reality there has only been one Christian, and he died on the Cross," clearly separating the Christ of history from the Christ of Christendom, Nietzsche also pursued his philosophical writing in the form or genre of a gospel in his book *Thus Spoke Zarathustra*. *Zarathustra* appears in many ways "to be a dialectical reversal and transformation of the Christian Gospel," though its protagonist, Zarathustra, while portrayed as an anti-Christ, is the "liberator who has come to free man from the life-negating power of guilt and revenge"—whose intent is strangely similar to the failed attempt of the historical Christ as Nietzsche similarly portrays in his final work, *The Anti-Christ* (*TNC* 81, *GCA* 60-61). In other words, Nietzsche's attack upon Christ is an attack upon the Christ of Christendom, and not the Jesus Christ of history—as Nietzsche draws a clear distinction between the two. The historical Jesus, according to Nietzsche, is tragically bound to nearly two thousand years of *resentiment*-driven misidentification, and therefore a new mythical liberator is needed; hence, *Zarathustra*.[51]

The Jesus Christ who is apart from the world, to both Nietzsche and Altizer, is a Christ who is "free of all *resentiment*," that is, disassociated with a God who is the 'No' to life; and, at least to Altizer, *is* the God who is the ultimate 'Yes' (*GCA* 60).[52] As evidenced in recent literature and philosophy—as Blake and Nietzsche are only two major examples—the traditional Christian God is a lifeless deity, as culture "has progressively but decisively dissolved every sign and image of the Christ who was once present in the Church." As long as Christ is perceived, however, as a continually kenotic presence in the world, the anonymous, even *"secular,"*

---

[50] McCullough, "Theology as the Thinking of Passion Itself" (2004), 38.
[51] Nietzsche, *The Anti-Christ* 39. Cf. *Thus Spoke Zarathustra*, trans. Walter Kaufmann (New York: Modern, 1995). Cf. *RT* 99-100.
[52] Grigg (2006), 8.

Jesus will "finally obliterate the God of a former faith," declaring a Christian atheism where the true God as Christ is the only God (74).[53]

---

[53] Altizer continually stresses this point, especially in his earlier work, as the central thesis of his theology: "at no time has [the Christological question] become so compelling as it has today, as Christianity is attempting to move beyond its past historical expression to a universal form, and is inevitably being forced to face the full scandal of its own particularity" (*GCA* 55).

Chapter 4

Transcendence and Immanence in Altizer

The Alien, Absolute, and Primordial

Philosopher John Caputo explains Altizer's views of transcendence and immanence as follows: "In Altizer the death of God primarily meant that the absolute center shifted its residence from a transcendence to immanence by means of a metaphysics of *kenosis*, by which the full presence of a transcendent God was transported to the plane of immanence."[1] For Altizer, transcendence cannot be eternal because a continuing alien transcendence contradicts any sense of divine kenotic process.[2] Transcendence and immanence are non-polar binaries. Transcendence is "the primary symbol of [the] symbolic point from which the eschatological movement of God originates"—this process "will culminate in pure immanence." "Accordingly," he continues, "the eschatological movement of God would occur by way of a continual passage or transition *from* transcendence *to* immanence" (*DH* 89). This is not a singular event and it is not one single, linear motion, it is a passage that is dialectical, continual and continued, reversing, and spirating. This movement *from* transcendence *to* immanence should "rather be conceived as a comprehensive process embodying the realization of its life and energy through a long and complex series of movements and countermovements between its respective poles" (90). Furthermore, by "[a]llowing this model to stand forth as a witness to the eschatological movement of God, we could then understand God as reaching or realizing the fullness and finality of His own immanence only be way of negating and reversing His own transcendent ground."

That said, Altizer's definitions of transcendence and immanence should be considered together as *nonpolar* binaries.[3] While "[t]ranscendence realizes or fulfills itself by passing into immanence"; "immanence," on the other hand, "is opposed to transcendence in the sense

---

[1] Caputo, in Caputo and Vattimo (2007), 68.
[2] Meyer (1971), 437.
[3] Theodore Runyon, "The Death of God: One Year Later," *Christian Advocate* ns 10.22 (17. Nov. 1966), 8.

that immanence *is* that which transcendence *was*" (*DH* 91). Altizer uses the term *primordial transcendence* to describe the totality of Godhead prior to the willed, spoken act of creation; pure immanence is enacted as the pole into which the perishing of Godhead moves in history (*GN* 7-8). While *alien transcendence* is a "wholly other" transcendence, immanence is also *other, othered,* and *othering* by virtue that it is a process by which Godhead apocalyptically self-exiles or "banishes" Godself into the self-embodiment of history.[4]

Absolute transcendence is "the absolute passivity and absolute immutability of God" as "absolute sovereignty." This is the position of traditional Christianity. Absolute transcendence is a nonprimordial, alien transcendence that is regarded to be presently existing outside of space and time. It is a "simplicity of God foreclosing all possibility of an actual transfiguration of Godhead itself, thereby making impossible the 'death' or transfiguration of Godhead in the Crucifixion" (*GN* 33). Therefore, an actual incarnated, kenotic, descending-into-Hell, transfiguring, resurrecting, and Christological Godhead can only be spoken of in empty terminology and meaning in a traditional Christian theology of God. A total transcendence of God as a primordial transcendence is only knowable, Altizer argues, through a fully incarnated Christian theology (4). Alien transcendence is not *only* a primordial or absolute transcencence as 'wholly other,' but also indicative of the ultimate actualization of transcendence in a pure immanence. Altizer writes in *The New Gospel of Christian Atheism*:

> With the full and final actualization of an ultimate death, all innocence disappears, every possible historical return is ended, transcendence itself does not simply vanish but becomes ultimately alien, and a new and total emptiness of nothingness is everywhere. For the death of God is inseparable from the advent of a truly new and even total nihilism, a truly new desert and abyss…and a consequence of the uniquely Christian God, that God who alone has made possible and made necessary our ultimate abyss. (*NGC* 31)

---

[4] Thomas Altizer, "The Challenge of Modern Gnosticism," *Journal of Bible and Religion* 30.1 (1962), 24. Altizer, "History as Apocalypse" (1982), 176: "History is the eschatological embodiment of that God, a God who becomes absolutely present in the Incarnation, and incarnate or self-conscious presence which releases the finality and irreversibility of history. That finality and irreversibility is actually itself, and actuality which is undeniable…and an actuality which is the kenotic emptying of everything which it enacts."

He further explains, returning to the kenotic Christology:

> That God only appears and is real in consciousness with the occurrence of the Incarnation, an incarnation ending in the beyondness of the beyond, and it is only an emptied beyondness that can appear and be real as absolute transcendence and absolute transcendence alone, a truly alien and empty transcendence that itself is a consequence of the Incarnation. So the Incarnation itself is a self-emptying of an absolute transcendence, or the self-emptying of God, and only as a consequence of that self-emptying is a truly alien and infinitely distant transcendence actually born, one genuinely absent from both Israel and the pre-Christian world. (54)

So the death of God, as a religious and metaphysical metaphor, describes a Christian ontology which has an historical aspect and is Christ-centered (*GA* 18). As such, in the *process* of kenotic, incarnational movement in history, the pole of transcendence changes and shifts with the pole of immanence, becoming increasingly transcendent or alien.[5]

Immanence is the pole against which transcendence dialectically moves, and *pure* or *absolute immanence* is the total presence of Godhead finally emptied out into a state of enfleshment. The final act of Spirit emptying into flesh is indicated in scripture, Altizer argues, in "Jesus' proclamation that the Kingdom of God is dawning in our midst" (Luke 17:21), "the expectation of the coming of the Paraclete" (John 14:16-17), and "Paul's hope and assurance that God will be all in all" (Heb. 10:22-23).[6] At the last remnant of transcendence in its final emptying of itself—symbolized by the descent into Hell and resurrection of Christ—is the ultimate "dissolution of an absolutely transcendent Godhead." In this final kenosis of transcendence into an absolute immanence, is a truly apocalyptic genesis, a New Creation (2 Cor. 5:17), as a "final apocalyptic negation"; where "an original Creator can be known as a truly negative or wholly alien Creator," transcending "both an original creation and an original Creator" (*GN* 91).

This enfleshment is a transfiguration of the movement of transcendence and immanence into an eschatological New Creation, as

---

[5] McCullough, "Theology as the Thinking of Passion Itself" (2004), 44.
[6] Thomas Altizer, "Response," *Theology of Altizer*, ed. John Cobb (Philadelphia: Westminster, 1970), 75.

symbolized by the resurrection of Christ. Altizer explains in *The Descent into Hell*:

> Let us first be fully aware that if we are to arrive at a truly eschatological understanding of resurrection, then we must be prepared to negate and annul the ancient mythical meaning of resurrection. Already we have come to the realization that the ascending movement from flesh to Spirit is a return to a primordial form of Spirit. Therefore it is a reversal of forward and final movement of an eschatological process. Can we now say that an eschatological movement of resurrection would be a *descending* movement from the "higher" level of Spirit to the "lower" level of flesh? This would mark an attempt to speak theologically about a divine movement from the "higher" form of Spirit to the "lower" form of flesh. In other words, it would be an attempt to understand resurrection as incarnation as the Word's becoming flesh. Here, the descending movement from Spirit to flesh would also be an eschatological movement from a primordial form of Spirit to an eschatological form of flesh. (*DH* 116-117)

"Thereby," Altizer concludes, "The process of divine process itself passes into a new identity and form: it is 'resurrected'" (117). This resurrection is the advent of an eternal death of Jesus, "an eschatological consequence of negating and reversing the distance and beyondness of Heaven"; in other words, "when Heaven has been emptied of Sprit," he argues, "eternal life can be actualized as eternal death." Heaven or Spirit—transcendence—is now "actualized" and kenoted "as flesh or Hell" (124). Resurrection, then, is a symbol of the reversal of transcendence into immanence, from exile into Kingdom, from Spirit into flesh. To be sure, this final self-embodiment and self-kenosis is also a change for flesh, as well; it is a New Creation where flesh is totally and finally transfigured as "simultaneously the body of Satan and the body of Christ."[7] This transfiguration between the *coincidentia oppositorum* of flesh and Spirit—the Pauline *sarx* and *pneuma*—is the radical immanence of ultimate enfleshment that is apprehended by orthodox Christianity and is the consequence of, as Lissa McCullough states, "the passionate realization and embodiment of Godhead" (*NGC* 19).[8]

---

[7] Altizer, "A Response" (2004), 223.
[8] McCullough, "Theology as the thinking of Passion Itself" (2004), 44.

Coincidentia Oppositorum

It is hopefully clear to my reader by now the dialectical, contrary, metonymical, semantic, and contradictory nature of Altizer's ideas within his systematic theology. In other words, in an ultimate sense the following theological terminologies are interrelated and in some cases appositional to each other, when considered in Altizer's apocalyptic reinterpretations: creation, incarnation, the 'Word,' 'I AM,' kenosis, Christ, passion, crucifixion, descent, resurrection, enfleshment, atonement, divine perishing (the death of God), life, death. These concepts are all *transfigurations* of each other in a grand history of Godhead in a forward-and-downward movement from a primordial transcendence into an absolute immanence.

Altizer calls the theological method implicit in his thinking *coincidentia oppositorum* or the coincidence of opposites. He describes *coincidentia oppositorum* in his 1955 doctoral dissertation, "A Critical Analysis of C. G. Jung's Understanding of Religion":

> The archetypal representation of...[the] resolution of the opposites—the *coincidentia oppositorum*—in a higher synthesis is the so-called reconciling or unifying symbol (*vereinigendes symbol*), representing the partial systems of the psyche integrated into the Self upon a transcending higher plane. Brahman, Rita, and Tao are all such unifying symbols which balance and reconcile two mutually contending tendencies of the psyche. All are irrational, and all stand beyond the conflict at hand. Yet, each mediates in this conflict by a dialectical process of unifying the tensions in a psychologically transcending synthesis. The unifying symbols represent and embody the "ways" to psychic and cosmic harmony. Psychologically, the problem becomes one of reducing the "mystery" of this process to terms which are more intelligible than those of dogmatic statement. (*CA* 215-216)

Altizer did not invent this concept, but he has taken it from a few other sources. In the Christian tradition, *coincidentia oppositorum* is attributed to three primary works: Nicholas of Cusa's *Of Learned Ignorance*, Bruno's *The Expulsion of the Triumphant Beast*, and Hegel's *Science of Logic*.[9] Bruno, for

---

[9] Ross (1969), 356; Cf. Nicholas of Cusa, *Of Learned Experience*, ii.2-3; Bruno, *The Expulsion of the Triumphant Beast*, i.I; G. W. F. Hegel, *Science of Logic*, trans. A. Miller (London: George

example, wrote in a dialectical style exhibiting the *coincidentia oppositorum*: "The beginning, the middle, and the end, the birth, the growth, and the perfection of all that we see, come from contraries, through contraries, into contraries."[10] *Coincidentia oppositorum* is a dialectical means by which a thinker, as David Jasper writes, "inhabits paradox."[11]

It is the historian of religions Mircea Eliade—the same Eliade that influenced Tillich at the end of his life—through whom Altizer receives his understanding of *coincidentia oppositorum*. Altizer writes in his memoir, *Living the Death of God*, of his profound respect for Eliade as a teacher and mentor; and it is apparent from Altizer's appearance in a few of Eliade's later works that Eliade respected and admired Altizer's intellectual project, as well (*LDG* 47). As it happens, the Altizer archive at Syracuse University has a letter from Eliade, offering suggestions for titles for Altizer's first book.[12] David Tracy calls Eliade's *coincidentia oppositorum* methodology a "morphology" (referring to Goethe) of what Eliade calls "the very nature of...divinity."[13] Eliade writes in his classic, *Patterns of Comparative Religion*:

> The *coincidentia oppositorum* is one of the most primitive ways of expressing the paradox of divine reality.... However, although this conception, in which all contraries are reconciled (or rather, transcended), consists what is, in fact, the most basic definition of divinity, and shows how utterly different it is from humanity, the *coincidentia oppositorum* becomes nevertheless an archetypal model for certain types of religious men, or for certain of the forms religious experience takes.

Coincidentia oppositorum is one of the primary means by which religion expresses itself to reconcile the paradoxes of human reality; divinity reflects these paradoxical elements. Eliade writes of its prevalence in "oriental" thought:

Allen and Unwin, 1969), 67; Young Chun, *A Conceptual Analysis of Religion in Paul Tillich (1886-1965)*, Ph.D. diss., Drew U. (1981), 96.

[10] Bruno, in Ross (1969), 356, quoting a 1964 translation by Arthur Imerti.

[11] Jasper (2007), 160.

[12] Mircea Eliade, Letter to Thomas Altizer (15. Jan. 1963). Consequently, the title Eliade suggested—*Mircea Eliade and the Dialectic of the Sacred*—was the one Altizer decided upon and is the inspiration of the title of this dissertation's title. See ibid., "Notes for a Dialogue," in *The Theology of Altizer*, ed. John Cobb (Philadelphia: Westminster, 1970): 234-241.

[13] David Tracy, *Dialogue with the Other* (Louvain: Pecteus, 1990), 55-56; Mircea Eliade, *Patterns of Comparative Religion*, trans. Rosemary Sheed (Lincoln, NB: U Nebraska P, 1996), §159 (p. 419).

> The oriental mind cannot conceive perfection unless all opposites are present in their fullness. The neophyte begins by identifying all his experience with the rhythms governing the universe (sun and moon), but once this "cosmisation" has been achieved, he turns all his efforts toward *unifying* the sun and moon, towards taking into himself the *cosmos as a whole*; he remakes in himself and for himself the primeval unity which was before the world was made; a unity which signifies not the chaos that existed before any forms were created but undifferentiated *being* in which all forms are merged.[14]

Coincidentia oppositorum is the process by which divinity is processed by the individual as the individual's religiously *processing* his reality. This processing culminates toward an ultimate *conjectio oppositorum*—a *conjunction* of opposites—through the relationality and movement of the *coincidence* of opposites.

Altizer appropriates Eliade's morphological methodology onto a modern vision of Christianity. "[T]he incarnation," Altizer writes, "is the final realization of the ancient symbol of the *coincidentia oppositorum*...but is unique—is Christian—insofar as it is a dialectical coming together of the most radical expression of the sacred and profane, a dialectical *coincidentia* of the totally sacred and the totally profane." The reclamation of a methodology of *coincidentia oppositorum* is, for Altizer, not a recognition of an implicit theory *of* Christian theology, but points to *the mistake* of orthodox Christianity. "Could it be," Altizer asks, "that Eliade has made possible for us an apprehension of the Christian identity of the uniquely modern symbol of the death of God?"[15] For Eliade, Altizer interprets, the *coincidentia oppositorum* in the present is a question of the collision of the sacred and the profane, that post-incarnation, the sacred is *hidden* in the profane: "If the incarnation is the supreme theophany, as Eliade affirms, and that here eternity is manifest precisely *in* the profane, then its identity *must* be camouflaged. And what could be a greater camouflage than the death God?" He explains:

> Remembering that for Eliade the sacred hides itself in showing itself, we can only conclude that in the supreme theophany God is totally hidden, and totally hidden precisely in that theophany itself.

---

[14] Eliade (1996), §159 (p. 419, 420).
[15] Altizer, "Mircea Eliade and the Death of God" (1979), 265.

> Above all it is in the Incarnation that the transcendent is unrecognizable and unrecognizable because here the sacred is wholly camouflaged in the profane. Or, and we say that here the life of God is meaningful and real in consciousness only by way of a realization of the death of God? Or that here the sacred shows itself only *in* the profane, or only *as* the profane? ....Not until religion is totally negated, or truly recognized as a consequence of the Fall, can the transcendent be known as by fully present and real in history and thereby truly unrecognizable as God.[16]

Coincidentia oppositorum is a process by which an actual apophasis or hiddenness is possible within an incarnational Christian theological context. Altizer continues that God's "unrecognizability makes possible the actual omnipresence of God, and from this point of view the actuality of the omnipresence of God can only be manifest in a purely profane history and consciousness," adding, "that consciousness can only know and experience the presence of God as the actuality of the death of God." Through Eliade's theological methodology, in other words, Altizer finds that the hiddenness of God in the profane is indicative of a radical divine immanence. Concluding, Altizer remarks that "[n]o one in our own time has given a fuller witness to this omnipotence than Mircea Eliade, and he has done so most fully by making God invisible as a sacred presence and identity, and therefore invisible and unrecognizable as God."[17]

Brian Schroeder suggests that for Altizer, *coincidentia oppositorum* is a theological concept of the highest first order, such as "atonement," as a means of explaining the connection between all of the other interrelated concepts.[18] (Many of these concepts are, again, as follows: creation, incarnation, the 'Word,' 'I AM,' kenosis, Christ, passion, crucifixion, descent, resurrection, enfleshment, atonement, divine perishing, life, and death.) The constant change, uncovering, and novelty of Godhead in the progress of *coincidentia oppositorum* is the apocalypse of history, moving dialectically with the forward-motion of time. Robert Ross suggests that Altizer's appropriation of Eliade's morphological concept is an *apocalyptic coincidentia oppositorum*, radically involving a perpetual "consummation" of Godhead, and is made immanent through the incarnation of Christ. In

---

[16] Ibid. 257.
[17] Ibid. 268.
[18] Brian Schroeder, "Absolute Atonement," *Thinking Through the Death of God*, ed. Lissa McCullough and Brian Schroeder (Albany, NY: SUNY UP, 2004), 65, referencing *NG* 104–105, *GA* 158, and *CJ* xxi.

comparison to Eliade, Ross argues, Altizer's *coincidentia* moves toward a pure immanence, as disclosed through the death of God in Christ.[19] The reversal of orthodox Christianity is implicit in the *coincidentia*; Altizer explains:

> Only Christianity knows an ultimate self-negation or self-emptying of the Godhead, but that is a self-negation inevitably realizing an absolute abyss, and an absolute abyss of Godhead itself. Therein and thereby the negative pole of the Godhead fully stands forth, and this is not an illusory negativity as it finally is in Gnosticism, nor a negative pole that is simply and only the pure "other" of the positive pole, but far rather a negative pole that is dialectically identical with the positive pole, as Godhead for the first time is fully actual as an ultimate *coincidentia oppositorum*. If Godhead here undergoes an absolute self-negation or self-emptying, this is not a primordial self-emptying, but rather an apocalyptic and historical self-emptying, one realizing itself in the actualities of history and consciousness.

As a result, this kenosis transfigures actuality and consciousness.

> Not only does an absolutely "new" dawn ever more fully, but an absolutely "old" is equally called forth, an "old" which apocalyptically can be named as the old aeon or even Satan, but an actualization of Satan and the old aeon or the old creation only possible as the consequence of an absolutely forward movement. Just as it was the prophetic revolution which first enacted the absolutely new, this is a revolution fulfilled in Jesus, and in that Jesus who enacted the final dawning of the Kingdom of God, a kingdom that is not a primordial or an ancient or eternal kingdom, but a kingdom that is and only is an apocalyptic kingdom, or that kingdom which *is* the absolutely new.

It is for this reason the language of the "Kingdom of God" is New Testament language and not the language of the Hebrew Bible. A *new* morphology of God emerges on the perpetuating *edge* of apocalypse in history—the eternal now—the *coincidentia oppositorum* of the absolute primordial Godhead (*GN* 148).

---

[19] Ross (1969), 355, 356; cf. Walter Love, "Mercy for Miss Awdy," *The Theology of Altizer*, ed. John Cobb (Philadelphia: Westminster, 1970), 245-246.

Coincidentia oppositorum for Altizer is a methodology for a truly realized dialectical theology that primarily operates between flesh and spirit that has largely remained dormant in orthodox Christian thought beyond Augustine (*NGT* 35, 39, 101ff., 117-119). Pushing dialectical thinking beyond Luther and Kant into a truly modern Christianity, Altizer believes that this dialectical *thinking* is, when it comes to the *coincidentia* of God and world, the form of "the fullness of eschatological faith."[20]

Paul Van Ness, in a 1972 dissertation at the University of Chicago, criticized Altizer's dialectical method as an inconsistent *coincidentia oppositorum* because it is a methodology that takes 'history' seriously as a theological process without taking seriously an actual dialectic between "Father" and "Son" as an incarnation, instead focusing upon "some very peculiar sense" of the idea of "Word."[21] Van Ness further criticizes Altizer's theology from an anti-feminist point of view; claiming that Altizer has appropriated Blakean feminine imagery of Godhead, which Altizer discusses in *The New Apocalypse* (see, for example, 96-99, and 102).[22] Van Ness suggests that in Altizer's use of feminine imagery in Blake, the gendered images of God which Blake uses are negated, "collapsed, abolished, or transcended....and therefore, *they constitute only a preliminary level of history or redemption.*" The dialectic for Altizer is *not* a dialectic between two poles which easily essentialize gendered tropes such as aggression and healing, and is, as a result, *not truly* a dialectic, according to Van Ness.

Van Ness' interpretation represents an interesting and common misreading of Altizer, namely, that Altizer is not really dialectical when he claims he in fact is. Rather, Altizer's methodology is dialectical *as* a *coincidentia oppositorum*.[23] As an actualized Hegelian methodology for dialectial thinking, it must betray its own teleology. Altizer maintains that his dialectical methodology is consistent with Hegel's logic; and Eliade

---

[20] Altizer, "Response" [Response A], 75-76; cf. William Beardslee, "Dialectic or Duality?" *The Theology of Altizer*, ed. John Cobb (Philadelphia: Westminster, 197): 58-67.

[21] Paul Van Ness, *Death of God theology and Freud*, Ph.D. diss., U. of Chicago (1972), 106.

[22] Ibid. 113-114. Altizer discusses this by some implication in his extraordinarily difficult essay, "Satan as the Messiah of Nature?" (in *The Whirlwind in Culture*, ed. Donald Musser and Joseph Price, [Bloomington, IN: Meyer-Stone,1988], 129), citing Blake's "Jerusalem" 93: 20-16.

[23] Van Ness, 114, 115-116; cf. 122. It is worth mentioning that for Van Ness, an immanence is regarded as a masculine trait and transcendence is a concept which contemporary feminism at the time was attempting to resurrect—perhaps influenced by de Beauvoir's criticism of immanence as stagnation, as discussed earlier in this dissertation (116).

wrote that Altizer was rooted in a tradition which interpreted a dialectical kind of thinking in a similar fashion, with "similar paradoxical recoveries of the sacred."[24] In other words, the Altizeran *coincidentia* is understood by Altizer to be a Hegelian dialectical methodology which remains its own fidelity to itself by ultimately betraying its own method.

Altizer's *coincidentia oppositorum* is a methodology by which he interprets the Bible. In some ways, it is a biblical theology by which coherence is discovered between the oldest texts of the Hebrew Bible and the modern epic and poetic voice, especially William Blake (*HA* 196-198, 201ff.). Namely, it describes the history of Godhead as a "destruction of transcendence," which makes possible for us to speak of epiphanies of the Word in the present.[25] At bottom, Altizer's theology points toward a theology of immanence. He wrote as a response to critics in 1970:

> I regard the Incarnation as a coming together of God and the world, as a *coincidentia oppositorum*, as a coincidence…of the opposites, God and world or creature and Creator. Moreover, I regard the Incarnation as a historical movement and process; it does not reveal the illusory opposition between God and the world, but rather effects an actual reconciliation between estranged and alienated opposites, between an alien transcendent form of God that is estranged from the world and a fallen and broken form of the world that is estranged from God. Thus I would insist that the Incarnation *is* a coincidence of real opposites. But as a consequence of the Incarnation, the real opposition between God and the world is negated and transcended.

"From this point of view," Altizer continues, "the scholastic principle that there is an essential *and* eternal difference between God and the world would not necessarily result in a denial of the event or reality of its Incarnation."[26] While the incarnation and the process of history *is* a process between two 'real' opposites—God and world—the process does not really work through a dialectic of 'real' opposites. It is a *process*. As a result, the 'world,' as a polar binary of 'God,' is the not-yet-God, the *not-yet-holy*.

---

[24] Eliade (1970), 235; cf. Hegel (1969) 431ff., 439ff., and 831ff. Lovejoy suggests that this kind of thinking (though not necessarily that of Altizer's) regarding *coincidentia oppositorum* is similar to a Neoplatonic scheme of logic (Lovejoy, 83). Clearly, this is not a *coincidentia* in a Cusan sense, but a strictly Hegelian—or even a distinctly Altizeran take on Hegel.
[25] Van Ness, 104, 105-106.
[26] Thomas Altizer, "Response" [Response B], *The Theology of Altizer*, ed. John Cobb (Philadelphia: Westminster, 1970), 114.

Traditional Christianity, John Cobb writes while describing Altizer, "apprehends the Kingdom of God as wholly other," whereas Altizer finds Godhead in the profane.[27]

Radical theology itself is a *coincidentia oppositorum* of orthodox Christianity. While Blake, for example, preached that the true Christianity is a reversal of practiced Christianity, it is telling that it is not so clean as a *simple* reversal or dialectic. Instead, for Altizer, it is a *coincidentia oppositorum*. Altizer writes in *The Genesis of God*:

> Virtually the whole body of Christian theology is grounded in the presumption that no new prophet arose in Jesus, and thus no truly new enactment or proclamation here which is not a repetition of an earlier revelation, and above all no truly new realization of God in the eschatological proclamation and parabolic enactment in Jesus. All too naturally that is a proclamation and enactment which is progressively dissolved in the Christian Church, and it is already forgotten by the second century, a negation which is the dissolution of the original Jesus. (*GG* 170-171)

While such a dissolution was a tragic failure, it was also necessary for its reversal. He continues:

> Even as ancient Christianity progressively came to know an absolute transcendence of God that was realized in the wake of the disappearance of an apocalyptic Kingdom of God, our history has ever more progressively come to know an absolute immanence which is realized in the wake of the disappearance of the transcendence of God. Each of these primal movements of our history is fully parallel to the other, and just as the apocalyptic ground of Christianity was only "discovered" in the wake of the uniquely modern realization of the death of God, the absolutely transcendent God of Christianity was only "discovered" in the wake of an ancient Christian dissolution and reversal of the Kingdom of God.
>
> Yet these very historical movements make fully manifest a dichotomy between "God" and the Kingdom of God, or between

---

[27] John Cobb, "Christianity and Myth," *Journal of Bible and Religion* 33.4 (1965), 320. Clearly, To be sure, "fundamental" accusation against "orthodox Christianity" is a straw man against popular Christianity of the 20th century (Altizer, "Response" [Respnse B, 1970], 114). It is, nevertheless, a crucial move within Altizer's development of his *coincidentia oppositorum*.

> the apocalyptic God and the God of Christendom, a dichotomy which is a pure dichotomy, and a dichotomy which has been actually realized in our history. All too significantly the God of Christendom is far more purely and more totally transcendent than is any epiphany or naming of God in Israel, and is even more transcendent and majestic than any naming of God in the New Testament. But what is most missing in the orthodox God of Christianity is that very movement of actualization which is so primary in prophetic Israel, a movement which is totally realized in an original Christian apocalypticism, and there realized as the absolute triumph of the Kingdom of God. That is the triumph which Christianity originally celebrated as the resurrection, a resurrection which is the initial realization of apocalypse, and whose very occurrence is a decisive sign of a dawning apocalyptic transformation, a transformation which is the absolute transformation of everything whatsoever. Only that reversal of that transformation made possible an apprehension of the absolute transcendence of God, an absolute transcendence which is the glory of God and the glory of God alone, and therefore an absolute transcendence which is finally manifest and real as an unmoving an inactual or passive transcendence. (*GG* 171)

Again, for all of its errors, orthodox Christianity is essential for a radical theology and it even serves a *didactic* purpose for Altizer, namely, it is a prime example of how radical theology makes sense within the scheme of his methodology of *coincidentia oppositorum*.

In the current situation, where transcendence is emptied out, "dismembered," and enfleshed, in the vacuousity of the present, Godhead is made actual through actualization. And as enfleshment, we actualize Godhead. "The very everydayness of true parabolic language," that is, the language of Jesus, Altizer writes: "bespeaks an immediate presence in a world of voice. Parabolic enactment occurs on earth and not in heaven, in 'flesh' as opposed to 'spirit.'" *Now* is the kingdom of God; "Now is the time of decision, and this nowness reverses every trace of a beyond which is only a beyond…likewise, there occurs here a reversal of a world which is merely and only world." This world "now stands forth in its immediacy, and that immediacy is itself the time of decision." The voice of Godhead transfigured through our flesh is "itself…praxis, the praxis of a world come of age" (*TP* 7). Speaking and actualizing Godhead out of enfleshment "stills the sound of speech by breaking up and dismembering a vertical immediacy into a horizontal presence," that is to say, "vertical presence recedes behind and before the impacting center of voice and in that expanding horizon an immediate identity passes into simile and metaphor" on the edge of language. It is to *dismember* and *reverse* vertical presence into an actual immanence (4). Altizer writes in *The Self-Embodiment of God:*

> The pure and emptying of voice is the pure transcendence of voice, a transcendence which is self-transcendence, for it is the self-enactment of the self-embodiment of voice. When the voice of "I AM" realizes itself as pure transcendence, it fully empties itself of its original voice and identity. That emptying is the self-embodiment of the voice of "I AM," a self-embodiment which is a self-transcendence of the original identity of "I AM." Now the voice of "I AM" is a wholly self-actualized immediacy, and an immediacy wherein voice is totally present in hearing. But this presence, this self-actualizing presence, is a self-negating presence. Only the self-negation of the original presence in the immediate actuality of hearing. Pure hearing is the total embodiment of voice, an embodiment wherein voice is the otherness of itself. That otherness is the pure otherness of the original presence of "I AM." Therefore, in that otherness, the original identity of "I AM" realizes itself as "I AM NOT." (*SEG* 70-71)

"'I AM NOT' can be the fully embodied identity of the voice of 'I AM'" (71). McCullough observes that "[i]f the death of God inaugurates the 'triumph' of the kingdom of God, that 'triumph' nonetheless feels like death, a totally consuming darkness, faith is a kingdom in which the Godhead is broken up."[28] Self-negation, kenosis, incarnation, self-transcendence: they all point toward a simple fact of reality of Altizer, namely, that in each moment we step into a new world, and this new world is a New Creation when we self-actualize or self-create such a New Creation. The final and total transfiguration of flesh into an immanence in a *coincidentia oppositorum* with Spirit is "only...resolved as such in our deepest theological vision" and is made actual through apocalyptic thinking.[29]

---

[28] McCullough, "Theology as the Thinking of Passion Itself" (2004), 44-45.
[29] Altizer, "A Response" (2004), 223. Perhaps a good criticism of Altizer at this point is to ask, *how exactly does this happen?* And further: *How should one act?* Without jumping ahead of ourselves, or Altizer, the sort of theological ethics implied by Altizer's system of theology is at once incarnational and apocalyptic. By this I suggest that Christian ethics be kenotic

Godhead as the *Nothing*[30]

As mentioned earlier, Altizer critic Ray Hart observed that Altizer's theology shifts the notion of *creatio ex nihilo* to *creatio ex nihilo sive Deo ipse*, which is to say, "God creates from nothing, that is, from God Godself."[31] The *nothing* is perhaps Altizer's most challenging theological concept; and, while it is one of the primary foci of his later work, it is surprisingly present and developed in some of Altizer's earlier works as well—the Syracuse Altizer archive holds notes for a lecture given in March, 1960, to the Emory University Student Colloquium titled "Faith and the Nothing."[32]

Altizer asks in *Godhead and the Nothing*: "[c]an theology truly be liberated by finally knowing the nothingness of nothingness, and thereby knowing that God *is* God only by knowing the nothingness of nothingness, and is that finally what the very word 'God' most truly and most actually means?" (*GN* 53) Answering, Altizer re-emphasizes the idea of the death of God from his earlier work: "[i]t is this negation [the death of God] and this negation alone which makes possible an epiphany or a realization of the actuality of nothingness, as the dissolution or self-emptying of that God whose 'isness' is the very annihilation of nothingness [which] inevitably and necessarily calls forth an absolute nothingness, an absolute nothingness which truly is the absolute 'other' of Godhead itself" (58). In other words, to think of an absolutely transcendent deity is to conversely equivocate an absolutely radical deity: if God is constantly kenotically self-negating, *the nothing* is at the end of Christian nihilism.

---

and self-subverting and radically subversive. Genuine, apocalyptic acts silently or loudly interrupt the banality of Nothingness.

[30] Cf. Christopher Rodkey, Revs. of *The New Gospel of Christian Atheism* and *Godhead and the Nothing* by Thomas Altizer, *Bulletin of the North American Paul Tillich Society* 31.2 (2006): 7-9. The author admits that he, in fact, misinterpreted the notion of the "Nothing" in Altizer's work in this unfortunate and thankfully unnoticed book review.

[31] Hart (2004), 51. Also: "If *indeterminate Godhead* does not equal cosmos, *determinate God* is not and cannot be a 'proper' name. Creation *ab origine*, however *sui generis*, does not close or exhaust the transformation of indeterminate Godhead; *creation continua* is the covenant of epiphantic transformation of the selfsame but redemptive Godhead the apocalypse of salvation for both humanity and God" (50). It is worth mentioning that the idea of the "nothing" is rooted in a deep impulse throughout the history of Jewish and Christian mysticism—which will be mentioned later—but particularly through Meister Eckhart.

[32] Altizer, "Faith and the Nothing," dated 3. March 1960, in the Syracuse Altizer archive (box 4, folio 4). He picks up this concept later, largely inspired by D. H. Leahy's work, in Altizer, "Modern Thought and Apocalypticism," in *Encyclopedia of Apocalypticism*, vol. 3, ed. Stephen Stein (New York: Continuum, 1998), esp. 345-356.

What does Altizer mean by *the nothing*? The nothing is the "deepest other...the opposite of everything which we once knew as God, and a Nothing whose full advent is inseparable from a uniquely modern realization of the death of God" (*GN* x). "This new nihilism in which the Nothing is fully embodied," Altizer writes, is "so fully embodied that the Nothing has ceased to be manifest as the Nothing and the Nothing alone" (x-xi). To be sure, the primordial Godhead—the primordial Nothing—is to be understood as "pure difference or pure otherness itself" (*GA* 47). In the immanence of the present, the transfigured Nothing is made actual in its implicit connection to a historical understanding of Godhead itself. This Nothing is not only a symbol of the New Creation and its creative potentiality but is a total *nihil*, a negated new beginning point, the "absence of everything we once knew as either world or humanity." This is a true abyss, an ultimate kenosis "that is cosmic and historical at once, interior and exterior at once.... A truly universal body and world that is precisely thereby a total *coincidentia oppositorum* of Satan and Christ" (*CJ* 204).

Altizer's understanding and usage of the Nothing is indicative of the shift from *creatio ex nihilo* to *creatio ex nihilo sive Deo ipse*, indicating a cyclical return to a new beginning, a New Creation. He writes in *Genesis and Apocalypse*, referring to the otherness of primordial transcendence:

> In the beginning, 'God?' Yes, for in the beginning is pure difference or pure otherness, an otherness which is 'God,' and an otherness apart from which beginning could not actually begin. That difference is what a postexilic Israel could name as the Creator, a Creator who alone is Creator, and a Creator who alone is finally actor, and who is finally actor only by being finally alone. The God who is God and only God is pure difference or pure otherness itself; that is a difference which is necessarily unreal in an eternity which is eternally the same, and therefore that is a difference which begins, and which actually begins, in 'God said.' If 'God said' is the self-naming of I AM, that is a self-naming which is the actualization of pure difference or pure otherness, and therefore the actualization of 'God.' (*GA* 47).

While Altizer is playing on a creation spirituality, he is clearly drawing upon Hegel's logic. For Hegel, being, as "the indeterminate immediate, is in fact *nothing*, and neither more or less than *nothing*" because "[i]t is pure indeterminateness and emptiness." Continuing, "*Nothing, pure nothing*" has a meaning in thinking and is "therefore the same determination, or rather absence of determination, and thus altogether the same as pure *being*." Hegel writes in the *Science of Logic*:

> *Pure being* and *pure nothing* are, therefore, the same.... But it is equally true that they are not undistinguished from each other, that, on the contrary, they are not the same, that they are absolutely distinct, and yet they are unseparated and inseparable and that each immediately *vanishes in its opposite*. Their truth is, therefore, this moment of the immediate vanishing of one in the other: *becoming*, a moment in which both are distinguished, but by a difference which has equally resolved itself.[33]

"For the mystic," Altizer observes, "Being is the Nothing: and to the extent that he is conscious of Being *qua* being he lives on this side of the sacred reality."[34] When such thinking is applied to creation spirituality, Altizer's ideas reside close to the apocalyptic sense of the "Primordial Nothingness" early in the Zohar, where the Nothing is "the highest point and the world that is coming" (Zohar 3:26b).[35] Richard Rubenstein made an early observation that Altizer's metaphysics was similar to the Lurianic Kabala, where the primordial nothingness of creation "was not exterior for God" and that, again, "God created the world out of *his own nothingness* through an act of self-diminution" akin to Altizer's notion of kenosis.[36] Beyond this, Rubenstein suggested that the Lurianic mystical worldview posits the world in a perpetual dialectic conflict "between the tendency toward self-maintenance and the yearning to return to the nothingness that is our true origin and our real essence." "Eventually, of course," Rubenstein writes: "God's nothing will be victorious" and "[w]ith the self-division of God, in Luria and as in Hegel, negation comes into existence. The price paid for

---

[33] Hegel (1869), 82-83. Further: "*Nothing* is usually opposed to *something*; but the being of *something* is already determinate and is distinguished from another something; and so therefore the nothing which is opposed to the something is also the nothing of a particular something, a determinate nothing. Here, however, nothing is to be taken in its indeterminate simplicity. Should it be held more correct to oppose to being, *non-being* instead of nothing, there would be no objection to this so far as the result is concerned, for in *non-being* the relation to *being* is contained: both being and its negation are enunciated in a *single* term, nothing, as it is in becoming" (83). Cf. 592, 829.
[34] Thomas Altizer, "The Religious Meaning of Myth and Symbol," *Truth, Myth, and Symbol*, ed. Thomas Altizer, William Beardslee, and J. Young (Englewood Cliffs, NJ: Prentice-Hall, 1962), 100.
[35] Zohar 3:26b (p. 87).
[36] Richard Rubenstein, "Thomas Altizer's Apocalypse," *The Theology of Altizer*, ed. John Cobb (Philadelphia: Westminster, 197), 129.

creation is negation."[37] The *coincidentia* of the immanence and transcendence of the primordial Godhead is for Altizer, following a spiritual spin of Hegel, not the *same* but a *return* for which no eternal return may ever follow (*GA* 47). Alien transcendence will never return in Altizer's eternal return of the same, even if it is an historical beginning point: primordial transcendence's primal kenotic action enacts the *coincidentia* of history, a beginning point to which reality itself will never return as a result.

This direction of thinking is consistent with the rest of Altizer's Christian theology. Jesus Christ, then, must be understood as "an ultimate and final sacrifice...releasing an absolutely sacrificial body, a body embodying apocalyptic sacrifice itself" (*GN* 152). Therefore, the emptied-out God is not really empty, but rather it is "the embodiment of a purely negative abyss, a negative abyss which is an absolutely negative body, but nevertheless one which is essential to the very actuality of the absolute sacrifice" (153). Altizer offers the following definition:

> [God's] self-negation realizes an absolutely actual dichotomy in the Godhead, a dichotomy in which Godhead itself is absolutely torn asunder, now absolutely divided between its positive and negative poles.... Now absolute beginning is and only can be an absolute ending, but that absolute transfiguration of the poles of the Godhead releases an absolute negativity which is absolutely new, and absolutely new as an absolutely transfiguring power.

> That transfiguring power is inseparable from that Nihil which it embodies, a Nihil which can be named as the dead body of God or the Godhead, an abysmal body of the Godhead which is the inevitable consequence of an absolute sacrifice of the Godhead. Now this is just the sacrifice that is refused in every Christian apprehension of the absolute sovereignty and the absolute transcendence of God. That refusal inevitably impels a radical movement away from that very actuality which is a necessary consequence of the absolute sacrifice of the Godhead, or that actuality which in full modernity realizes itself as an absolute immanence, and an absolute immanence that is the necessary consequence of the pure reversal of an absolute transcendence. That reversal can be understood as occurring in the full sacrifice

---

[37] Ibid. 130.

of the Godhead, for if that sacrifice is the absolute negation of absolute transcendence, its inevitable consequence is the realization of the very opposite of that absolute transcendence, an opposite which is absolute immanence itself, and an immanence only possible by way of the negation and reversal of absolute transcendence. The very advent of that immanence is inseparable from the realization of the full and actual emptiness of absolute transcendence, an emptiness that is truly alien emptiness, and one which is realized as the Nihil itself. (154)

The Nothing, then, is an alien Nihil, and is a challenge to the contemporary human situation. Within the Nihil the dialectic of the *coincidentia* continues and culminates:

> Only Christianity knows an ultimate self-negation or self-emptying of the Godhead, but that is a self-negation inevitably realizing an absolute abyss, and an absolute abyss of Godhead itself. Therein and thereby the negative pole of the Godhead fully stands forth, and this is not an illusory negativity as it finally is in Gnosticism, or a negative pole that is simply and only the pure "other" or the positive pole, but far rather a negative pole that is dialectically identical with the positive pole, as Godhead for the first time is fully actual as an ultimate *coincidentia oppositorum*. If Godhead here undergoes an absolute self-negation or self-emptying, this is not a primordial self-emptying, but rather an apocalyptic and historical self-emptying, one realizing itself in the actualities of history and consciousness. Therein it profoundly transforms both consciousness and history, a transformation inseparable from the transformation or transfiguration of Godhead itself. Not only does an absolutely "new" dawn ever more fully, but an absolutely "old" is equally called forth, and "old" which apocalyptically can be named as the old aeon or even Satan, but an actualization of Satan and the old aeon or old creation only possible as the consequence of an absolutely forward movement. Just as it was the prophetic revolution which first enacted the absolutely new, this is a revolution fulfilled in Jesus, and in that Jesus who enacted the final dawning of the Kingdom of God, a kingdom that is not a primordial or an ancient or an eternal kingdom, but a kingdom that is and only is an apocalyptic kingdom, or that kingdom which *is* the absolutely new. (148)

Thus, in an apocalyptic sense, the spirating and generating aspects of Trinitarian theology are perpetuated by the *coincidentia oppositorum*, and made new and transfigured into the Nothing by the ultimate self-emptying of Godhead into the immanence of the present. In other words, as a rejection of the "unoriginate" orthodox Christian trinity, Father and Son are generated anew by an "unoriginate" Godhead, the dead God, fully pouring forth Son and Spirit (149).[38]

In this situation, we are too called forth to become enfleshed by this kenosis of the apocalyptic trinity as "a voyage realizing a new responsibility," that is, Altizer writes, "creating a new world."[39] Apple Igrek asks of Altizer, "[i]f the affirmation of nothingness cannot be fully subordinated to our selfish interests, if it exceeds calculative potentiality, then how do we move beyond the 'total immanence' of postmodernity if the aimlessness of that age remains…is in the absolute circling of the apocalypse?" She answers that "[i]t may be that the realization of the absolute abyss is a moment of transformation which cannot be separated from its antithetical negations: the immanence of the abyss is perhaps…included within its teleological actualization."[40] As a *coincidentia oppositorum*, the negation is always defined and shaped by its prior figuration prior to transfiguration. Similarly, we stand in a New World where the actuality of Godhead can only be manifest in our own actualizations, and a new ethics reflecting this apocalyptic immanence is demanded.

Apocalyptic Thinking: *Reputo-Ipsum*

Steven Smith observes in a review of *The New Gospel of Christian Atheism* that at bottom, Altizer leaves his readers with an ethical decision. Despite this, Smith observes, Altizer "is unwilling to speak 'ethically.'"[41] Like Tillich, Altizer points toward an ethics of a Nietzschean eternal recurrence, but Altizer appropriates it within a methodological context of *coincidentia oppositorum*. In Hegel's logic, Altizer writes, there "is a radically and comprehensively forward movement from absolute beginning to absolute ending, a movement that is seemingly reversed" in Nietzsche's notion of

---

[38] J. Nelson, "A Misuse of Kenosis," *Christian Advocate* 10.11 (2. June 1966), 15.
[39] Thomas Altizer, Introduction to "To Create the Absolute Edge" by D. G. Leahy, *Journal of the American Academy of Religion* 57.4 (1989), 778.
[40] Apple Igrek, Book Profile of *Godhead and the Nothing* by Thomas Altizer, *Journal of Cultural and Religious Theory* 6.2 (2003), 145.
[41] Smith, 892.

the eternal return (*GN* 59). "Yet that reversal certainly is not the primordial movement of eternal return, but rather its very opposite, and thereby it is in deep continuity with Hegelian thinking, for Nietzsche and Hegel alike transformed an absolute transcendence into an absolute immanence" (59-60). The eternal return is not a *literal* eternal return but an *actualized* and *enacting* understanding of ethics.[42] The eternal recurrence is *not* "the recurrence of full and actual events" or "simply the return of such events," but rather "a transfiguration of these events, for now all events are realized in an absolute immanence, and immanence that is only possible as a consequence of the death of God, an immanence that now *is* that which a pure transcendence *was*, which is to say eternity itself" (*GA* 140-141).

D. G. Leahy writes that in Altizer there is "not the eternal recurrence of all things, but the *end of the eternal recurrence of all things*," that is, a reversal of "the Nietzschean abyss."[43] In some ways, Altizer is rejecting Nietzsche by affirming his ideas by at once acknowledging and refusing the "most brutal and savage" sense of nihilism which inevitably "broke" Nietzsche.[44] "The idea of Eternal Recurrence is the supreme challenge we can face, the ultimate test of courage, or life, for it poses the question whether we can affirm life, *our* life, here and now," Altizer writes in his contribution to the important collection *The New Nietzsche*. "Here is Nietzsche's categorical imperative—the most awful and awesome that man has ever faced, for it calls for an act of total affirmation."[45] He continues:

> The death of God, which brings to an end the transcendence of being, the beyondness of eternity, makes Being manifest in every Now. Being assumes a totally new meaning and identity: no longer is it eternal; rather, it begins or dawns in every actual moment. Here the verb *begins* is all-important, for it defines or establishes both the subject and the predicate. We might even say that in this affirmation the subject ceases to be, with the result that it is no longer possible to say that being *is*, or that anything whatsoever

---

[42] Altizer, "Nietzsche's Understanding of Christianity" (1958/1960), 5. Cf. Marion (1991), 30.
[43] D. Leahy, "The Diachrony of the Infinite in Altizer and Levinas," *Thinking Through the Death of God*, ed. Lissa McCullough and Brian Schroeder (Albany, NY: SUNY UP, 2004), 106.
[44] Thomas Altizer, Rev. of *Nietzsche's Existential Imperative* by Bernd Magnus, *Journal of the American Academy of Religion* 47.4 (1979), 697; ibid. "The Challenge of Nihilism," *Journal of American Academy of Religion* 62.4 (1994), 1016.
[45] Ibid., "Eternal Recurrence and the Kingdom of God," *The New Nietzsche*, ed. David Allison (Cambridge, Mass.: MIT UP, 1977) 241.

is, as everything *begins* in every Now. Thereby, it is revealed that the proposition "Being *is*" is a product of the detachment of the speaker from the immediate moment: to be totally immersed in the Now is to be free of a permanent existence of any kind.[46]

Different from a Stoic notion of eternal return, Altizer's appropriation of Nietzsche's return is *apocalyptic* and Christian. It is at once an eternal death and an eternal transfiguration.[47] "Only the final ending of eternal recurrence or eternal return makes possible a once and for all and irreversible beginning, an actual beginning which is absolutely new, and is absolutely new only by way of the absolute ending of an eternity which is eternally the same" (*GA* 47). As Nietzsche wrote in *Thus Spoke Zarathustra*, "Being begins in every now," Altizer suggests "that beginning is the ending of transcendence or the death of God, a death which occurs in every full and actual moment, and therefore a death releasing a total immanence, a pure immanence which is a reversal of every moment which is open to transcendence," that is, a reversal of anything resembling an orthodox Christianity which apprehends the historical progression of Godhead (128).[48] And this absolute immanence is an "absolute nothingness" through which we must pass (*GN* 58).

Because there is not a literal eternal return of the same for Altizer, but rather, the eternal return is reversed in the New Creation of the Nothing. He writes that on this point "it becomes overwhelmingly important to understand an eternal death of God which is not the eternal resurrection," instead it is "a death of God finally shattering every possible movement of eternal return, and a death of God absolutely reversing to apocalypse itself, and an apocalypse wholly and totally transcending genesis itself" (*LDG* 133). The immanence of the Nothing in which we now habituate is one of darkness, but it is one of ultimate joy; the only meaningful way in which to live in the Nothing is to, as Steven Smith

---

[46] Ibid. 243.
[47] Ibid. 241.
[48] Altizer is here is quoting *Thus Spoke Zarathustra*, III §2 ("The Convalescent"). Altizer writes elsewhere, quite poignantly, on "The Convalescent": "Note the order of the images establishing the new meaning of reality or being: *Rad* ('wheel, 'cycle'), *Jahr* ('year'), *Haus* ("house,' "home," 'family,' 'race'), and *Ring* ('ring,' 'circle,' 'cycle'). The imagery itself is cyclical, moving to and from the image and idea of the circle, and comprehending first a cyclical image of time (*Jahr*), and that what can only be intended as a cyclical image of space (*gleich Haus*).... When manifest and known in total affirmation, the abyss of the eternal round of suffering and pain is transformed into the highest order of perfection, as symbolized by the circle" ("Eternal Recurrence and the Kingdom of God" [1977], 242).

writes, "live forward *into* a genuinely open future with commensurate optimism," observing that to so do "would be the life of hope, love, and faith."[49] But it is a qualified joyfulness, Altizer warns, impelling that "[w]e are called upon not to will an eternity of joy, but rather to will the world with all its sorrow, transfigured in the act of willing it."[50]

We will, or transfigure, the world 'with all its sorrow' as an act of joyfulness when enacting the eternal return as a moral imperative that is reversed. It is an affirmation or Yes or *theology* of "absolute death that is precisely a theology of absolute life," that is "a theology of the death of God that is purely apocalyptic and even thereby a theology of absolute resurrection."[51] As a Yes that names "our darkness" the false, Satanic vision that must be transfigured not only in deed but in time and space, this willed sorrow of immanence is a perpetual ritual that must be enacted constantly.[52] That is to say, the eternal return, and its reversal, not only suggests a moral imperative but a ritualistic understanding of ethics that is open to its own reversal.[53] In other words, it is to *think apocalyptically.*

Thinking apocalyptically is at once an acknowledgement of the Nothing and a genuine attempt to kenotically pour oneself out as an act of joyfulness. It is to unmask the "world of forgetfulness" that forgets the primordial Godhead as a primordial Godhead.[54] The 'world of forgetfulness' is the same world where, as Blake wrote in "The Marriage of Heaven and Hell," "All deities reside in the human/ breast."[55] The human breast, the body, is the ground for God-thought and God-talk, and it arises more specifically through human thinking. Like Tillich, theology begins with being-itself, *esse-ipsum*, which occurs in thinking, but for Altizer apocalyptic thinking is not just human thought itself but the thinking itself now occurring: *reputo ipsum iam evulsum. Reputo ipsum iam evulsum* is not just thought itself but the *apocalyptic* thought perpetually

---

[49] Smith, 892. Cf. Wyschogrod (2004), 101.
[50] Altizer, "Nietzsche's Understanding of Christianity," (1958/1960).
[51] Ibid., "A Response" (2004), 219.
[52] Ibid., "Satan as the Messiah of Nature" (1998), 129.
[53] Mircea Eliade, *The Myth of the Eternal Return*, trans. Willard Trasnk (New York: Pantheon, 1954), 143-144, citing Hebrews 9 and 1 Peter 3:18 as examples where there are events not "subject to repetition" (143).
[54] Thomas Altizer, "The Otherness of God as an Image of Satan," *The Otherness of God*, ed. Orrin Summerell (Charlottesville, VA: UP of Virginia, 1998), 207.
[55] Blake, "The Marriage of Heaven and Hell," pl. 11, ln. 15 (p. 186).

now-occurring; it cannot be divorced from the now nor from the human. It occurs within the space of *vita-ipsum*, in the immanent Nothing of the now.

Altizer's faith is a faith in the value of *reputo-ipsum*, in apocalyptic thinking. The value of apocalyptic thinking is that it establishes the ultimacy of the Tillichian *vita-ipsum*, that is, that every will has the potentiality to participate in the apocalyptic history of Godhead. Altizer writes in *Living the Death of God*:

> There is no greater challenge to faith than the pervasive judgment that faith is a flight from life, an evasion of pain and suffering, a refusal of the burden and the anguish of the human condition, or a capitulation to the passivity which is the very reversal of human freedom and responsibility. Certainly I have always known faith as an ultimate challenge, and an ultimate challenge inseparable from a profound conflict, one which could be understood as an ultimate conflict between a pure activity and a pure passivity, or between a genuine freedom and a fully actual impotence. Insofar as Stonewall Jackson has been a model for my life, I have thought of this conflict as war itself, a deeply interior and yet violent war, one finally allowing no hostages or slackers, and demanding a ruthless discipline, and yet a discipline allowing if not impelling truly innovative tactics and strategy, for here the odds are overwhelmingly against victory, and even the very meaning of victory is deeply in question. While ultimately faith is a gift of grace, humanly it is an ultimate struggle, and the absence of struggle can be understood as an absence of faith, but the struggle itself can only be a truly individual struggle. Hence this is a struggle transcending any possible guidelines or rules, and wholly inseparable from one's unique condition and situation. (*LDG* 155)

Faith is a struggle, perhaps seemingly fruitless and nonsensical, but nonetheless ultimately important and requiring the greatest risk or *courage*. Altizer continues, writing that in his conversation with other theologians, the greatest test of a theology is whether it "meets the challenge" of an "ultimate courage," an *existential* courage *to be*:

> If only through my fellow theologians I became persuaded that such a courage is now a truly necessary theological discipline, and while I am alone in centering my work upon damnation and Satan, I certainly am not alone in centering theology upon an absolute nothingness, and just as Hell can be known as a primal symbol of

absolute nothingness, damnation can be known as a deeply modern if not universal condition, and one that becomes truly meaningful to us all through the language and imagery of an absolute nothingness. (156-57)

Faith is the ultimate courage to unmask, as Blake did, Christ for Satan, "the Ratio" for "the Infinite," resurrection as descent, apprehended life as meaningless death, as the affirmation of life as an eternal and ultimate death.[56] It is a "voyage into darkness, and into the depths of darkness," where "the theologian must know that darkness as Godhead itself, and not a Godhead whose darkness is only the consequence of an epiphany of an absolute glory to us, but far rather a darkness which is Godhead itself, and is Godhead itself in the depths of its absolutely negative abyss" (161). Reflecting upon a eulogy delivered for Charles Winquist, Altizer affirms: "Yes, we are celebrants of Joy, but only by being celebrants of Darkness, and if our deepest desire is for Joy, that desire can be only realized through the deepest darkness" (179). This celebration of a luminous darkness is not a worship of darkness, or even of Satan, but is an consequent of the *coincidentia oppositorum* occurring between "light" and "darkness."

Thinking apocalyptically, as *reputo ipsum iam evulsum*, is for Altizer a faith in his own methodology, but is more specifically a faith in the value of oneself and others. To think apocalyptically, that is, to have faith, is to have the courage to live in *vita-ipsum*, in life itself, and burden oneself with the darkness of life. While Altizer's vision is very much a kenotic Christian vision, it is post-Christian in that it requires an exodus from the apprehensions of orthodox Christianity.

---

[56] Blake, "There Is No Rational Religion" (p. 76).

CHAPTER 5

THE DIALECTIC OF THE SACRED

Tillich's Influence on Altizer

It is perhaps obvious that Tillich had a profound influence on Altizer, even though their theological systems are in many ways quite different. Tillich's central notion of existential courage is essential to Altizer's understanding of faith; that Altizer shifts Tillich's ontological thinking away from a strict *ontology* to an *etiological ontology*, an ontology with a historical and causal aspect.[1] While Altizer's heavy reliance upon a Christology might surprise many of his critics, the *givenness* of Christ as New Being as "paradox" and "good news" has a similar salience within Tillich's systematic theology.[2] That said, perhaps the biggest difference between Tillich and Altizer is what connects the two. While both Tillich and Altizer are surprisingly systematic theologians, Tillich *poses himself* as a traditional philosophical theologian in terms of methodology, while Altizer's approach is more implicitly modern and uniquely his own. While I might suggest that Tillich is *systematic* where Altizer is *constructive*, yet Altizer's theology is far more systematic than one might assess at first glance. Clearly different, the two thinkers are similar in tone and breadth because, I suggest, they are both rooted in an explicit Christian radicalism and their theological thinking operates upon a *boundary* between this religious radicalism and post-Christian exoditic thinking. It is, to use William Hamilton's terminology, *expatriate* theology.[3]

Terrance Thomas has suggested that while Altizer—along with every other Protestant theologian and pastoral minister trained in the 1950s and 1960s—was influenced by Tillich, Altizer's first published book, *Mircea Eliade and the Dialectic of the Sacred*, very well might have introduced Mircea Eliade's ideas to Tillich as a subject of importance to the systematic theologian.[4] In this book Altizer systematically appropriates Tillichian

---

[1] Rubenstein (1970), 126; Hartshorne, 259.
[2] Winquist, "Untimely History," *Truth and History: A Dialogue with Paul Tillich/ Warheit and Geschichte*, ed. Gert Hummel (Berlin: Walter de Gruyter, 1998), 75.
[3] W. Hamilton (1974), 44. Cf. Greenfield, 87.
[4] T. Thomas, 244.

theological thinking for the means of exposing Eliade, as well as Tillich, as *not yet* "fully dialectical." The two thinkers, when taken radically, however, according to Altizer, are "complimentary" and take each other to each thinkers' radical ends (*ME* 86). As mentioned before, the final product of Tillich and Eliade's collaboration ended with Tillich's lecture, "The Significance of the History of Religions for the Systematic Theologian," which was delivered with Altizer in the audience the night before Tillich's death.

Following this, it is perhaps the "radical Tillich" that Tillich himself so infamously affirmed to Altizer during the end of Tillich's life and seemed to propose in his 'Religion of the Concrete Spirit' in this final lecture that defines the ethos of Altizer's own radicalism.[5] Altizer has written that the last weeks of Tillich's life were an intensive period of theological breakthrough for him and that in the small community of radicals, including Tillich, in Chicago at the time shaped the radical theological vision he had only begun to mold at that point—as a reaction to his own Satanic *theosis* at the University of Chicago campus a few years before. At the same time, the radical Tillich that Altizer claims that he knew in Tillich's final weeks stands in sharp contrast to the "late Tillich" handed to the public in the form of the third volume of his *Systematic Theology*. In his forward to Mark C. Taylor's *Deconstructing Theology* Altizer charged that the third volume was a rejection of the "dialectical and mediational theology" which made Tillich's earlier work worthwhile and that the book pandered to "a traditional ecclesiastical or church theology"; and in *Living the Death of God* Altizer further calls the work "not only truly conservative but derivative and unoriginal as well" (*LDG* 133).[6] More specifically, Richard Grigg observes that for Altizer, Tillich was simply unable to correlate the "contemporary *Existenz* and biblical eschatological faith."[7]

It is the radical ethos of Tillich which Altizer has channeled or divinated in his own theology. While "Tillich didn't start a 'school' of thought," Altizer writes, "he had a deep impact, indeed, and perhaps most so in the birth of a uniquely American atheistic theology," namely, *death of God theology* (*LDG* 53). Beyond this influence, however, according to

---

[5] D. Foster, 23.
[6] Thomas Altizer, "Forward," *Deconstructing Theology* by Mark C. Taylor (New York: Crossroad, 1982), xi-xv.
[7] Richard Grigg, "Tillich's Ontological Eschatology," *New Creation or Eternal Now*, ed. Gert Hummel (Berlin: Walter de Gruyter, 1991), 154, citing *RT* 10-11, 105-109.

Altizer, Tillich's great failure was caused by his own apprehension of a truly radical Christianity, that is, to initiate a larger movement of radical faith (*GN* xi-xii).

At the same time, Tillich's ideas are the roots of Altizer's radical theology, even if Tillich wasn't entirely comfortable with Altizer's direction.[8] William Hamilton has suggested that Tillich's few documented comments on Altizer or the death of God theology reflect that Tillich did not or could not understand it.[9] In *Genesis and Apocalypse*, Altizer charges that Tillich was unable to recognize the true nihilism of the present and was thus ultimately unable to "incorporate the apocalyptic or eschatological ground of Christianity" (*GA* 11, 23). I suggest that a better way to approach the intellectual relationship between Altizer and Tillich is to render Tillich's Religion of the Concrete Spirit as a post-theological—or *metatheological*—move away from the particularizations of Christian theology toward a universal, non-tribal world theology. To this end, we may consider Altizer's Christian Atheism as a *metatheological return* to Christianity. We will return to this idea later in the dissertation. Even if Altizer's theology is a post-Christian return from a Tillichian trajectory *away* from Christianity, the radical Tillich's ethos remains within Altizer's ideas.

While not fully or actually apocalyptic, Tillich's theology is a "Dionysiac Theology" in the sense of Jacob Taubes' use of the terms. To recall, Altizer reminds us, "Taubes is astute in recognizing that Dionysiac theology" which has the potential to be *against the Crucified* but at the same time dangerously affirms the self in demonic ways by closing itself to apocalyptic revelation.[10] Altizer rejects any apprehension of a church theology in Tillich to achieve what is perhaps a theology completely removed from the church or *ecclesia*. It is a theology which requires and demands solitude.

Richard Feero, in a 1993 dissertation on American radical theology, suggested that Tillich's true influence on Altizer was a rebirth of language in the Tillichian method of correlation.[11] Like Tillich, Altizer

---

[8] Crockett, "Contact Epistemology for the Sites of Theology" (2001), 206; Grigg (2006), 152 n. 14. Cf. Eigi Hibino, *The Sacred and the Holy*, Ph.D. diss., Drew U. (1989), 152-154; Steve Odin, "Kenosis as a Foundation for Buddhist-Christian Dialogue," *Eastern Buddhist* ns 20.1 (1987), 34.
[9] W. Hamilton (1961), 57.
[10] Altizer, "Nietzsche's Understanding of Christianity" (1958/1960), 258-259.
[11] Richard Feero, *Radical Theology in Preparation*, Ph.D. diss., Syracuse U. (1993), 72.

appropriates nearly every historical theological category, but voyages beyond Tillich by using the theological concepts themselves to *violate* theology; where Tillich redefined and reappropriated theological language, it was understood within the context that theological language is by its nature paradoxical, and as such Tillich shifted toward a use of ontological language to reflect this.[12] In the same sense, Altizer's language and writing subverts and "violates language" itself.[13] For example, Altizer's affirmation of resurrection is at once Biblical and dependent upon a historical reality, because it is a historical event for Godhead, which is, in this sense, a more conservative position than Tillich's, but the *meaning* of resurrection for Altizer within his apocalyptic methodology reverses not only the traditional sense of 'resurrection' and reverses his own methodology—and as such it affirms *both*, even if they are contrary (*GA* 70-71). Through the *coincidentia oppositorum* methodology, Altizer affirms the same Anselmian ontology of language which Tillich also affirms, as an "auto-deconstructive" process of using language at the *edge* of language.[14] Perhaps for Altizer it is the *center* of language where language itself fragments, rather than the *edge*, as the *nihil* of center-language reveals the impending *einstürzende* implicit in his theological 'violation.'

This *violation*, subversion, repetition, and reversal reveals the *liturgical* nature of Altizer's use of language.[15] This is not only because of Altizer's exegetical and homiletical tenor of his writing, but more importantly because of the Eucharistic shift to an enfleshed immanence enacted in his preached voice, which demands a willed and actual response without necessarily charging a *benidictio*. Yet the *exitus* from the church is implicit in the preaching.[16] Trevor Greenfield has suggested that Altizer's writing is, on the whole, a liturgical meditation on Matthew 27:51, a "literal tearing of the curtain that breaks down the barrier between God and the Universe" in the new implicit immanence.[17] One should recall that in Nietzsche's aphorism of the madman, after announcing the death of God

---

[12] T. Thomas, 252-253.
[13] Charles Winquist, Revs. *The Self-Embodiment of God* and *Total Presence* by Thomas Altizer, *Religious Studies Review* 8 (1982), 339.
[14] Caputo, in Caputo and Vattimo (1977), 147. Cf. T. Thomas, 261.
[15] David Jasper, "In the Wasteland," *Thinking Through the Death of God*, ed. Lissa McCullough and Brian Schroeder (Albany, NY: SUNY UP, 2004), 185. A critique is found in Robert Corrington, Rev. *Genesis and Apocalypse* by Thomas Altizer, *Theology Today* 49.1 (1992), 135.
[16] Santiago Zabala, "Introduction," *The Future of Religion* by Gianni Vattimo and Richard Rorty, ed. Santiago Zabala (New York: Columbia UP, 2005), 2.
[17] Greenfield, 88.

the madman "forces his way into several churches and there struck up his *requiem aeternam deo.*"[18]

In doing so, Altizer affirms the Tillichian *vita-ipsum* as the *novum* of the present as the reversal of subjectivity, but yet a solipsistic and solitary journey. It is in this immanence of the Nothing where the *reputo ipsum iam evulsum*, the apocalyptic possibility of the thinking now occurring, occurs. *Reputo-ipsum* requires *esse-ipsum*. Altizer writes in *History and Apocalypse*:

> Now origin ends as a human or natural source, for "I AM" is the sole source of every "I," and the only source of every true or primal ground of meaning and identity. But only an interior and exterior loss of every given and manifest source or origin makes possible this radical and revolutionary opening* to a wholly and totally transcendent God. (*HA* 54)

The Altizeran tetragrammaton is congruent to the Tillichian *esse-ipsum*, but for Altizer it is much clearer that the ground of the "I AM" is the human and the human imagination. While Tillich's theology pointed toward an erasure of subjectivity through the dissolution of grammatical boundaries enforced by an ontology, Altizer affirms this dissolution but in the dissolution is a stronger, solipsistic affirmation of the self.[19] Again, *esse-ipsum* as *reputo ipsum iam evulsum* is only possible within an immanence of *vita-ipsum*, where the novum of the present calls us individually forth to *think apocalyptically* to give meaning and joy in the Nothing. This requires an ultimate existential courage to voyage through the Nothing, and if this demands an exitus out of anything remotely "Christian," so be it. At the same time, confessing this *exitus* and the death of God is regarded by Altizer as nothing less than a profession of authentic Christian faith.[20]

To return to Tillich's final lecture, for which Altizer was in the audience, The Religion of the Concrete Spirit called for a post-Christian shift *by means of* a religious atheism. More specifically, this atheism is post-Christian most prominently as a turn against the theological theism of Christendom: in Tillich's words, "a fight of God against religion within

---

[18] Nietzsche, *Gay Science*, §125 (p. 182).
[19] John Corrington, "Thomas Altizer Talks with *NOR*'s Editor-at-Large," *The New Orleans Review* 1.1 (Fall 1968): 26-35+.
[20] Eric Meyer, "Catholic Theology and the Death of God," *The Theology of Altizer*, ed. John Cobb (Philadelphia: Westminster, 1970), 89.

religion" (*FR* 88). Altizer's theology takes this post-Christian move *into account*, but then *returns*. This return is a post-Christian, *metatheological*, return: after moving beyond a localized theology and into a more general, non-tribal religious paradigm of the Concrete Spirit, Altizer *returns* to Christian theology, but this Christianity is now very different than before. While Tillich self-transcended his own Christian theology in his proposal for the Religion of the Concrete Spirit, Altizer has dialectically negated Tillich's new paradigm in a *coincidentia oppositorum*.

As such, the Altizeran move is not a move *further away* from Christianity, but is, in essence, *rebounded* by its own logos: a passage of return "by another path," but still, it is a return that is unquestionably Christian, even if it may be unrecognizable to Christendom. Altizer's Christian *rebound* is not a clear movement in an opposing direction, but rather a *carom* against a movement away. Ironically enough, Tillich's lecture, proposing the Religion of the Concrete Spirit, began with a general critique of the death of God movement at the time: Tillich *could not have* understood Altizer. Even though Tillich's proposal of a Religion of the Concrete Spirit is a self-transcendence of his own Christian theology in some ways, it is not a *betrayal* of his own systematic thinking in its radical expression. In fact, Tillich's proposed Religion of the Concrete Spirit is an expression of *fidelity* to his own ideas. While Altizer's theology might be considered Christian by virtue of its betrayal of Christianity, Altizer's theology is more immediately a betrayal of Christianity *qua* Tillichianism.

Critiques of Altizer

Almost every response to Altizer's theology misses the *point* of his theology, which is that he is attempting to develop a distinct, relevant, and original Christianity, even if it is no longer recognizable as "Christianity."[21]

---

[21] The most notable of Altizer's published academic critics are Bernard Murchland's *The Meaning of the Death of God* (New York: Vintage, 1967), Charles Sabatino's "The Death of God: A Symbol for Religious Humanism" (in *Horizons* 10.2, 288-303), Charles Butler's excellent "Hegel, Altizer and Christian Atheism" (in *Encounter* 41, 103-128), and William Beardslee and Charles Long in *Criterion* 7.3. All commonly dodge Altizer's Christology by matter-of-factly mentioning it or ignoring it altogether; a common theme in almost every response, summary, or criticism of the theologian's thought. Even more recently, Theodore Jennings in a 20th Century Handbook of Contemporary Theology in a chapter only mentions the centrality of Christ in the thought of Altizer (Jennings, 17). The only exceptions that I am aware of are Thomas Ogletree, Mark C. Taylor, and Charles N. Bent (*The Death of God Movement* (New York: Paulist, 1967), 174-179. Ogletree, in *The Death of God Controversy* (Nashville: Abingdon, 1966), explicates Altizer's Christology as a primary tenet of the theologian's thought (86-95).

Much of the early criticism of Altizer from evangelical sources borders on the ridiculous, even accusing Altizer's theology of perpetuating a neo-Nazism, since Altizer was fond of Bonhoeffer, whose radical writings were believed by some to have been tainted by NAZI censors.[22] Even more sophisticated approaches to Altizer accuse Altizer of, for example, not taking the Holocaust seriously, even though Altizer was one of the first theologians to take the Holocaust seriously as an ontotheological event.[23] Liberation theologians in particular have charged that radical theology is not politically radical enough; in fact, some arguments have even emerged that suggest that radical theology is in fact politically conservative.[24] Even the most detailed critique of Altizer's early work, the severely outdated anthology *The Theology of Altizer* (1970, ed. John Cobb), largely skirts Altizer's understanding of Christ, which is obviously very central to Altizer's thought, as conveyed by Altizer in his response to his critics in that volume, though the theologian's sentiments seem to remain generally ignored.[25] Like Nietzsche, a thoughtful approach to the death of God is also saying something about Christology.[26]

The most significant problem with Altizer's theology, in my view, is perhaps the polemic tone of his earlier writings, which imply a false *either/or* dichotomy, when Altizer is really writing about a *coincidentia oppositorum* between a Hegelian *both/and* and a Kierkegaardian *either/or*.[27] Speaking polemically, Altizer believes that there are two distinct choices

---

[22] John Paton, "Is God Dead," *Good News Broadcaster* (Feb. 1966), 5.
[23] Stephen Haynes, "Christian Holocaust Theology," *Journal of the American Academy of Religion* 62.2 (1994), 559; McCullough, "Historical Introduction" (2004), xxi-xxii, xxv.
[24] Nick Brown, "The Conservatism of Radical Theology," *Political Theology* 4.1 (2002). See also Jeff Robbins' brief discussion of this issue in "Terror and the Postmodern Condition," in *Religion and Violence in a Secular World*, ed. Clayton Crockett (Charlottesville, VA: U. Virginia P, 2006), 195-196.
[25] John Cobb, ed., *The Theology of Altizer: Critique and Response* (Philadelphia: Westminster, 1970). William Hamilton comments: "For Altizer men do not solve the problem of the death of God by following Jesus, but, it seems, by being liberated from history by him. In spite of [Altizer's] insight that ethics (or transforming the profane) can be a real war of handling the problems of the ambiguity of the profane realm, Altizer ultimately prefers the categories of neither Christology nor ethics but of mysticism" (*RT* 30-31).
[26] Altizer states in the opening remarks of a debate, in introducing his thought, that "I would like to ask you to remember—since we're so wont to forget it—that in one sense, at least, Christianity has always been grounded in a faith in the death of God. That is to say, Christianity in its orthodox and normative expressions has affirmed that Jesus Christ is fully God and fully man, while at the same time affirming that Christ has died and has died redemptively for man. It certainly has affirmed, if only implicitly, that God has died in Christ" (*AM* 8).
[27] Mark C. Taylor and Carl Raschke, "About *About Religion*," *Journal of Cultural and Religious Theory* 2.2 (2001), online.

in Christology, rhetorically stated: *either* Altizer's proposed kenotic Christ *or* a dead, empty Christ.[28] While Altizer in his work does not *explicitly* state this dualistic choice, he certainly implies it by concluding that only through a kenotic, apocalyptic Trinitarian portrayal of Christ can salvation or redemption be possible; and furthermore, to disagree with Altizer's proposed changes are to sink "ever more deeply into the darkness of an irrecoverable past" (*GC* 74, 76).[29] Following this, Altizer argues that to subscribe to any form of orthodox Christology would be heretical in a most primitive sense, proposing that "the Christian must betray his faith if it refuses the forward movement of the divine process" (*GC* 92).

For example, in a dialogue with a more traditional theological thinker in the *Journal of the American Academy of Religion*, Altizer charges that traditional theological attacks on radical expressions of faith are the content of the death of God—a (bad) Satanic worship of an idol long dead. Furthermore, to criticize the radical from any traditional argument places "pre-historic, non-historical or post-historical categories" upon Christian theology to "have [one's] transcendent cake and most immanently eat it, too."[30] While Altizer's rhetoric does set a reader up for a false choice to be made between two extremes, this (self-negating) choice is necessary for Altizer's "kenotic Christology" to be completely consistent while maintaining a distinct Christian *uniqueness* to his portrayal of Jesus Christ.[31] It is, as Mark C. Taylor and Carl Raschke discuss in a 2001 interview, neither a *both/and* nor an *either/or*, but rather a *neither/nor* in Altizer's thought. This *neither/nor* skirts theological attempts to talk *about* theology or Christology, instead, one has no option left but to *think* and *do*

---

[28] Montgomery, in *AM* 59-60.

[29] For example: "the Christian discipline cannot seek the presence of Christ in a moment of time that is irrevocably past; he might open himself to the Incarnate Word that is present in his own time and space. Faith in Jesus Christ demands a response to a Word that is present in the life of every human hand and face" (*RT* 123). Furthermore, to "cling to...traditional images of Jesus is to place an insuperable barrier to the appearance of Jesus in our flesh. Jesus can appear neither as an apocalyptic Son of Man nor as an eternal Son of God, nor can we isolate the historical Jesus from the 'mythological' categories of the New Testament" (125). Such thinking, he suggests, is "primitive" (*GC* 66).

[30] Thomas Altizer, "From Death into Life," *Journal of the American Academy of Religion* 41.2 (1973), 239.

[31] To his credit, Altizer recognizes that he does set up a false choice, as the Christological questions "each man is called to answer for himself" (*AM* 71). Altizer's rhetoric throughout his body of work, however, suggests otherwise.

theology.³² To do otherwise would be to simply speak *about* theology or to remain silent.

Another problem with Altizer's Christology is that, at least in a traditional theological sense, a theology which remains bound to the language and imagery of the New Testament should also consider the relations described in the scripture between God and Jesus, specifically *paternity* (Father to Son), *filiation* (Son to Father), *active spiration* (Father and Son to Spirit), and *passive spiration* (Spirit to Father and Son).³³ These four relations are partially a foundation for the Trinitarian Christology which Altizer wishes to reject; however, in his rejection of the Trinity he invariably ignores the scriptural basis for *these* traditionally-understood relations. While these relations are also based upon orthodox understandings of the proper attributes of God—namely, ingenerate, generating, generated, spirating, and spirated—Altizer is correct to claim that a kenotic attribute is ignored; however, Altizer, in making a legitimate argument against orthodox Trinitarian formulation rejects the other processional descriptions of God's movement in the New Testament. Instead, the focus is an *apocalyptic* understanding of the trinity which has little connection to traditional Trinitarian thought or formulae. While this thinking is consistent with Altizer's larger project of reappropriating traditional theological categories as a rejection of traditional understandings of theology, the Trinity arose as a highly sophisticated, politically relevant, and in some ways *radical* theological development rooted in a close reading of scripture. It is possible that a fully developed Altizeran theology of the Trinity may be possible, but only glimpses of it have yet to be seen in Altizer's work.³⁴

As a provocative call for reform, Altizer's Christology, as a primary component of his larger project of 'Christian atheism,' is also an *apologetic* theology for Christianity in culture. It is a theology of culture in a more subtle sense than a Tillichian theology of culture.³⁵ The only way to rediscover the living Christ in our culture, Altizer says, is to reverse the "religious forms of Christianity" and discern a spiritual, mystical Christ in culture (*GC* 56). The radical Christian who "lives in Christ must refuse every image of the preincarnate God insofar as such images are

---

³² M. Taylor and Raschke (2001), online.
³³ See Richard Norris, ed., *The Christological Controversy* (Philadelphia: Fortress, 1980).
³⁴ Altizer has worked on a text with a working title of *The Apocalyptic Trinity* which addresses these concerns. [Which would be published in 2012.]
³⁵ Georgia Harkness, *The Fellowship of the Holy Spirit* (Nashville: Abingdon, 1966), 186, 189.

transfigured by the self-sacrifice or self-negation of God himself," the theologian writes, calling for a massive reform of the basis of the theology in which the churches are grounded (92). Following this, to reject the Christ of Christendom is an act of faith or conviction of the reality of Christ's presence in the world as the incarnate Word in the present, as "the Christian who comes to understand God as a kenotic and forward-moving process will be delivered from the temptation to think of God as a wholly other and autonomous Being, just as he will be freed from any form of theological dualism" (25, 90). This proposed negation of 'orthodox' Christianity follows the negated forms of Christ in culture while simultaneously (and inevitably) liberating the Christian from the institutional constraints of the church, hence the title 'Christian atheism.'[36] The Christo-centric nature of Altizer's theology, especially his earlier work, led theologian Georgia Harkness to even accuse the death of God theology of being the most "ultraconservative" of conservative religious movements of the time; in fact, one that may have even generated the *coincidentia oppositorum* that led to the new Christian fundamentalism that emerged in the 1970s.[37] To this end, Harkness wrote elsewhere, the death of God theology is at the same time a reaction to the failure of the American mainline church to fully accept liberal theology.[38]

In some ways, to attack Altizer's theological position is little more than a personal attack on Altizer himself. Even Harkness reduces her critique of Altizer in her 1969 *Stability Amid Change* to an *ad hominem* attack on the prayer lives of the death of God theologians.[39] American Academy of Religion President Nathan Scott even offered a Kafkaesque parody of Altizer in the *Journal of the American Academy of Religion*, claiming him to be like a royal courier, "whose king no longer exists, but who...nevertheless insist[s] most adamantly that they are *royal* couriers,"

---

[36] Cf. *GC* 56. There are some other more obvious problems which stem out of these basic flaws in Altizer's Christology. Most explicitly, where there is some scriptural basis for language that implies an Altizeran kenotic Christology; such as, "Do you not believe that I am in the Father and the Father is in me?" (John 14:10ff.). Statements of Jesus Christ in the Gospels contradict Altizer's Christology as well, for example: Jesus prays to the "Father" in Gethsemane (Matt. 26:39, Mark 14:36, Luke 22:42, John 12:27).
[37] Georgia Harkness, *Understanding the Kingdom of God* (Nashville: Abingdon, 1974), 17-18, 19.
[38] Ibid., *Stability Amid Change* (Nashville: Abingdon, 1969), 87. Cf. Herberg, "Death of God Theology."
[39] Ibid., 60.

implying a clear *pretentiousness* about Altizer.⁴⁰ These *ad hominem* arguments probably emerge because for Altizer the theological vision is uniquely his own, in solitude, and perhaps can be no one else's but his. It is a personal response to a Satanic *theosis* and an apologetic Christianity that will follow itself out of the churches and outside of Christianity if necessary. John Cobb writes that "I have never been able to respond to Altizer in an adequate way," but to engage Altizer keeps him honest. "What I learn from him enters deeply into my psyche and over the years bears fruit," continuing, Altizer "forces me to examine what I truly believe, what I affirm with conviction, in its distinction from beliefs that I continue to hold but which no longer move me."⁴¹ Altizer's theology is a *radical* invitation to Christianity for those willing to *exodus* out of Christianity for the sake of religion.⁴²

As a post-Christian Christian theology, Altizer has also been criticized as being "too theological" and even not radical enough for remaining lodged as a *Christian* post-Christian *exoditic* thinker.⁴³ Philosopher John Caputo criticized Altizer in his book *After the Death of God* (written with Gianni Vattimo) that Altizer offers a "thinly disguised *grands récits*" who simply concocts a new "Big Story" or "Final Story" theology to replace an older "Big Story" that is deemed as false. Further, Caputo charges that Altizer's theology, taken as a whole, "is quite a Tall Tale to be telling in the name of deconstruction, a story of how consciousness or history traverses from transcendence to immanence, from alienation to homecoming, in which Judaism, as the religion of the Father or of alienation, plays the bad guy."⁴⁴

---

⁴⁰ Nathan Scott, "On the Fallacies of a 'Close Reader,'" *Journal of the American Academy of Religion* 39.1 (1971), 82. One must wonder if Scott was taking notes during Horace Freeman's Sunday School class at First Methodist Church in Brunswick, GA, on February 13, 1966, since, in his published lecture lesson for that day made a shockingly similar argument! See: Horace Freeman, *An Address on the Sunday School Lesson Before the Together Class of First Methodist Church, Brunswick, GA, Sunday, February 13, 1966* (Brunswick, GA: First Methodist Church, 1966), 6. Cf. A. Foster, "The Resurrection of God," *Religion in* Life 38.1 (1969), 144. Anthony Towne parodied Altizer as "God's surgeon" in "God is Dead in Georgia," *Motive* 26.5 (Feb. 1966): 74.
⁴¹ John Cobb, "Responses to Critiques," *John Cobb's Theology in Process*, ed. David Griffin and Thomas Altizer (Philadelphia: Westminster, 1977), 158.
⁴² W. Hamilton (1961), 59.
⁴³ M. Taylor and Raschke (2001), online; John Caputo and Carl Raschke, "Loosening Philosophy's Tongue," *Journal of Cultural and Religious Theory* 3.2 (2002), online.
⁴⁴ Caputo, in Caputo and Vattimo (2007), 68-69.

Similarly, Nathan Scott—in his 1986 AAR Presidential Address—makes a similar charge, namely, that theologies such as Altizer's simply replace one "absolutism" which is deemed "unsuccessful" with a new "absolutism," which Scott claims is similarly "uncalculated to facilitate any vital dialogue between religious thought and other modes of cultural discourse."[45] Of course, any full consideration of Altizer understands that Altizer's vision is, again, a solitary vision but yet one that is rooted in the Bible.[46]

Although this may be a flippant response to this criticism, how does any theology that is in fact *a theology* resist being *theological*, unless it is simply *about theology*? Caputo, for example, criticizes Altizer more specifically for his use of the terminology of death without having a theology of "mourning," and that death is never grieved for Altizer but only an "empty death." Caputo offers his theology of the Cross instead, that Jesus was killed for mainly political reasons, "murdered because of the menace he posed to the powers that be, Roman powers and Temple powers."[47] While Caputo's story is not as big as a story as Altizer's, it's still a story with significant theological implications.

Immanence and Fantasy

All theologies are rooted in a Big Stories.

Another critic of Altizer, Brian Hancock, asks similarly, almost flippantly (and written both out of respect and disrespect of Altizer), in a review of *Living the Death of God*, does "he [write] this with a straight face?"[48] Steven Smith similarly observes in a review of *The New Gospel of Christian Atheism* that "[a] highly abstract, formal appeal like Altizer's provokes basic questions about the relation between gesture and life."[49] In other words, how does this death-of-God business have anything to do with real life and living? Even in reviews and responses to Altizer's earlier

---

[45] Scott (1987), 8. Cf. Frances Cunningham, "Altizer's Understanding of the Death of God," *Philosophy Today* 13 (1969): 48-49; Colin Lyas, "On the Coherence of Christian Atheism," *Philosophy* 45.171 (Jan. 1970): 1-19.
[46] Altizer, "Introduction," *John Cobb's Theology in Process*, ed. David Griffin and Thomas Altizer (Philadelphia: Westminster, 1977), 1.
[47] John Caputo, "The Desire for God, the God of Desire," unpublished essay, p. 15, 16. This paper is the lecture given by Caputo at a public dialogue with Altizer at Lebanon Valley College (Annville, PA), on September 23, 2004. The debate was titled "The Death of God vs. The Desire for God."
[48] Hancock, 163.
[49] Smith, 892.

work, this question has emerged. John Cobb wrote in a 1965 essay that Altizer's theology subverts or "threatens" the then-recent trend of "demythologizing" because Altizer is re-mythologizing, reconstructing mythology.[50] Allan Denison's 1966 review of *Mircea Eliade and the Dialectic of the Sacred* criticizes Altizer's ideas, that a Christian non-transcendent theism "seems incredible."[51]

Beyond these, David Tracy wrote in his *Blessed Rage for Order* that the weakness of Altizer's theology is his own methodological ability to perpetuate a "meaningful way to affirm the reality of God" that likely only has meaning to the local one with the metatheological ability to think in this way.[52] Terrance Tilley, in a review of a book by Charles Winquist, wrote that theologies such as Altizer's have an "apparent absence of anyone" who might find the ideas useful or even insightful.[53] Richard Rubenstein simply called Altizer's apocalypticism "the false illusion of...hope."[54] Altizer's theology is clearly a theology of hope, despite its affinity for the darker areas of theology; in fact, it is hopefulness that seems to be Altizer's primary attraction to Hegelian metaphysics. However, Rubenstein's charge of a "false illusion" points toward the fact that Altizer's theology did not manifest itself into a meaningful religious tradition or community of faith.

I return to this question: again, is not all theology *illusory* in the sense that it engages, imposes, extrapolates, poaches, and desires meaningfulness in the desert of *vita-ipsum*, of life itself? *Reputo-ipsum* brings about meaningfulness in the immanence of life, and Altizer's sense of the *thinking now occurring* apocalyptically spawns the New Being and calls forth the New Creation of an absolute edge. Paul Kuntz suggested an Anselmic reading of Altizer in a 1970 essay in the *Journal of the American Academy of Religion*, and proposed the following scheme of Altizer against the ontological argument:

---

[50] Cobb (1965), 320.
[51] Allan Denison, Rev. *Mircea Eliade and the Dialectic of the Sacred* by Thomas Altizer, *Interpretation* 20 (1966), 361. He writes: "Finally, that the sacred should luminously but mysteriously engage into the present moment without a transcendent Value Source seems incredible" (361). What Denison didn't follow—likely because Altizer's ideas were not yet fully developed—is that for Altizer, the *moment itself* is the so-called "Value Source."
[52] Tracy (1996), 32.
[53] Terrence Tilley, Rev. *The Surface of the Deep* by Charles Winquist, *Theological Studies* 66.2 (2005), 495.
[54] Rubenstein (1970), 133.

1. Altizer moves dialectically from faith to faith, and it is not a linear process, where as the onto-logician...trusts reason and he trusts reasoning independent of sensory observation. [Altizer] is an extreme rationalist.

2. The onto-logician insists upon objectively defining his terms, asking questions and answers and conclusions of arguments.... In saying that God died he is saying something about the person in our age. No definition or argument can justly convey what the prophet is proclaiming.

3. [O]n the level of theory.... [Altizer] is deeply involved in the mixture of sacred and secular aspects of his culture.... The dialectician is deciding his future of his whole being in society. He provides a myth for guiding action and he opens an apocalyptic vision of how we will act and feel as well as how we should think.

4. While there is a similar desire for truth between Altizer and the onto-logician, the "truth" that is sought is different. The onto-logician seeks truth in things that are true, but for Altzier truth is a profession, an act of saying, "yes." However, the person belongs to a historical age and he may as truly at one time say "yes" as at another time say "no." We must study circumstances to discover he has acted appropriately.

5. The onto-logician tries to avoid contradiction, the "reductio ad absurdum," whereas Altizer welcomes the *coincidence of opposites*. To have *yes* and *no* together...is, of course, logical nonsense, but the dialectician finds it more revealing of the age in which the one who was believed never to be able to die![55]

For Knutz, the ontological argument is at odds with Altizer, but Knutz is appropriating the traditional interpretation of the ontological argument that is, as Tillich and van Buren have pointed out, an appropriation.[56] Following van Buren and Tillich—as discussed in the Introduction and Part One—Anselmic ontological thinking points toward *boundary* or *edge* language and thinking, ideas that occasionally push, transcend, shatter, and mend boundaries from the outside. Sometimes it leads to *expatriate* thinking and language, just beyond the *edge*. A theology such as Altizer's

---

[55] Quoted and paraphrased from Paul Kuntz, "the Ontological Argument and 'God is Dead,'" *Journal of the American Academy of Religion* 38.1 (1970), 69-70.
[56] Ibid. 69.

requires a methodology such as the *coincidentia oppositorum* for it to retain any cohesion as a consistent theological system—even if this methodology is subversive to itself and ultimately contradictory.

Theology, then, is more than just an *illusion* or even a "mystical assumption"; from an Anselmic perspective it is *fantasy*, and further, it is *madness*.[57] Following Tillich, as long as theological symbols—even if they are fantastical—are in fact *symbols*, they are rooted the ultimate and point toward the immanence of *vita-ipsum*.[58] Recall that for Anselm, even in the traditional appropriation of the *Proslogium*, God occurs *in the mind* and it is out of the presence *in the mind* that the *necessity* of divinity emerges (symbolically stated, from Chapter 1, $\Box p \rightarrow p$, or $\Diamond p$). More specifically, in the Amselmian scheme, God occurs in the *imagination*: 'we can conceive of a greatest conceivable being.' Its residence is in the mind. The *necessity* of *reputo ipsum iam evulsum*, the thinking-itself now occurring, which occurs in the *mind*, is the *ground* of theology. Even for Eliade, the *meaning* of the sacred is the absolute for the individual practitioner, in all of its morphological manifestation—that is, religion has meaning when it is "cosmisated" by the *individual*.[59] In Altizer's doctoral dissertation the *coincidentia oppositorum* is a "pan-psychic" process leading to religious meaning which not even Nietzsche escapes (*CA* 172, 215-216, 228). Even Altizer inadvertently acknowledges that his kind of thinking is a "higher form of myth," a "vehicle for a new epiphany of the sacred, an epiphany which draws all things into itself' in an early essay on myth and symbol.[60] It is my position that Altizer would disagree with this assessment of his own work, because it is clear that to him his theology is *the* correct and *the* absolute theology—*at least for him*.[61]

---

[57] Karras, 53.
[58] Cf. Feero, 17-18; Thomas Altizer, "Spiritual Existence as God-Transcending Existence," *John Cobb's Theology in Process*, ed. David Griffin and Thomas Altizer (Philadelphia: Westminster, 1977), 54ff.
[59] Eliade (1996) §159 (p. 420). Cf. *GN* 117; Sabin, 61-62.
[60] Altizer, "The Religious Meaning of Myth and Symbol" (1962), 105.
[61] While there is a clear openness to his theology based on his collegiality with other thinkers who have seriously engaged, disagreed, and even rejected his work, such as Mark C. Taylor, D. G. Leahy, John Cobb, and Charles Winquist (and perhaps even Tillich, as well), these thinkers have taken up Altizer's project as "the possibility that the radical expressions of the profane in their total negation of the sacred openly coincide with the radical movement of the sacred" differently (Altizer, in Edward DeBary, "Interview with Dr. Thomas Altizer," *St. Luke's Journal* 10.2 [1967], 35).

Altizer calls this *gesture* from a position of *vita-ipsum* a "voyage" occasionally his writing. This voyage, he writes in *The Genesis of God*, as exhibited by the "apocalyptic prophets" Milton, Dante, and Blake, is a "cosmic voyage and an interior voyage simultaneously, and a voyage which embodies a truly new historical world," which is "ever more fully an apocalyptic world" (*GG* 165). Altizer prefaces the first page of his memoir that the theological journey toward a "new theology" is "a universal one, truly embodied in each of us, whether directly or indirectly, or consciously or unconsciously." Continuing, "This is a voyage that every more comprehensively has occurred throughout our history, and if that voyage is ending today, its very ending has created a new call" (*LDG* ix). He writes at the end of *Living the Death of God*:

> As my theological work approaches its culmination, I can see that the transfiguration of the Godhead has become its deepest center, and if its previous center was a *coincidentia oppositorum* of Christ and Satan, that, too, can be understood as a transfiguration of the Godhead. So perhaps this has always been the deep center of my work…and has been hidden and obscured by conflicting turns and moves, perhaps these were necessary to this theological voyage, and necessary if only because of the weakness of this voyager. Certainly this has been a genuine voyage for me, whether pathological or not, and so, too, it has been a genuine theological voyage, *whether illusory or not.* For a theological voyage is truly a voyage, one realizing whatever depths are possible for us, and one occurring not in heaven or in a dreamy world of innocence, but in the very actualities of our time in world. I deeply believe that each and every one of us is called to a theological voyage, and that it inevitably occurs whether or not we are aware of it, *so that in this sense theology is our most universal way,* and even if theology has never been so invisible as it is today, that invisibility could be a necessary mask for its contemporary actuality, and my gravest fear about my own work is that it is an irresponsible dislodging of that mask, and one only unveiling a hollow and artificial theology. Perhaps any such unveiling will inevitably suffer this consequence, or any unveiling of our lesser voyages, but even those voyages challenge that deep silence that reigns among us, and while many can know silence as a deep theological virtue, it can no less so be an ultimate theological veil and curse. (168-169, emph. add.)

Theology is our most universal way, even if it is a madness: we are all called to make meaning for our lives, seek justice for others: in the immanence of the now we are all called to place ultimacy on the presence of the present. If theology is a madness, this *madness* has saturated Altizer's own being, from the Satanic *theosis* to his own fear that his theology, done in a public way, is irresponsible to its public, even if it is his own.[62] This madness is not entirely different from the madness related to memory, as discussed earlier, in Plato's *Phaedrus*. If Altizer's theology is an absolutized absolution, closed off from the rest of Christian theology as an *either/or*, its absolutizing is indicative of its localized significance and vivaciousness of its vision.[63]

In some sense, one might speak of Altizer's theology as *metatheological*, in that his theology, more so than Tillich (though it might have progressed *dialectically* from Tillich), points to the very nature, meaning, methodology, and *madness* of theology. He asks in a 1994 article in the *Journal of the American Academy of Religion*, regarding the nature of theology, "[a]re our academic games only innocent play, a play inflicting no real injury, and yet one effecting a release from drab anonymity of our lives, and doing so in such a way as to make possible understanding of our nihilistic world?"[64] How can theology be possible if the theologian no longer believes in his own theology? Recall that for Nietzsche, after the death of God is declared, the madman asks, "what sacred games shall we have to invent?"[65] Nearly every one of Altizer's books begins with a criticism of the state of modern theology and its inability to speak of God: in the advent of the death of God, not even the theologian 'believes in' his own theology. Altizer wrote in an "Apocalyptic Creed" (with my emphasis):

> *I* believe in the triumph of the Kingdom of God, in that Kingdom which is the final life of the spirit, a life incarnate in Jesus, and consummated in his death. That death is the self-embodiment of the Kingdom of God, and a death which is the resurrection of incarnate body, a body which is a glorified body, but glorified only in its crucifixion, which is the death of all heavenly spirit, and the life of a joy which is grace incarnate. That joy and grace are all in all, offered everywhere and to everyone, and invisible and unreal

---

[62] Jasper (2007), 160.
[63] Tom Driver, "From Death into Life," *Journal of the American Academy of Religion* 41.2 (1973), 237. Cf. 232.
[64] Altizer, "The Challenge of Nihilism" (1994), 1016.
[65] Nietzsche, *Gay Science*, §124 (p. 181).

only to those who refuse them, *a refusal which is everyone's* but a refusal which is annulled in the death of the incarnate and crucified God, and transfigured in that resurrection, a resurrection which is the actual and present glory of the Kingdom of God. (*GG* 185)

In this revealing creed—and perhaps in astonishment of the *coincidentia oppositorum* at work for Altizer to commit to any sort of creed—the unique role of the heretic is stated (in italics, above) as the *I* of the "I believe." Those who refuse the call of the voyage are ultimately offered a Barthian annulment, in "a refusal which is everyone's." At the same time, there is the "joy and grace" that "are all in all, offered everywhere" at stake. This is not an inclusivistic creed, it is an inclusivistic exclusivism, making the Augustinian "I" all-important in its self-subjective proclamation. The author, Altizer, *really believes* what he has written. Yet it is mindful of its own *subjectivity*.

Theology for Altizer is the *reputo ipsum iam evulsum*, the *thinking now occurring* within the ultimacy of the *vita-ipsum*, the present. But beneath this, theology is the desire to stir up meaning within a world which no longer leaves meaning with a transcendent God. It is, at bottom, a *constructive* attempt to make meaning in a godless world; a theology which *masks* the atheism of *vita-ipsum*, life-itself. To theologize, to voyage, to make meaning of the atheism is "the advent of metaphor and allegory, for metaphor and allegory break of the immediacy of a totally actual present by establishing a horizontal distance between language and world" (*TP* 7). It is in finding one's own Voyaging Voice—to use Mary Daly's words—that reality is shattered, constructed, and appropriated. It requires courage, especially as one's voice becomes progressively heretical and radical (*GG* 166). It is to find joy in a world of darkness and to preach that Gospel, even if it remains Christian, of Atheism, of the immanence of life itself (*GN* 4).

It is on this point where we may enter into a dialogue with Mary Daly, whose theology is quite different from Altizer.

Bibliography

In The Horizon of the Infinite

All Biblical quotations are taken from the New Revised Standard Version (NRSV).

Bibliographic references marked by an asterisk (*) were referenced in editorial notes or changes to the original work.

"A Cook for All Seasons." *Time* (4. April 1969). Online. Accessed 19. June 2008.
Acorn, Wallace. "A God is Dead Professor and a Gospel Preacher." *The Baptist Bulletin* 32.2 (July 1966): 10-13. Thomas Altizer Archive, Syracuse University, Box 2, Folder 7.
Adams, James. *Paul Tillich's Philosophy of Culture, Science and Religion.* New York: Harper, 1965.
Aichele, George. "Fantasy and Myth in the Death of Jesus." *Cross Currents* 44.1 (1994): 85-96.
—. "Literary Fantasy and Postmodern Theology." *Journal of the American Academy of Religion* 59.2 (1991): 323-337.
Allen, E. "The Challenge of Nietzsche." *The London Quarterly and Holborn Review* 178 (July 1953) 266-210+.
Alster, B. "Taimat." *Dictionary of Deities and Demons in the Bible (DDD).* Ed. Karel van der Toorn, Bob Beeking, and Pieter van der Horst. Leiden: Brill, 1995. 1634-1639.
Althaus-Reid, Marcella. *Indecent Theology: Theological Perversions in Sex, Gender and Politics.* London: Routledge, 2000.
Alston, William. "Being-Itself and Talk about God." *Center Journal* 3.3 (1984): 9-25.
Altizer, Thomas. "Absolute Nothingness and Taylor's Imagology." *Journal of Cultural and Religious Theory* 2.2 (2001). Online. Accessed 26. October 2007.
—. "Altizer on Altizer." *Literature and Theology* 15.2. (2001).
—. *The Apocalyptic Trinity.* New York: Palgrave Macmillan, 2012.*
—. "Catholic Philosophy and the Death of God." *Cross Currents* 17.3 (1967): 271-282.
—. "The Challenge of Modern Gnosticism." *Journal of Bible and Religion* 30.1 (1962): 18-25.
—. "The Challenge of Nihilism." *Journal of the American Academy of Religion* 62.4 (1994): 1013-1022.
—. *The Contemporary Jesus.* Albany, NY: SUNY UP, 1997.
—. "To Create the Absolute Edge." *Journal of the American Academy of Religion* (1989).

—. *A Critical Analysis of C. G. Jung's Understanding of Religion.* Unpublished Ph.D. diss., U. Chicago, 1955.
—. "The Death of God: Is This Our Situation?" *Christian Advocate* ns 9.19 (7. Oct. 1965): 9-10. United Methodist Archives, GBHA/Drew University, Madison, NJ. Accessed 24. Oct. 2007.
—. *The Descent into Hell.* Philadelphia: Lippincott, 1970.
—. "The Dialectic of Ancient and Modern Apocalypticism." *Journal of the American Academy of Religion* 39 (1974): 312-320.
—. "Dialectic vs. Di-Polar Theology." *Process Studies* 1.1 (1971): 29-37.
—. "Eternal Recurrence and the Kingdom of God." *The New Nietzsche.* Ed. David Allison. Cambridge, Mass.: MIT UP, 1977.
—. "Faith and The Nothing." Transcript of Emory Student Colloquium lecture (Atlanta, GA), 3. March 1960. Thomas Altizer Archive, Syracuse University, Box 4, Folder 4.
—. "Forward." *Deconstructing Theology* by Mark Taylor. AAR Studies in Religion. Vol. 28. New York: Crossroad, 1982. xi-xv.
—. "From Death Into Life: Are Theologians Free Simply To *Choose?*" *Journal of the American Academy of Religion* 41.2 (1973): 238-242.
—. *Genesis and Apocalypse.* Louisville, KY: Westminster, 1990.
—. *The Genesis of God.* Louisville, KY: Westminster, 1993.
—. "God as Holy Nothingness." *What Kind of God?: Essays in Honor of Richard L. Rubenstein.* Ed. Betty Rubenstein and Michael Berenbaum et al. Studies in the Shoah. Ser. ed. Zev Garber. Lanham, MD: UP America, 1995. 347-356.
—. *Godhead and the Nothing.* Albany, NY: SUNY UP, 2003.
—. *The Gospel of Christian Atheism.* London: Collins, 1967.
—. "Hegel and the Christian God." *Journal of the American Academy of Religion* 59.1 (1991): 71-91.
—. "History as Apocalypse." *Deconstruction and Theology* by Thomas Altizer et al. New York: Crossroad, 1982. 147-177.
—. *History as Apocalypse.* Albany, NY: SUNY UP, 1985.
—. "The Holocaust and the Theology of the Death of God." *The Death of God Movement and the Holocaust: Radical Theology Encounters the Shoah.* Ed. Stephen Haynes and John Roth. Contributions to the Study of Religion. Vol. 55. Christianity and the Holocaust—Core Issues. Ser. ed. Carol Rittner. Westport, CT: Greenwood, 1999. 17-23.
—. "Introduction: A Holistic, Non-Alienated Theologian." *John Cobb's Theology in Process.* Ed. David Griffin and Thomas Altizer. Philadelphia: Westminster, 1977. 1-4.
—. Introduction to "To Create the Absolute Edge" by D. G. Leahy. *Journal of the American Academy of Religion* 57.4 (1989): 773-779.
—. "Is the Negation of Christianity the Way to Its Renewal?" *Religious Humanism* 24.1 (1990): 10-16.
—. Letter to the Editor. *Time* (29. Oct. 1965). Online. Accessed 19. June 2008.
—. *Living the Death of God: A Theological Memoir.* Albany, NY: SUNY UP, 2006.
—. "Mircea Eliade and the Death of God." *Cross Currents* 29 (1979): 257-268.
—. *Mircea Eliade and the Dialectic of the Sacred.* Philadelphia: Westminster, 1963.

—. "Modern Thought and Apocalypticism." *Encyclopedia of Apocalypticism.* Vol. 3. 3 vols. Ed. Stephen Stein. New York: Continuum, 1998. 325-359.
—. *Nature and Grace in the Theology of Saint Augustine, With Special Reference to the Confessions and the Anti-Pelagian Writings.* Unpublished M.A. thesis, University of Chicago, 1951.
—. *The New Apocalypse: The Radical Christian Vision of William Blake.* Ann Arbor, MI: Michigan State UP, 1967.
—. *The New Gospel of Christian Atheism.* Aurora, CO: Davies, 2002.
—. "Nietzsche's Understanding of Christianity and Its Influence Upon Contemporary Theology." Manuscript with handwritten notes, 1958/1960. Altizer Archive, Syracuse University, Syracuse, NY. Box 4.
—. *Oriental Mysticism and Biblical Eschatology.* Philadelphia: Westminster, 1961.
—. "The Otherness of God as an Image of Satan." *The Otherness of God.* Ed. Orrin Summerell. Studies in Religion and Culture. Ed. Robert Scharlemann, et al. Charlottesville, VA: UP Virginia, 1998. 206-195.
—. "Overt Language about the Death of God." *The Christian Century* 95.21 (1978).
—. "Paul and the Birth of Self-Consciousness." *Journal of the American Academy of Religion* 51.3 (1983): 359-370.
—. "A Radical Theologian's Response to 'The Sea of Faith.'" Sea of Faith Annual Conference, Leichester, England, Aug. 1997. Published on-line under a different title, "Why So Conservative?" Sea of Faith Network. Online. Accessed 8 October 2007.
—. "Radical Theology and Political Revolution." *Criterion* 7.3 (Spring 1968) 5-10.
—. "The Religious Meaning of Myth and Symbol." *Truth, Myth, and Symbol.* Ed. Thomas Altizer, William Beardslee, and J. Young. Englewood Cliffs, NJ: Prentice, 1962. 87-108.
—. "Response." *The Theology of Altizer: Critique and Response.* Ed. John Cobb. Philadelphia: Westminster, 1970. 68-76. ["Response A."]
—. "Response." *The Theology of Altizer: Critique and Response.* Ed. John Cobb. Philadelphia: Westminster, 1970. 112-124. ["Response B."]
—. "Response." *The Theology of Altizer: Critique and Response.* Ed. John Cobb. Philadelphia: Westminster, 1970. 138-146. ["Response C."]
—. "A Response." *Thinking Through the Death of God: A Critical Companion to Thomas J. J. Altizer.* Ed. Lissa McCullough and Brian Schroeder. SUNY Series in Theology and Continental Thought. Ser. ed. Douglas Donkel. Albany, NY: SUNY UP, 2004. 213-229.
—. "Response to David Jasper." *Contributions in Religion and Theology* 5.2 (2007): 169-172.
—. "A Response to Stanley Romaine Hopper." *Eastern Buddhist,* ns 4.1 (1971): 150-161.
—. Rev. *Blake and the Assimilation of Chaos* by Christian Galant. *Journal of the American Academy of Religion* 47.3 (1979): 485-486.
—. Rev. *Blessed Rage for Order* by David Tracy. *Journal of the American Academy of Religion* 44.2 (1976): 372-373.
—. Rev. *Christ Proclaimed* by Franz Josef van Beek. *Journal of the American Academy of Religion* 50.1 (1979): 136.

—. Rev. *Nietzsche's Existential Imperative* by Bernd Magnus. *Journal of the American Academy of Religion* 47.4 (1979): 697.
—. Rev. *The Radical Kingdom* by Rosemary Ruether. *Journal of the American Academy of Religion* 39.4 (1971): 569.
—. "Satan as the Messiah of Nature." *The Whirlwind in Culture: Frontiers in Theology, In Honor of Langdon Gilkey.* Ed. Donald Musser and Joseph Price. Bloomington, IN: Meyer-Stone, 1988. 119-133.
—. *The Self-Embodiment of God.* New York: Harper, 1977.
—. "Spiritual Existence as God-Transcending Existence." *John Cobb's Theology in Process.* Ed. David Griffin and Thomas Altizer. Philadelphia: Westminster, 1977. 54-66.
—. "A Theonomy in Our Time?" *Christian Scholar* 46.4 (1963): 356-362.
—. "The Triumph of the Theology of the Word." *American Academy of Religion* 54.3 (1986): 525-529.
—. *Total Presence.* New York: Seabury, 1980.
—, and William Hamilton. *Radical Theology and the Death of God.* (1966)
—, and John Montgomery. *The Altizer-Montgomery Dialogue: A Chapter in the God is Dead Controversy.* Chicago: Intervarsity, 1967.
—, et al. *Deconstruction and Theology.* New York: Crossroad, 1982.
—, ed. *Toward a New Christianity: Readings in the Death of God Theology.* New York: Harcourt, 1967.
"A Man of Ultimate Concern." *Time* 29. Oct. 1965. Online. Accessed 19. June 2008.
Ambruster, Carl. *The Vision of Paul Tillich.* New York: Steed, 1967.
Anselm of Canterbury. *Basic Writings.* 2nd ed. Trans. S. Deane. Chicago: Open Court, 1962. 47-80.
Aquinas, Thomas. *The 'Summa Theologica.'* Vol. 1. 2nd and rev. ed. Trans. English Dominican Province. London: Burns Oats and Washborne, 1970.
Aschrich, Klaus. *Theologie schreiben: Dorothee Sölles Weg zu einer Mystik der Befreiung.* Symbol-Mythos-Medien. Vol. 14. Ser. ed. Klaas Huizing, Michael Meyer-Blanck, Hermann Timm. Berlin, LIT, 2006.
Axtell, G. "Logicism, Pragmatism, and Metascience: Towards a Pancritical Pragmatic Theory of Meta-Level Discourse." *PSA: Proceedings of the Biennial Meeting of the Philosophy of Science Association* 1 (1990): 39-49.
Baard, Rachel. "Original Grace, Not Destructive Grace: A Feminist Appropriation of Paul Tillich's Notion of Acceptance." *Bulletin of the North American Paul Tillich Society* 30.4 (2004): 4-15.
Baker, Barry. *The Mystical Theology of Paul Tillich.* M.Th. thesis, University of Trinity College (Toronto School of Theology), Toronto, 1970.
Ball, Virginia. *The Godless Christians.* Atlanta: Pendulum, 1966.
Barber, Dorothy. "The Meaning of *The Lord of The Rings*." *Mankato State College Studies* 2 (1967): 38-50.
Baum, Gregory. *The Future of Belief Debate.* New York: Herder and Herder, 1967.
—. "Orthodoxy Recast." *The Future of Belief Debate.* Ed. Gregory Baum. New York: Herder and Herder, 1967. 103-108.
Beardslee, William. "A Comment on the Theology of Dr. Altizer." *Criterion* 7.3 (1968): 11-14.

—. "Dialectic or Duality?" *The Theology of Altizer: Critique and Response.* Ed. John Cobb. Philadelphia: Westminster, 1970. 58-67.
Bent, Charles. *The Death of God Movement.* New York: Paulist, 1967.
Berry, Wanda. "Feminist Theology: The 'Verbing' of Ultimate/Intimate Reality in Mary Daly." *Feminist Interpretations of Mary Daly.* Ed. Sarah Lucia Hoagland and Marilyn Frye. Re-Reading the Canon. Ser. ed, Nancy Tuana. University Park, PA: Pennsylvania State UP, 2000. 26-55.
Biesecker-Mast, Gerald. "Psyched Over Žižek, Disturbed by Derrida, and Running from Rorty." *Brethren Life and Thought* 48.3-4 (2003): 204-211.
Bischoff, Paul. "*Participation:* Ecclesial Praxis with a Crucified God for the World." *Journal for Christian Theological Research* 8 (2003): 19-36.
Blake, William. *The Complete Poems.* Ed. Alicia Ostriker. London: Penguin, 1977.
Blavatsky, H. *An Abridgement of the Secret Doctrine.* Ed. Elizabeth Preston and Christmas Humphreys. Wheaton, IL: Theosophical, 1966.
Bonhoeffer, Dietrich. *Letters and Papers from Prison.* Enlarged ed. Ed. Eberhard Bethage. London: SCM, 1971. Orig. pub. *Widerstand und Ergebung: Briefe und Aufzeichnangen aus der Haft.* Munchen: Christian Kaiser, 1970.
Braaten, Carl. "Paul Tillich and the Classical Christian Tradition." *Perspectives on 19th and 20th Century Protestant Theology* by Paul Tillich. Ed. Carl Braaten. New York: Harper, 1967.
Brassier, Ray, and Alberto Toscano. "Postface: Aleatory Realism." In *Theoretical Writings* by Alain Badiou. Ed. and trans. Ray Brassier and Alberto Toscano. London: Continuum, 2006. 260-286.
Brauer, Jerald. "Editor's Preface." *The Future of Religions* by Paul Tillich. New York: Harper, 1966. 7-11.
—. Letter to the Editor. *Life* 59.22 (26 Nov. 1965): 25.
Brindle, Susan. "No Man's Land." *What Is Enlightenment?* 16 (Fall/Winter 1999). Online. Accessed 18. April 2008.
Brown, D. *Ultimate Concern: Tillich In Dialogue.* New York: Harper, 1965.
Brown, Norman. *Love's Body.* Berkeley: U. California UP, 1966.
Brown, Nick. "The Conservatism of Radical Theology." *Political Theology* 4.1 (2002): 81-90.
Brueggemann, Walter. "The Triumphalist Tendency of Exegetical History." *Journal of the American Academy of Religion* 38.4 (1970): 367-380.
Bulman, Raymond. *A Blueprint for Humanity: Paul Tillich's Theology of Culture.* New York: Harper, 1965.
Buri, Fritz. *How Can We Still Speak Responsibly of God?* Philadelphia: Fortress, 1968.
Bush, George W. "Transcript of Bush Speech." CNN.com. Online. Accessed 18. December 2005.
Burkhart, John. "Mary Daly: Theological Orphan?" *Horizons* 2 (1975): 119-120.
Butler, Clark. "Hegel, Altizer and Christian Atheism." *Encounter* 41 (Spring 1980) 103-128.
Calvin, John. *Institutes of the Christian Religion.* 2 vols. Trans. Ford Battles. Ed. John McNeill. Library of Christian Classics. Vols. 20-21. 26 vols. Ser. ed. John Baille, John McNeill, Henry van Dusen. Philadelphia: Westminster, 1960.

Campbell, Debra. "Be-ing Is Be/Leaving." *Feminist Interpretations of Mary Daly*. Ed. Sarah Lucia Hoagland and Marilyn Frye. Re-Reading the Canon. Ser. ed, Nancy Tuana. University Park, PA: Pennsylvania State UP, 2000. 164-193.

Campbell, James. "Van Buren: The Background of an Approach." *Continuum* 4 (1966): 63-75.

Caputo, John. "The Desire for God, the God of Desire." Unpublished paper. Based upon a debate with Thomas Altizer, "The Death of God vs. The Desire for God," Lebanon Valley College, Annville, PA (23. September 2004).

—. *The Weakness of God: A Theology of the Event*. Indiana Series in the Philosophy of Religion. Ser. ed. Marold Westphal. Bloomington, IN: Indiana UP, 2006.

—, and Carl Raschke. "Loosing Philosophy's Tongue." *Journal of Cultural and Religious Theory* 5.2 (2002). Online. Accessed 26. October 2007.

—, and Gianni Vattimo. *After the Death of God*. Ed. and trans. Jeffrey Robbins. Insurrections: Critical Studies in Religion, Politics, and Culture. New York: Columbia UP, 2007.

Carey, John, "The Death of God Movement and Twentieth-Century Protestant Theology." *The Death of God Movement and the Holocaust: Radical Theology Encounters the Shoah*. Ed. Stephen Haynes and John Roth. Westport, CT: Greenwood, 1999.

Carr, Anne. "Is a Christian Feminist Theology Possible?" *Theological Studies* 43.2 (1982): 279-297.

—. "Starting with the Human." *A World of Grace: An Introduction to the Themes and Foundations of Karl Rahner's Theology*. Ed. Leo O'Donovan. Washington, DC: Georgetown UP, 1995. 17-30.

Carter, Robert. "The Nothingness Beyond God." *Eastern Buddhist*, ns 18.1 (1985): 120-130.

Casey, Edward. "Abysmal Absences: Body and Place in Altizer's Theology." *Thinking Through the Death of God: A Critical Companion to Thomas J. J. Altizer*. Ed. Lissa McCullough and Brian Schroeder. SUNY Series in Theology and Continental Thought. Ser. ed. Douglas Donkel. Albany, NY: SUNY UP, 2004. 125-145.

Charry, Ellen. "Heart of Integrity." *The Christian Century* 122.4 (Feb. 22, 2005): 31+.

Christ, Carol. *She Who Changes: Re-Imagining the Divine in the World*. New York: Palgrave Macmillan, 2003.

Choi, Du Loi. *Transcendence and Immanence in Paul Tillich's Theology and Chutisi's Neo-Confucian Philosophy*. Ph.D. diss., Drew U., Madison, NJ, 2000.

Chun, Young. *A Conceptual Analysis of Religion in Paul Tillich (1886-1965) with Particular Reference to his Positive Contribution Towards a Theology of World Religions*. Ph.D. diss., Drew U., Madison, NJ, 1981.

Clarke, Bowman. "God and the Symbolic in Tillich." *Anglican Theological Review* 43.3 (1961): 302-311.

Clyburn, David. Letter to Thomas Altizer (Nov. 11, 1965). Thomas Altizer Archive, Syracuse University, Box 1, Folder 6.

Cobb, John. "Altizer and Christian Theology." *Clio* 16.4 (1987): 331-344.

—. "Christianity and Myth." *Journal of Bible and Religion* 33.4 (1965): 314-320.
—. "Preface." *The Theology of Altizer: Critique and Response*. Ed. John Cobb. Philadelphia: Westminster, 1970. 7-10.
—. "Responses to Critiques." *John Cobb's Theology in Process*. Ed. David Griffin and Thomas Altizer. Philadelphia: Westminster, 1977. 150-192.
—, and Nicholas Gier. "Introduction." *The Theology of Altizer: Critique and Response*. Ed. John Cobb. Philadelphia: Westminster, 1970. 11-44.
—, and David Griffin. *Process Theology: An Introductory Exposition*. Philadelphia: Westminster, 1976.
—, ed. *The Theology of Altizer: Critique and Response*. Ed. John Cobb. Philadelphia: Westminster, 1970.
Coburn, Robert. "Revelation and Religious Truth: Some Themes and Problems in the Theology of Paul Tillich." *Faith and Philosophy* 13.1 (1996): 3-33.
Cole, Dan. "The Death of God Can be Christian Affirmation." *Christian Advocate* ns 10.17 (8. September 1966): 9-10. United Methodist Archives, GBHA/Drew University, Madison, NJ. Accessed 24. Oct. 2007.
Coleridge, Samuel Taylor. *Biographia Literaria*. 1817. Project Gutenberg Online. Accessed 17. March 2008.
"Comment." *Christian Advocate* ns 9.19 (7. Oct. 1965): 2. United Methodist Archives, GBHA/Drew University, Madison, NJ. Accessed 24. Oct. 2007.
"Contemporary Religion: The Position of Dr. Paul Van Buren." *The New Perspective* 1.1 (August 1966): 1-5. Thomas Altizer Archive, Syracuse University, Box 1, Folder 15.
Corner, Martin. "Christianity for the Multiverse: The Uses of Heresy in the Writings of Joseph Smith." "Introduction: The Necessity of Heresy." *Figures of Heresy: Radical Theology in English and American Writing, 1800-2000*. Ed. Andrew Dix and Jonathan Taylor. Brighton, England: Sussex Academic, 2006. 21-36.
Corrington, John. "Thomas Altizer Talks with *NOR*'s Editor-at-Large." *The New Orleans Review* 1.1 (Fall 1968): 26-35+. Thomas Altizer Archive, Syracuse University, Box 3, Folder 4.
Corrington, Robert. "Being and Faith: *Sein und Zeit* and Luther." *Anglican Theological Review* 70 (1988): 16-31.
—. "The Christhood of Things." *Drew Gateway* 52.1 (1981): 41-47.
—. *Ecstatic Naturalism: Signs of the World*. Advances in Semiotics. Gen. ed. Thomas Sebeok. Bloomington, IN: Indiana UP, 1994.
—. Rev. of *Genesis and Apocalypse* by Thomas Altizer. *Theology Today* 49.1 (1992): 134-135.
—. *Riding the Windhorse: Manic-Depressive Disorder and the Quest for Wholeness*. Lanham, MD: Hamilton, 2003.
Covino, William. "Walt Disney Meets Mary Daly: Invention, Imagination, and the Construction of Community." *JAC: A Journal of Composition Theory* 20.1 (2000): 153-165.
Cox, Harvey. *The Feast of Fools*. Cambridge, MA: Harvard UP, 1969.
—. *God's Revolution and Man's Responsibility*. Valley Forge: Judson, 1965.
—. *The Secular City: Secularization and Urbanization in Theological Perspective*. New York: Collier, 1965.

—. *Religion in the Secular City: Toward a Postmodern Theology*. New York: Simon and Schuster, 1984.
Crockett, Clayton. "Contact Epistemology for the Sites of Theology." *Secular Theology: American Radical Theological Thought*. Ed. Clayton Crockett. London: Routledge, 2001. 198-211.
—. "Introduction." *Secular Theology: American Radical Theological Thought*. Ed. Clayton Crockett. London: Routledge, 2001. 10-25.
Cupitt, Don. *After God: The Future of Religion*. New York: Basic, 1997.
—. *Radical Theology: Selected Writings*. Santa Rosa, CA: Polebridge, 2006.
—. *Reforming Christianity*. Santa Rosa, CA: Polebridge, 2001.
Cunningham, Frances. "Altizer's Understanding of the Death of God." *Theology Today* 13 (Spring 1969): 48-59.
Cunningham, Valentine. "Introduction: The Necessity of Heresy." *Figures of Heresy: Radical Theology in English and American Writing, 1800-2000*. Ed. Andrew Dix and Jonathan Taylor. Brighton, England: Sussex Academic, 2006. 1-18.
Cyrill, Saint. *Liturgia*. In *Liturgiarum Orientalium Collectio*. Ed. Eusebe Renaudot. London: Joannem Leslie Bibliopolam, 1847.
Daly, Mary. "Abortion and Sexual Caste." *Commonweal* 95 (1972): 415-419.
—. "After the Death of God the Father: Women's Liberation and the Transformation of the Christian Consciousness." *Commonweal* 94 (1971): 7-10.
—. *Amazon Grace: Re-Calling The Courage to Sin Big*. New York: Palgrave, 2006.
—. *Beyond God the Father: Toward a Philosophy of Women's Liberation*. Boston: Beacon, 1973.
—. "A Call for the Castration of Sexist Religion." *Unitarian Universalist Christian* 27 (1972): 23-37.
—. "Be-Friending: Weaving Contexts, Creating Atmospheres." *Weaving the Visions*. Ed. Judith Plaskow and Carol Christ. New York: Harper, 1989. 199-207.
—. *The Church and the Second Sex*. Harper Colophon ed. New York: Harper, 1975.
—. "The Courage to Leave: A Response to John Cobb's Theology." *John Cobb's Theology in Process*. Ed. David Griffin and Thomas Altizer. Philadelphia: Westminster, 1977. 84-98.
—. "The Courage to See." *The Christian Century* 83 (1971): 1108-1111.
—. "Dispensing with Trivia." *Commonweal* 88 (1968): 322-325.
—. *Gyn/Ecology: The Metaethics of Radical Feminism*. 1991 ed. Aylesburg, England: Women's, 1991.
—. "Mary Daly on the Church." *Commonweal* 91 (1969): 215.
—. *Outercourse: The Be-Dazzling Voyage*. New York: Harper San Francisco, 1992.
—. "The Problem of Hope." *Commonweal* 92 (1970): 314-317.
—. "The Problem with Speculative Theology." *The Thomist* 29 (1965): 177-216.
—. *Pure Lust: Elemental Feminist Philosophy*. New York: Harper San Francisco, 1984.
—. "Return of the Protestant Principle." *Commonweal* 90 (1969): 338-341.
—. "A Short Essay on Hearing and on the Qualitative Leap of Radical Feminism." *Horizons* 2 (1975): 120-124.

—. "The Spiritual Revolution: Women's Liberation as Theological Re-Education." *Andover Newton Quarterly* 12.4 (1972): 163-176.

—. "The Spiritual Dimension of Women's Liberation." *A Reader in Feminist Knowledge.* Ed. Sneja Gunew. London: Routledge, 1991. 335-341. Rpt. *Radical Feminism.* Ed. A. Koedt, E. Levine, and A. Rapone. New York: Quadrangle, 1973.

—. *Quintessence... Realizing the Archaic Future: A Radical Elemental Feminist Manifesto.* Boston: Beacon: 1998.

—. "The Women's Movement: An Exodus Community." *Religious Education* 67 (1972): 327-335.

—, and Jane Caputi. *Webster's First New Intergalactic Wickedary of the English Language.* Boston: Beacon, 1987.

—, and Aquinas Ferrara. "'Underground Theology': An Exchange of Views." *Commonweal* 88 (1969): 531-534.

Dawes, Gregory. "God Beyond Theism?: Bishop Spong, Paul Tillich, and the Unicorn." *Pacifica* 15 (Feb. 2002): 65-71.

De Haven, Steven, and John King-Farlow. "Metaphilosophy and Religious Disagreements." *Noûs* 13.4 (1979): 511-516.

De Bary, Edward. "Interview with Dr. Thomas Altizer." *St. Luke's Journal* 10.2 (1967): 32-42. Thomas Altizer Archive, Syracuse University, Box 3, Folder 4.

De Beauvoir, Simone. *The Second Sex.* Trans. and ed. H. Parshley. New York: Knopf, 1953. Orig. pub. *Les Deuxième Sexe.* Librarie Gallihard: 1949.

Demos, Raphael. Rev. of *Systematic Theology, Vol. 1* by Paul Tillich. *The Journal of Religion* 46.1.ii (Jan. 1966): 205-214.

Denison, Allan. Rev. of *Mircea Eliade and the Dialectic of the Sacred* by Thomas Altizer. *Interpretation* 20 (1966): 360-361.

Depoortere, Frederick. "*Jouissance feminine*?: Lacan on Bernini's 'The Ecstasy of Saint Teresa' Versus Slavoj Žižek on Lars von Trier's 'Breaking the Waves.'" *Encountering Transcendence: Contributions to a Theology of Christian Religious Experience.* Ed. Lieven Boeve, Hans Geybels, and Stijn Van den Bossche. Annua Nuntia Lovaniensia. Vol. 53. Leuven: Peeters, 2005. 21-37.

Derrida, Jacques. *A Derrida Reader: Between the Blinds.* Ed. Peggy Kamup. New York: Columbia UP, 1991.

—. *On The Name.* Trans. David Wood, John Leavey, Ian McLeod. Ed. Thomas Dutoit. Meridian Crossing Aesthetics. Ser. ed. Werner Hamacher and David Wellberg. Stanford, CA: Stanford UP, 1995.

de Schutter, Dirk. "Zarathustra's Yes and Woe: Nietzsche, Celan, and Eckhart on the Death of God." *Flight of the Gods: Philosophical Perspectives on Negative Theology.* Ed. Ilse Bulhof and Laurens ten Kate. Perspectives on Continental Philosophy. Ser. ed. John Caputo. New York: Fordham UP, 2000. 121-143.

De Vaux, Alexis. *Warrior Poet: A Biography of Audre Lorde.* New York: Norton, 2004.

Dewart, Leslie. *The Future of Belief: Theism in a World Come of Age.* New York: Herder and Herder, 1966.

—. "Neo-Thomism and the Continuity of Philosophical Experience." *The Future of Belief Debate*. Ed. Gregory Baum. New York: Herder and Herder, 1967. 211-229.

Dicenso, James. "Anxiety, Risk and Transformation: Re-Visiting Tillich with Lacan." *Secular Theology: American Radical Theological Thought*. Ed. Clayton Crockett. London: Routledge, 2001. 51-72.

Dourley, John. "The Problem of Essentialism: Tillich's Anthropology Versus His Christology." *Paul Tillich's Theological Legacy: Spirit and Community*. Ed. Frederick Parrella. Theologische Bibliothek Töpelmann. Vol. 73. Ser. ed. O. Bayer, W. Härle, H. Müller. Berlin: Walter de Gruyter, 1995. 125-141.

Dreisbach, Donald. *Symbols & Salvation: Paul Tillich's Doctrine of Religious Symbols and His Interpretation of the Symbols of the Christian Tradition*. Lanham, MD: UP America, 1993.

Driver, Tom. "From Death Into Life: Altizer Challenged." *Journal of the American Academy of Religion* 41.2 (1973): 229-237.

Durandeaux, Jacques. *Living Questions to Dead Gods*. Trans. William Whitman. New York: Sheed and Ward, 1968. Trans. of *Question vivante à un Dieu mort*. Paris: Descleé de Brouwer, 1967.

Dych, William. "Theology in a New Key." *A World of Grace: An Introduction to the Themes and Foundations of Karl Rahner's Theology*. Ed. Leo O'Donovan. Washington, DC: Georgetown UP, 1995. 1-16.

Dyck, Arthur. "A Comment on the Distinction between Normative Theology and Metatheology." *The Harvard Theological Review* 63.3 (1970): 453-456.

Eckhart, Meister. *Meister Eckhart: The Essential Sermons, Commentaries, Treatises, and Defense*. Trans. Edmund Collegde and Bernard McGinn. Classics of Western Spirituality. Ser. ed. Richard Payne et al. Mahwah, NJ: Paulist, 1981.

Edwards, Clifford. "Altizer Speaks to the Scholars." *Christian Advocate* ns 10.10 (19. May 1966): 11. United Methodist Archives, GBHA/Drew University, Madison, NJ. Accessed 24. Oct. 2007.

—. "Grokking the Church of A.D. 2000." *Motive* 38.3 (Dec. 1967): 45-47. United Methodist Archives, GBHA/Drew University, Madison, NJ. Accessed 24. Sept. 2007.

Edwards, David, ed. *The Honest to God Debate: Some Reactions to the Book 'Honest to God.'* Philadelphia: Westminster, 1963.

Eggan, Weil. Rev. of *Paul Tillich and the New Religious Paradigm* by Gabriel Vahanian. *Exchange* 34.1 (2005): 81.

Eliade, Mircea. Letter to Thomas Altizer (Jan. 15, 1963). Thomas Altizer Archive, Syracuse University, Box 1, Folder 4.

—. *The Myth of the Eternal Return*. Trans. Willard Trask. Bollingen Series. Vol. 46. New York: Pantheon, 1954. Org. pub. *Le Mythe de l'éternal retour: archetypes et répétition* (Paris: Gallimard, 1949).

—. "Notes for a Dialogue." *The Theology of Altizer: Critique and Response*. Ed. John Cobb. Philadelphia: Westminster, 1970. 234-241.

—. *Patterns in Comparative Religion*. Trans. Rosemary Sheed. Bison Books ed. London, NB: U. Nebraska UP, 1996.

Elshtain, Jean. *Public Man, Private Women: Woman in Social and Political Thought*. Princeton, NJ: Princeton UP, 1981.
Emmet, Dorothy. "The Ground of Being." *Journal of Theological Studies*, ns 15.2 (1964): 280-292.
Evans, John Charles. "Nietzsche on Christ vs. Christianity." *Soundings* 78 (Fall/Winter 1996): 571-588.
Fancher, Betsy. "Altizer: Two Years After the Death of God." *Atlanta* 7.7 (Nov. 1967): 48-51. Thomas Altizer Archive, Syracuse University, Box 3, Folder 4.
Feero, Richard. *Radical Theology in Preparation: From Edwards to Altizer*. Ph.D. diss., Syracuse U., Syracuse, NY, 1993.
Ferré, Nels. *The Christian Understanding of God*. New York: Harper, 1957.
—. "Three Central Issues in Tillich's Philosophical Theology." *Scottish Journal of Theology* 10 (1957): 225-238.
—. "Tillich and the Nature of Transcendence." *Paul Tillich: Retrospect and Future* by Nells Ferré, Charles Hartshorne, John Dillenberger, James Livingston, and Joseph Haroutunian. Nashville: Abingdon, 1966. 7-18.
Field-Bibb, Jacqueline. "From *The Church* to *Wickedary*: The Theology and Philosophy of Mary Daly." *Modern Churchman* 30 (1989): 35-41.
Finch, William. *The Descent into Hades: An Exegetical, Historical, and Theological Study*. Ph.D. diss., Drew University, Madison, NJ, 1940.
Fitzer, Joseph. "Paul J. Tillich on Natural Theology." *God in Contemporary Thought: A Philosophical Perspective*. Ed. Sebastian Matczak. Philosophical Questions. Vol. 10. Ser. ed. Sebastian Matczak. New York: Learned, 1977. 643-664.
Fjeld, Darla. *Gender and Divine Transcendence: Preface for a Philosophy of Religion*. Ph.D. diss., Drew U., Madison, NJ, 1974.
Ford, Lewis. Rev. of *Panentheism in Hartshorne and Tillich* by David Nikkel. *Encounter* 57 (1996): 398-401.
—. "Tillich's Tergiversations Toward the Power of Being." *Scottish Journal of Theology* 28.4 (1975): 323-340.
Foster, A. "The Resurrection of God." *Religion in Life* 38.1 (1969): 131-147. United Methodist Archives, GBHA/Drew University, Madison, NJ. Accessed Sept. 24, 2007.
Foster, Durwood. "Tillich and the Personal God." *Bulletin of the North American Paul Tillich Society* 33.2 (Spring 2007): 21-25.
Foster, Kenlem. "Paul Tillich and St. Thomas." *Paul Tillich in Catholic Thought*. Ed. Thomas O'Meara and Celestin Weisser. Dubuque: Priory, 1964. 97-105.
Fox, David. *Beyond Secularism: The Theological Vision of Fr. Alexander Schmemann*. Ph.D. diss., Drew U., 2006.
Fox, Marvin. "Tillich's Ontology and God." *Anglican Theological Review* 43.3 (1961): 200-267.
Frame, John. "Rev. of *The Edges of Language* by Paul M. van Buren." *Westminster Theological Journal* 36 (1973): 106-111.
Freeman, Horace. *An Address on the Sunday School Lesson Before the Together Class of First Methodist Church, Brunswick, GA, February 13, 1966*. Brunswick,

GA: First Methodist Church, 1966. Thomas Altizer Archive, Syracuse University, Box 1, Folder 13.

Friedman, Susan. *Mappings: Feminism and the Cultural Geographies of Encounter.* Princeton, NJ: Princeton UP, 1998.

Frye, Marilyn. "Famous Lust Words." *The Women's Review of Books* 1.11 (Aug. 1984): 3-4.

Fulkerson, Mary. "Sexism as Original Sin: Developing a Theacentric Discourse." *Journal of the American Academy of Religion* 59.4 (1991): 653-675.

Gage, Matilda. *Woman, Church and State: A Historical Account of the Status of Woman Through the Christian Ages: With Reminiscences of the Matriarchate.* Chicago: Kerr, 1893.

Gaiser, Fredrick. "The Christian Story as Fantasy? No! Do Not 'Potter' with The Gospel." *Word & World* 26.2 (2006): 214+.

Gallagher, Martin. "Paul Tillich, The Mystical Overcoming of Theism, and the Space for the Secular." *Bulletin of the North American Paul Tillich Society* 31.2 (2005): 7-14.

Gardner, Martin. *The Flight of Peter Fromm: A Novel.* 1994 ed. Amherst, NY: Prometheus, 1994.

Gellman, Jerome. "The Meta-Philosophy of Religious Language." *Noûs* 11.2 (1977): 151-161.

Gillett, Carl. "Physicalism and Panentheism: Good News and Band News." *Faith and Philosophy* 20.1 (January 2003): 3-23.

Gilkey, Langdon. *Blue Twilight: Nature, Creation, and American Religion.* Minneapolis: Fortress, 2001.

—. *Gilkey on Tillich.* New York: Crossroad, 1990.

—. Rev. of *The Secular Meaning of the Gospel* by Paul M. van Buren. *Journal of Religion* 44 (1964): 238-243.

"God is Dead." Wikipedia Online. Accessed 8. September 2007. [http://en.wikipedia.org/wiki/Death_of_God]

"The 'God is Dead' Movement." *Time* (22. Oct. 1965), online. Accessed 19. June 2008.

Goldenberg, Naomi. *Changing of the Gods.* Boston: Beacon, 1979.

Graham, Billy. "Is God Dead?" *The Godless Christians.* Ed. Virginia Ball. Atlanta: Pendulum, 1966. 91-96.

Granrose, John. "Normative Theology and Meta-Theology." *The Harvard Theological Review* 63.3 (1970): 449-451.

Gray, Frances. "Elemental Philosophy: Language and Ontology in Mary Daly's Texts." *Feminist Interpretations of Mary Daly.* Ed. Sarah Lucia Hoagland and Marilyn Frye. Re-Reading the Canon. Ser. ed, Nancy Tuana. University Park, PA: Pennsylvania State UP, 2000. 222-245.

Gray, Wallace. "God is Dead—Or is He?: Nels Ferré and Paul van Buren (Dialogue and Analysis)." *Communio Viatorum* 11 (1968): 39-60.

"The Great Radical Theologian Was 'Apostle to the Skeptics': Paul Tillich (1886-1965)." *Life* 59.19 (5. Nov. 1965): 40D.

Greenfield, Trevor. *An Introduction to Radical Theology: The Death and Resurrection of God.* Winchester, UK: O Books, 2006.

Grigg, Richard. *Gods After God: An Introduction to Contemporary Radical Theologies.* Albany, NY: SUNY UP, 2006.

—. "Remaking Tillich as a Pragmatist: From Foundationalist Ontology to Pragmatic Construction." *Bulletin of the North American Paul Tillich Society* 30.2 (2004): 36-39.

—. *Symbol and Empowerment: Paul Tillich's Post-Theistic System.* Macon, GA: Mercer UP, 1985.

—. "Tillich's 'Ontological Eschatology.'" *New Creation or Eternal Now: Is there an Eschatology in Paul Tillich's Work?/ Neue Schöpfung oder Ewiges Jetzt: Hat Paul Tillich Eine Eschatologie?* Ed. Gert Hummel. Theologische Bibliothek Töpelmann. Vol. 54. Ser. ed. K. Aland et al. Berlin: Walter de Gruyter, 1991. 151-162.

Grimshaw, Jean. *Feminist Philosophers: Women's Perspectives on Philosophical Traditions.* London: Wheatsheaf, 1986.

Grimshaw, Mike. "Did God Die in *The Christian Century*?" *Journal of Cultural and Religious Theory* 6.3 (2005): 7-23.

Gruber, Tom. "Toward Principles for the Design of Ontologies Used for Knowledge Sharing." *International Journal of Human-Computer Studies* 45.4/5 (1995): 907-928. [Accessed online.]

—. "A Translation Approach to Portable Ontologies." *Knowledge Acquisition* 5.2 (1993): 199-200. [Accessed online.]

—. "What is Ontology?" Online. Accessed 21. August 2007. [http://www-ksl.Stanford.edu/kst/what-is-ontology.html]

Gudmarsdottir, Sigridur. *Abyss of God: Flesh, Love and Language.* Ph.D. diss., Drew U., 2007.

—. *Tillich and the Abyss.* New York: Palgrave Macmillan/Springer, 2016.*

Hall, Bennett. *An Experiment Communicating the Numinous through Preaching.* D.Min. diss., Drew University, Madison, NJ, 1979.

Hardwick, Charley. *Faith and Objectivity: Fritz Buri and the Hermeneutical Foundations of a Radical Theology.* The Hague: Martinus Nijhoff, 1972.

Harkness, Georgia. *Beliefs that Count.* Ed. Henry Bullock. Nashville: Graded, 1961.

—. *The Fellowship of the Holy Spirit.* Nashville: Abingdon, 1966.

—. *The Recovery of Ideals.* New York: Scribner's, 1937.

—. *The Resources of Religion.* New York: Henry Holt, 1936.

—. *Stability Amid Change.* Nashville: Abingdon, 1969.

—. *Understanding the Kingdom of God.* Nashville: Abingdon, 1974.

Hamilton, Kenneth. "On Having Nothing to Worship: The Divine Abyss in Paul Tillich and Richard Rubenstein." *God and the Good: Essays in Honor of Henry Stob.* Grand Rapids, MI: Eerdmans, 1975. 150-164.

—. *God is Dead: The Anatomy of a Slogan.* Grand Rapids, MI: Eerdmans, 1966.

—. *The System and the Gospel: A Critique of Paul Tillich.* Grand Rapids, MI: Eerdmans, 1963.

—. "Verifiable Christianity: From Arnold to van Buren." *Canadian Journal of Theology* 11 (1965): 3-16.

Hamilton, Peter. *The Living God and the Modern World: Christian Theology Based on the Thought of A. N. Whitehead.* Philadelphia: United Church Press, 1967.

Hamilton, William. "Can the Death of God Die?" *Religious Humanism* 24.1 (1990): 3-9.

—. "*Im Piam Memoriam*—The Death of God After Ten Years." *The Christian Century* 92.32 (8. Oct. 1975): 872-873.

—. "Ingmar Bergman on the Silence of God." *Motive* 27.2 (Nov. 1966): 36-41. United Methodist Archives, GBHA/Drew University, Madison, NJ. Accessed Sept. 24, 2007.

—. *The New Essence of Christianity*. Rev. ed. New York: Association, 1966.

—. *On Taking God out of the Dictionary*. New York: McGraw-Hill, 1974.

—. "The Shape of Radical Theology." *The Christian Century* (1965): 1221-1222. Will Herberg Archive, Drew University, Folio 186.

Hammond, Guyton. *A Comparison of the Thought of Paul Tillich and Erich Fromm*. Nashville: Vanderbilt UP, 1965.

—. "Paul Tillich's Impact Upon American Life." *Motive* 26.8 (May 1966): 26-30. United Methodist Archives, GBHA/Drew University, Madison, NJ. Accessed Sept. 24, 2007.

—. *The Power of Self-Transcendence: An Introduction to the Philosophy of Paul Tillich*. St. Louis: Bethany, 1966.

—. "Tillich on the Personal God." *Journal of Religion* 44.4 (1964): 289-293.

Hampton, Hayes. "Secondary Sources on Mary Daly." *Feminist Interpretations of Mary Daly*. Ed. Sarah Hoagland and Marilyn Frye. Re-Reading the Canon. Ser. ed. Nancy Tuana. University Park, PA: Pennsylvania State UP, 2000. 429-433.

Hancock, Brian. Rev. *Living the Death of God* by Thomas Altizer. *Contributions to Religion and Theology* 5.2 (2007): 162-168.

Hart, Ray. "Godhead and God." *Thinking Through the Death of God: A Critical Companion to Thomas J. J. Altizer*. Ed. Lissa McCullough and Brian Schroeder. SUNY Series in Theology and Continental Thought. Ser. ed. Douglas Donkel. Albany, NY: SUNY UP, 2004. 47-63.

—. "To Be *and* Not to Be: *Sit Anlem Sermo (Lógos) Vester, Eest, Est; Non, Non....*" *Journal of the American Academy of Religion* 53.1 (1985): 5-22.

Hartshorne, Charles. "Tillich and The Other Great Tradition." *Anglican Theological Review* 43.3 (1961): 245-259.

Haynes, Stephen. "Christian Holocaust Theology: A Critical Reassessment." *Journal of the American Academy of Religion* 62.2 (1994): 553-585.

—, and John Roth, ed. *The Death of God Movement and the Holocaust*. 1999.

Hegel, G. W. F. *Phenomenology of Spirit*. Trans. A. Miller. Oxford: Oxford UP, 1977. Rpt. *Phänomenologie des Geist*. 5th ed. Ed. J. Hoffmeister. Philosophische Bibliothek. Vol. 14. Hamburg: Feliz Meiner, 1952.

—. *Science of Logic*. Trans. A. Miller. Muirbead Library of Philosophy. Ser. ed. H. Lewis. London: George Allen and Unwin, 1969.

Heidegger, Martin. *Contributions to Philosophy (From Enowning)*. Trans. Parvis Emad and Kenneth Maly. Studies in Continental Thought. Ser. ed. John Sallis. Bloomington, IN: Indiana, 1989.

Henking, Susan. "The Personal is the Theological: Autobiographical Acts in Contemporary Feminist Theology." *Journal of the American Academy of Religion* 59.3 (1991): 511-525.

Henry, Granville. "Mathematics, Phenomenology, and Language Analysis in Contemporary Theology." *Journal of the American Academy of Religion* 35.4 (1967): 337-349.
Heraclitus. *Fragments: The Collected Wisdom of Heraclitus*. Trans. Brooks Haxton. New York: Viking, 2001.
Herberg, Will. "The 'Death of God' Theology: What it Is—What's Wrong with It." Handwritten lecture notes, c. 1967-1968. Will Herberg Archive, Drew University, Folio 186.
—. "The Problem of Faith in a Godless World." Handwritten and typed lecture notes, c. 1966. Will Herberg Archive, Drew University, Folio 186.
—. The Will Herberg Archive. Drew University, Madison, NJ. Folios 169 ("Paul Tillich") and 186 ("Death of God Theology").
Heyward, Carter. "Reuther and Daly: Theologians Speaking and Sparking, Building and Burning." *Christianity and Crisis* 39.5 (2. April 1979): 66-72.
Hick, John. Rev. of *The Edges of Language* by Paul van Buren. *The Journal of Theological Studies* 24.2 (1973): 633-635.
Hibino, Eiji. *The Sacred and the Holy: An Investigation of Thomas J.J. Altizer's Dialectic of the Sacred*. Ph.D. diss., Drew U., Madison, NJ, 1989.
Hoagland, Sarah, and Marilyn Frye. "Introduction." *Feminist Interpretations of Mary Daly*. Ed. Sarah Lucia Hoagland and Marilyn Frye. Re-Reading the Canon. Ser. ed. Nancy Tuana. University Park, PA: Pennsylvania State UP, 2000. 1-25.
Hoitenga, Dewey. "Tillich's Religious Epistemology." *God and the Good: Essays in Honor of Henry Stob*. Grand Rapids, MI: Eerdmans, 1975. 140-149.
Houtman, C. "Queen of Heaven." *Dictionary of Deities and Demons in the Bible (DDD)*. Ed. Karel van der Toorn, Bob Beeking, and Pieter van der Horst. Leiden: Brill, 1995. 1278-1283.
Hubben, William. *Dostoevsky, Kierkegaard, Nietzsche, and Kafka: Our Prophets of Our Destiny*. New York: Collier, 1952.
Hudson, Fred. "Four Meanings of the Death of God." *Motive* 26.7 (Apr. 1966): 20-23. United Methodist Archives, GBHA/Drew University, Madison, NJ. Accessed Sept. 24, 2007.
Hughes, G. Rev. of *Religious Belief* by C. Martin. *Australasian Journal of Philosophy* 40 (1962): 211-219.
Humm, Maggie. *The Dictionary of Feminist Theory*. Columbus, OH: Ohio State UP, 1990.
Igrek, Apple. Book profile of *Godhead and the Nothing* by Thomas Altizer. *Journal of Cultural and Religious Theory* 6.2 (2003): 142-145.
"In Memory of Roy Eckhardt and Paul van Buren." *The Institute* 8 (1999). Accessed online, 3. Nov. 2004.
Irigaray, Luce. *Marine Lover of Friedrich Nietzsche*. Trans. Gillian Gill. New York: Columbia UP, 1991.
Irwin, John. *Psychoanalysis in Christian Thought: In Search of Man Through the Gestalkreis*. Ph.D. diss., Drew U., Madison, NJ, 1974.
"Is 'God is Dead' Dead?" *Time* (2. May 1969). Online. Accessed 19. June 2008.
James, T. "The Agony of Religious Doubt." *Cosmopolitan* (Dec. 1959): 86-93.
Jameson, Fredric. *Marxism and Form*. Princeton, NJ: Princeton UP, 1971.

Jantzen, Grace. *Becoming Divine: Towards a Feminist Philosophy of Religion.* Bloomington, IN: Indiana UP, 1999.

Jasper, David. "In the Wasteland: Apocalypse, Theology, and the Poets." *Thinking Through the Death of God: A Critical Companion to Thomas J. J. Altizer.* Ed. Lissa McCullough and Brian Schroeder. SUNY Series in Theology and Continental Thought. Ser. ed. Douglas Donkel. Albany, NY: SUNY UP, 2004. 185-195.

—. Rev. *Living the Death of God* by Thomas Altizer. *Contributions in Religion and Theology* 5.2 (2007): 160-162.

Jaspers, Karl. *Nietzsche: An Introduction to the Understanding of His Philosophical Activity.* Trans. Charles Wallraff and Frederick Schmitz. Baltimore, MD: Johns Hopkins UP, 1965.

Jay, Eric. "Transcendence: A Concept under Attack." *The Church in the Modern World: Essays in Honour of James Sutherland Thomson.* Ed. George Johnston and Wolfgang Roth. Toronto: Ryerson, 1967.

Jellema, Roderick. "On the Death of God." *The Reformed Journal* 16 (Sept. 1966): 21.

Jennings, Theodore. "Thomas J. J. Altizer." *A New Handbook of Christian Theologians.* Ed. Donald Musser and Joseph Price. Nashville, TN: Abingdon, 1996. 15-21.

Johnson, Elizabeth. *She Who Is: The Mystery of God in Feminist Theological Discourse.* New York: Crossroad, 1992.

Jones, Serene. *Feminist Theory and Christian Theology: Cartographies of Grace.* Guides to Theological Inquiry. Ser. ed. Kathryn Tanner and Paul Lakeland. Minneapolis: Fortress, 2000.

Jones, Tony. *The New Christians: Dispaches from the Emergent Frontier.* A Living Way: Emergent Visions. San Francisco: Jossey-Bass, 2008.

Kant, I. "Prolegomena to Any Future Metaphysics." *Philosophers Speak for Themselves: Berkeley, Hume, and Kant.* Ed. T. Smith and Majorie Greene. Chicago: U. Chicago P, 1957.

Karras, Ray. Reviews of *The Gospel of Christian Atheism* and *The New Apocalypse. Motive* (Nov. 1967): 52-54. Thomas Altizer Archive, Syracuse University, Box 2, Folder 9.

Katherine, Amber. "'A Too Early Morning': Audre Lorde's 'An Open Letter to Mary Daly' and Daly's Decision Not to Respond in Kind." *Feminist Interpretations of Mary Daly.* Ed. Sarah Lucia Hoagland and Marilyn Frye. Re-Reading the Canon. Ser. ed, Nancy Tuana. University Park, PA: Pennsylvania State UP, 2000. 266-297.

—. "(Re)reading Mary Daly as a Sister Insider." *Feminist Interpretations of Mary Daly.* Ed. Sarah Lucia Hoagland and Marilyn Frye. Re-Reading the Canon. Ser. ed, Nancy Tuana. University Park, PA: Pennsylvania State UP, 2000. 298-321.

Kaufmann, Walter. *Existentialism from Dostoevsky to Sartre.* Rev., expanded ed. New York: Meridian, 1975.

—. *Nietzsche: Philosopher, Psychologist, Antichrist.* 4th ed. Princeton, NJ: Princeton UP, 1974.

—. "Nietzsche's Attitude Toward Socrates." *Nietzsche: A Critical Review*. Ed. Peter Sedwick. Oxford: Blackwell, 1995. 123-143.
Keating, AnaLouise. "Back to the Mother? Feminist Mythmaking with a Difference." *Feminist Interpretations of Mary Daly*. Ed. Sarah Lucia Hoagland and Marilyn Frye. Re-Reading the Canon. Ser. ed, Nancy Tuana. University Park, PA: Pennsylvania State UP, 2000. 349-388.
Kee, Alistair. *Nietzsche Against the Crucified*. London: SCM, 1999.
Keller, Catherine. *Apocalypse Now and Then: A Feminist Guide to the End of the World*. Boston: Beacon, 1996.
—. "Feminism and the Ethic of Inseparability." *Weaving the Visions*. Ed. Judith Plaskow and Carol Christ. New York: Harper, 1989. 256-265.
—. *Face of the Deep: A Theology of Becoming*. London, Routledge, 2003.
—. *From a Broken Web: Separation, Sexism, and Self*. Boston: Beacon, 1986.
—. *God and Power: Counter-Apocalyptic Journeys*. Minneapolis: Fortress, 2005.
—. "Goddess, Ear, and Mother: On the Journey of Nelle Morton." *Journal of Feminist Studies of Religion* 4.2 (1988): 51-67.
—. "Mary Daly." *A New Handbook of Christian Theologians*. Ed. Donald Musser and Joseph Price. Nashville: Abingdon, 1996. 127-134.
Kelsey, George. George Kelsey Archive. Drew University. Box 34, Folio 2 ("Paul Tillich").
Kierkegaard, Søren. *Attack Upon 'Christendom.'* 1968 ed. Trans. Walter Lowrie. Princeton, NJ: Princeton UP, 1968.
Killen, Allen. "Tillich, The Trinity and Honest to God." *Bulletin of the Evangelical Theological Society* 7.1 (1964): 22-27.
Kimberling, Clark. "Paul Johannes Tillich (1886-1965)." Online. Accessed 7. April 2008. [http://faculty.evansville.edu/ck6/bstud/tillich.html]
Klemm, David. "Open Secrets: Derrida and Negative Theology." *Negation and Theology*. Ed. Robert Scharlemann. Studies in Religion and Culture. Ser. ed. Robert Scharlemann. Charlottesville, VA: UP Virginia, 1992. 8-24.
Kliever, Lonnie and Hayes, John. *Radical Christianity: The New Theologies in Perspective*. Anderson, SC: Droke, 1968.
Knutsen, Mary. *Beyond God the Father—Toward a Trinitarian Theology of the Cross: The Challenge of Mary Daly and Resources in the Works of Jürgen Habermas and Paul Ricoeur for Contemporary Christian Theology*. 2 vols. Ph.D. dissertation, University of Chicago, 1996.
Korte, Anne-Marie. "Deliver Us From Evil: Bad Versus Better Faith in Mary Daly's Feminist Writings." Trans. Micha Hoyinck. *Feminist Interpretations of Mary Daly*. Ed. Sarah Lucia Hoagland and Marilyn Frye. Re-Reading the Canon. Ser. ed, Nancy Tuana. University Park, PA: Pennsylvania State UP, 2000. 76-111.
—. "Just/ice in Time: On Temporality in Mary Daly's *Quintessence*." Trans. Fischa Hoyinck. *Feminist Interpretations of Mary Daly*. Ed. Sarah Lucia Hoagland and Marilyn Frye. Re-Reading the Canon. Ser. ed, Nancy Tuana. University Park, PA: Pennsylvania State UP, 2000. 418-428.
Kuntz, Paul. "The Ontological Argument and 'God is Dead:' Some Questions about God; Ways of Logic, History, and Metaphysics in Answering Them." *Journal of the American Academy of Religion* 38.1 (1970): 55-78.

Kvanig, Jonathan. "Divine Transcendence." *Religious Studies* 20 (1984): 377-387.

Lämmermann-Kuhn, Heidermarie. *Sensibilität fürden Menschen: Theologie und Anthropologie bei Dorothee Sölle*. Würzburger Studien zur Fundamentaltheologie. Vol. 4. Ser. ed. Elmar Klinger. Frankfurt: Peter Lang, 1988.

Lane, Belden. "Fantasy and The Geography of Faith." *Theology Today* 50.3 (1993): 397-408.

Lash, Nicholas. "For God Read Red Ink." *Frontier* 16 (1973): 56-57.

Leahy, D. G. *Beyond Sovereignty: A New Global Ethics and Morality*. Unpublished manuscript. New York Philosophy Corporation, 2008.

—. "The Diachrony of the Infinite in Altizer and Levinas." *Thinking Through the Death of God: A Critical Companion to Thomas J. J. Altizer*. Ed. Lissa McCullough and Brian Schroeder. SUNY Series in Theology and Continental Thought. Ser. ed. Douglas Donkel. Albany, NY: SUNY UP, 2004. 105-124.

—. *Faith and Philosophy: The Historical Impact*. Burlington, VT: Ashgate, 2003.

—. *Foundation: Matter the Body Itself*. Albany, NY: SUNY UP, 1996.

—. *Novitas Mundi: Perception of the History of Being*. New York: New York UP, 1980.

Levinas, Emmanuel. *Totality and Infinity: An Essay on Exteriority*. Trans. Alphonso Lingis. Pittsburgh: Duquesne UP, 1969. Org. pub. *Totaite et Infini*. The Hague: Martinus Nijoff, 1961.

Lewis, C. S. *The Complete Chronicles of Narnia*. New York: HarperCollins, 2000.

—. "Preface." *George MacDonald, An Anthology*. Ed. C.S. Lewis. London: Bles, 1947.

"Literature in the Divinity School." *Time* (22. Dec. 1967). Online. Accessed 19. June 2008.

Lonergan, Bernard. *Method in Theology*. Toronto: U. Toronto P, 1971.

Longfellow, Henry. "I Heard the Bells on Christmas Day." Cyberhymnal.org. Online. Accessed December 19, 2005.

Loomer, Bernard. "Tillich's Theology of Correlation." *Journal of Religion* 35 (1956): 150-156.

Lorde, Audre. *Sister Outsider: Essays and Speeches*. Crossing Press Feminist Series. Trumansbury, NY: Crossing, 1984.

Losce, John. *A Comparison of Methodology and Principles Basic to the Quantum Mechanics of Bohr and Heisenberg, The Metaphysics of Emmet, and the Theology of Tillich*. Ph.D. diss., Drew U., Madison, NJ, 1961.

Lose, David. "The Christian Story as Fantasy? Yes! Do Not Domesticate the Gospel." *Word & World* 26.2 (2006): 214+.

Love, Walter. "Mercy for Miss Awdy." *The Theology of Altizer: Critique and Response*. Ed. John Cobb. Philadelphia: Westminster, 1970. 243-266.

Lovejoy, Arthur. *The Great Chain of Being: A Study of The History of an Idea*. Cambridge, MA: Harvard UP, 1936.

Lueke, Richard. "Two New Hermeneutics: Some Practical Reflections." *Dialog* 4 (1965): 283-291.

Lyas, Colin. "On the Coherence of Christian Atheism." *Philosophy* 45.171 (Jan. 1970): 1-19.

MacGregor, Geddes. *The Sense of Absence*. Philadelphia: Lippincott, 1968.

Mackler, Aaron. "Symbols, Reality, and God: Heschel's Rejection of a Tillichian Understanding of Religious Symbols." *Judaism* 40 (1991): 290-300.

Mahan, Wayne. *Tillich's System*. San Antonio, TX: Trinity UP, 1974.

Maher, Mary. Rev. *Pure Lust* by Mary Daly. *Women & Therapy* 4 (1985): 76-78.

Maly, Eugene. "The Secular and the Sacred." *Transcendence and Immanence: The Papin Festschrift: Essays in Honor of Joseph Papin*. Ed. Joseph Armenti. 2 vols. Vol. 2. Villanova, PA: Villanova UP, 1976. 206-213.

Manschreck, Clyde. "Nihilism in the 20th Century: A View From Here." *Church History* 45 (1976): 85-90.

Marion, Jean-Luc. *God Without Being: hors-texte*. Trans. Thomas Carlson. Religion and Postmodernism. Ser. ed. Mark C. Taylor. Chicago: U. Chicago UP, 1991.

—. *In Excess: Studies of Saturated Phenomena*. Trans. Robin Horner and Vincent Berraud. Perspectives in Continental Philosophy. Vol. 27. Ser. ed. John Caputo. New York: Fordham UP, 2002. Orig. pub. *De Sarcoît: Études sur les phénomènes saturés*. Paris: Presses Universitaires de France, 2001.

Mark, James. "The Challenge of Nietzsche's Atheism." *Theology* 88 (July 1985) 272-281.

Martin, J. A. "St. Thomas and Tillich on the Names of God." *Journal of Religion* 37.4 (1957): 253-259.

Marty, Martin, and Jonathan Moore. *Politics, Religion and the Public Good*. San Francisco: Jossey-Bass, 2000.

Mascall, E. "Rev. of *The Edges of Language* by Paul M. van Buren." *Downside Review* 91 (1973): 70-71.

Matt, Daniel, trans., ed., and comp. *Zohar: Annotated & Explained*. SkyLight Illuminations. Ser. ed. Andrew Harvey. Woodstock, VT: SkyLight Paths, 2002.

Maziarz, Edward. "A Proposal for Metatheology." *Zygon* 7.2 (1972): 125-134.

McCullough, Lissa. "Historical Introduction." *Thinking Through the Death of God: A Critical Companion to Thomas J. J. Altizer*. Ed. Lissa McCullough and Brian Schroeder. SUNY Series in Theology and Continental Thought. Ser. ed. Douglas Donkel. Albany, NY: SUNY UP, 2004. xv-xxvii.

—. "Theology as Thinking of Passion Itself." *Thinking Through the Death of God: A Critical Companion to Thomas J. J. Altizer*. Ed. Lissa McCullough and Brian Schroeder. SUNY Series in Theology and Continental Thought. Ser. ed. Douglas Donkel. Albany, NY: SUNY UP, 2004. 29-46.

—, comp. "Comprehensive Bibliography: Thomas J. J. Altizer." *Thinking Through the Death of God: A Critical Companion to Thomas J. J. Altizer*. Ed. Lissa McCullough and Brian Schroeder. SUNY Series in Theology and Continental Thought. Ser. ed. Douglas Donkel. Albany, NY: SUNY UP, 2004. 231-244.

McCutcheon, Russell. *Critics Not Caretakers: Redescribing the Public Study of Religion*. Albany: SUNY UP, 2001.

—. "A Gift with Diminished Returns." *Journal of the American Academy of Religion* 76.3 (2008): 428-265.

McLean, George. "Paul Tillich's Existential Philosophy of Protestantism." *Paul Tillich in Catholic Thought.* Ed. Thomas O'Meara and Celestin Weisser. Dubuque: Priory, 1964. 42-84.

—. "Symbol and Analogy: Tillich and Thomas." *Paul Tillich in Catholic Thought.* Ed. Thomas O'Meara and Celestin Weisser. Dubuque: Priory, 1964. 145-483.

McKelway, Alexander. *The Systematic Theology of Paul Tillich.* Richmond, VA: Knox, 1965.

Merton, Thomas. *Faith and Violence: Christian Teaching and Christian Practice.* Notre Dame, IN: Notre Dame UP, 1968.

The Methodist Church, Southeastern College of Bishops. "Statement of the College of Bishops, Southeastern Jurisdiction." *The Mississippi Methodist Advocate* ns 19.17 (2. Feb. 1966): 6. United Methodist Archives, GBHA/Drew University, Madison, NJ. Accessed 24. Oct. 2007.

Meyer, Eric. "Catholic Theology and the Death of God: A Response." *The Theology of Altizer: Critique and Response.* Ed. John Cobb. Philadelphia: Westminster, 1970. 77-11.

—. *A Critical Analysis of the Death-of-God Theology of Thomas J. J. Altizer in Its Origins and Development.* Ph.D. diss., Wilhelms-Universität Münster (Westfalen, Germany), 1971.

—. "Death of God Theology." *God in Contemporary Thought: A Philosophical Perspective.* Ed. Sebastian Matczak. Philosophical Questions. Vol. 10. Ser. ed. Sebastian Matczak. New York: Learned, 1977. 775-812.

Meynell, Hugo. "Gospel Without God." *Theology* (1968): 361-367.

Miller, Alan and Donald Arther. *Paul Tillich's Systematic Theology.* North American Paul Tillich Society,1979.

Miller, Arthur. *The Crucible.* New York: Penguin Classics, 2003.

Miller, Walter. *A Canticle for Leibowitz.* New York: Bantam, 1980.

Mitchell, Julia. "The Theist-Atheist Controversy: From Theology to Phenomenology." *Religious Humanism* 17 (1983): 163-172+.

Morasa, Cherrie, and Gloria Anzaldua, ed. *This Bridge Called My Back: Writings by Radical Women of Color.* San Francisco: Aunt Lute Press, 1981.

Morton, Nelle. *The Journey is Home.* Boston: Beacon, 1985.

Mueller, Philip. *The Centrality and Significance of the Concept of Ecstasy in the Theology of Paul Tillich.* Ph.D. diss., Fordham U., New York, 1972.

Mulder, M. "God of Fortresses." *Dictionary of Deities and Demons in the Bible (DDD).* Ed. Karel van der Toorn, Bob Beeking, and Pieter van der Horst. Leiden: Brill, 1995. 700-701.

Murchland, Bernard, ed. *The Meaning of The Death of God: Protestant, Jewish, and Catholic Scholars Explore Atheistic Theology.* New York: Vintage, 1967.

Na, Huyng Suk. *Paul Tillich's Theology of Preaching: Boundary Preaching.* Ph.D. diss., Drew U., Madison, NJ, 1996.

Nhat Hanh, Tich. *Living Buddha, Living Christ.* London: Rider, 1995.

Nancy, Jean-Luc. *The Inoperative Community.* Trans. Peter Connor, Lisa Garbus, Michael Holland, and Simona Sawhney. Ed. Peter Connor. Theory and History of Literature. Vol. 76. Ser. ed. Wlad Godzich and Jochen Schulte-Sasse. Minneapolis: U. Minnesota UP, 1991.

Nelson, J. "A Misuse of Kenosis." *Christian Advocate* ns 10.11 (2. June 1966): 15. United Methodist Archives, GBHA/Drew University, Madison, NJ. Accessed 24. Oct. 2007.

Newmann, Glass. "Splits and Gaps in Buddhism and Postmodern Theology." *Journal of the American Academy of Religion* 63.2 (1992): 303-319.

"The New Ministry: Bringing God Back to Life." *Time* (26. Dec. 1969). Online. Accessed 19. June 2008.

Niebuhr, H. *Christ and Culture*. New York: Harper, 1951.

Niehr, H. "God of Heaven." *Dictionary of Deities and Demons in the Bible (DDD)*. Ed. Karel van der Toorn, Bob Beeking, and Pieter van der Horst. Leiden: Brill, 1995. 702-705.

Nielsen, Kai. "Is God So Powerful that He Doesn't Even Have to Exist?" *Religious Experience and Truth: A Symposium*. Ed. Sidney Hook. New York: New York UP, 1961. 270-281.

—. "Some Meta-Theological Remarks about Reductionism." *Journal of the American Academy of Religion* 42.2 (1974): 336-338.

Nietzsche, Friedrich. *The Anti-Christ*. In *Twilight of the Idols/The Anti-Christ*. Trans. R. Hollingdale. London: Penguin, 1990.

—. *Beyond Good and Evil*. Trans. Walter Kaufmann. New York: Vintage, 1966.

—. *The Birth of Tragedy*. Rpt. in *The Birth of Tragedy/The Case of Wagner*. Trans. and ed. Walter Kaufmann. New York: Vintage, 1967.

—. *The Birth of Tragedy and the Genealogy of the Morals*. Trans. F. Golffing. Garden City, NY: Doubleday, 1956.

—. *The Case of Wagner*. Rpt. in *The Birth of Tragedy/The Case of Wagner*. Trans. and ed. Walter Kaufmann. New York: Vintage, 1967.

—. *Daybreak*. Trans. R.J. Hollingdale. Cambridge: Cambridge UP, 1982.

—. *Ecce Homo*. Trans. Walter Kaufmann. In *The Genealogy of Morals/Ecce Homo*. Ed. Walter Kaufmann. New York: Vintage, 1967. 199-335.

—. *The Gay Science*. Trans. Walter Kaufmann. New York: Vintage, 1974.

—. *On the Genealogy of Morals/Ecce Homo*. Trans. Walter Kaufmann and R. J. Hollingdale. Ed. Walter Kaufmann. New York: Vintage, 1967.

—. *Thus Spoke Zarathustra: A Book for All and None*. Trans. Walter Kaufmann. New York: Modern, 1995.

—. *Twilight of the Idols*. Trans. R.J. Hollingdale. Rpt. in *Twilight of the Idols/The Anti-Christ*. London: Penguin, 1990.

—. *Unmodern Observations*. Trans. and ed. William Arrowsmith. New Haven, CT: Yale UP, 1990.

Njarakunnel, George. "Religion Beyond Religions in Nietzsche." *Journal of Dharma* 5.4 (Oct. 1980): 99-405.

Nogar, Raymond. *The Lord of the Absurd*. New York: Herder and Herder, 1966.

—. "The Lord of the Absurd: A Non- Teilhardian View." *The Mystery of Suffering of Death*. Ed. Michael Taylor. Garden City, NY: Image, 1974. 101-107.

Norris, Richard, ed. *The Christological Controversy*. Philadelphia: Fortress, 1980.

O'Connor, June. "Liberation Theologies and the Women's Movement: Points of Comparison and Contrast." *Horizons* 2 (1975): 103-124.

O'Connor, Timothy. "'And This All Men Call God.'" *Faith and Philosophy* 21.4 (Oct. 2004): 417-435.

Oden, Thomas. "Radical Theology: Which Way Now?" *Motive* 28.3 (Dec. 1967): 14-17. United Methodist Archives, GBHA/Drew University, Madison, NJ. Accessed Sept. 24, 2007.

Odin, Steve. "Kenōsis as a Foundation for Buddhist-Christian Dialogue." *Eastern Buddhist*, ns 20.1 (1987): 34-61.

Ogden, Schubert. *On Theology*. Dallas: Southern Methodist UP, 1986.

—. "Theology and Objectivity." *Journal of Religion* 45 (1965): 175-195.

Ogletree, Thomas. *The Death of God Controversy*. Nashville: Abingdon, 1966.

Olds, Linda. "Metaphors of Hierarchy and Interrelatedness in Hildegard of Bingen and Mary Daly." *Listening* 24.1 (1989): 54-66.

"The Ontological Argument: The Modal Ontological Argument." Online. Philosophy of Religion . Info. [http://philosophyofreligion.info/modalontological.html]

Osborne, Kenan. *New Being: A Study on the Relationship Between Conditional and Unconditional Being According to Paul Tillich*. The Hague: Martinus Nijoff, 1969.

Otto, Randall. "The Doctrine of God in the Theology of Paul Tillich." *Westminster Theological Journal* 52 (1980): 303-323.

Otto, Rudolf. *The Idea of the Holy: An Inquiry into the Non-Rational Factor in the Idea of the Divine and Its Relation to the Rational*. Trans. John Harvey. London: Oxford UP, 1923.

Owen, H. *Concepts of Deity*. New York: Herder, 1971.

Padovano, Anthony. *The Estranged God*. New York: Sheed and Ward, 1966.

Painadath, Sebastian. "Paul Tillich's Theology of Prayer: An Indian Perspective." *Paul Tillich: A New Catholic Assessment*. Ed. Raymond Bulman and Frederick Parrella. Collegeville, MN: Liturgical, 1994. 218-240.

Pangerl, Susann. *Radical Feminism and Self Psychology in Dialogue: A Critical Evaluation of the Models of Women's Experience in the Works of Mary Daly and Heinz Kohut*. 2 vols. Ph.D. dissertation, U. Chicago, 1992.

Parsons, Susan. "Conceiving of God: Theological Arguments and Motives in Feminist Ethics." *Ethical Theory and Moral Practice* 4.4 (2001): 365-382.

Paton, John. "Is God Dead." *Good News Broadcaster* (Feb. 1966) 3+. Thomas Altizer Archive, Syracuse University, Box 2, Folder 3.

Patricca, Nicholas. *God and the Question of Being: An Analytical Comparison of the Thinking of Martin Heidegger and Paul Tillich*. Ph.D. dissertation, U. Chicago, 1972.

Penington, Chester. "Is God Dead or Hidden?" *Christian Advocate* ns (2. Dec. 1965): 11-12. United Methodist Archives, GBHA/Drew University, Madison, NJ. Accessed 24. Oct. 2007.

Peterson, Daniel. "Speaking of God after the Death of God." *Dialog* 44.3 (2005): 207-226.

Phillips, D. "Rev. of *The Edges of Language* by Paul van Buren." *Theology* 76 (1973): 152-153.

Picknett, Lynn. *The Secret History of Lucifer*. New York: Carroll & Graf, 2005.

Pike, James. *A Time for Christian Candor*. New York: Harper, 1964.

—, and Diane Kennedy. *The Other Side*. Garden City, NY: Doubleday, 1968.

Pippin, Tina. *Apocalyptic Bodies: The Biblical End of the World in Text and Image.* London: Routledge, 1999.
Pittenger, W. "Paul Tillich as a Theologian: An Appreciation." *Anglican Theological Review* 43.3 (1961): 260-267.
Plantinga, Alvin. "Aquinas and Anselm." *God and the Good: Essays in Honor of Henry Stob.* Grand Rapids, MI: Eerdmans, 1975. 122-139.
—, ed. *The Ontological Argument: From St. Anselm to Contemporary Philosophers.* Garden City, NY: Doubleday, 1965.
Plato. *Phaedrus.* Trans. Alexander Nehamas and Paul Woodruff. Indianapolis: Hackett, 1995.
—. *The Republic.* 2nd ed. Trans. Allan Bloom. New York: Basic, 1991.
Pojman, Louis. "Religion Within the Limits of Language Alone." *Theology* 75 (1975): 544-553.
Pseudo-Dionysius. *Pseudo-Dionysius: The Complete Works.* Trans. Colm Laibheid and Paul Rorem. Classics of Western Spirituality. Ser. ed. John Farina et al. New York: Paulist, 1987.
Rahner, Karl. *Foundations of Christian Faith: An Introduction to the Idea of Christianity.* Trans. William Dych. New York: Crossroad, 2000.
—. "Jesus Christ." *Sacramentum Mundi.* Burns and Oats, 1969.
—. *Karl Rahner: Theologian of the Graced Search for Meaning.* Ed. Geoffrey Kelly. The Making of Modern Theology. Ser. ed. John de Gruchy. Minneapolis: Fortress, 1994.
Rahner, Karl, and Herbert Vorgrimler. *Theological Dictionary.* Trans. Richard Strachan. Ed. Cornelius Ernst. New York: Herder, 1965.
Raphael, Melissa. "Theology, Redemption and the Call of the Wild." *Feminist Theology* 15 (May 1997): 55-72.
Raschke, Carl. "The Death of God the Father." *Iliff Review* 35 (1978): 55-64.
—. *Painted Black: The Chilling True Story of the Wave of Violence Sweeping Through Our Hometowns.* New York: Harper, 1990.
—. "Rending the Veil of the Temple: The Death of God as Sancrificium Representationis." *Thinking Through the Death of God: A Critical Companion to Thomas J. J. Altizer.* Ed. Lissa McCullough and Brian Schroeder. SUNY Series in Theology and Continental Thought. Ser. ed. Douglas Donkel. Albany, NY: SUNY UP, 2004. 1-10.
—. "The Weakness of God...And of Theological Thought for That Matter: *Acta est fibula Plaudite.*" *Journal of Cultural and Religious Theory* 8.1 (2006): 1-9.
Randall, John. "The Ontology of Paul Tillich." *The Theology of Paul Tillich.* Library of Living Theology 1. Ed. Charles Kegley and Robert Betalles. New York: Macmillan, 1951. 132-161.
Reager, Jennifer. "Mother Teresa's Anguish Made Towey's Jaw Drop." *Pittsburgh Tribune Review* (Aug. 31, 2007). Online. Accessed Oct. 8, 2007.
Reilley, R. *Romantic Religion: A Study of Barfield, Lewis, Williams, and Tolkien.* Atlanta, GA: U Georgia P, 1971.
Reimer, A. "The Kingdom of God in the Thought of Emmanuel Hirsch and Paul Tillich." *New Creation or Eternal Now: Is there an Eschatology in Paul Tillich's Work?/ Neue Schöpfung oder Ewiges Jetzt: Hat Paul Tillich Eine*

Eschatologie? Ed. Gert Hummel. Theologische Bibliothek Töpelmann. Vol. 54. Ser. ed. K. Aland et al. Berlin: Walter de Gruyter, 1991. 44-56.

—. "Prayer as *Unio Mystica*: Tillich's Concept of Prayer in Contrast to Barth's Christological Realism and Hirsch's Pietistic Personalism." *Das Gebet als Grundakt des Glaubens*. Ed. Werner Schüßler and A. Reimer. Tillich-Studien. Ser. ed. Werner Schüßler and Erdmann Sturm. Münster: LIT, 2004. 109-135.

Richard, Jean. "My Journey into the Work of Paul Tillich." *Bulletin of the North American Paul Tillich Society* 30.1 (2004): 2-7.

—. "The Roots of Tillich's Eschatology in his Religious-Socialist Philosophy of History." *New Creation or Eternal Now: Is there an Eschatology in Paul Tillich's Work?/ Neue Schöpfung oder Ewiges Jetzt: Hat Paul Tillich Eine Eschatologie?* Ed. Gert Hummel. Theologische Bibliothek Töpelmann. Vol. 54. Ser. ed. K. Aland et al. Berlin: Walter de Gruyter, 1991. 26-43.

Ristiniemi, Jari. *Experiential Dialectics: An Inquiry into the Epistemological Status and Methodological Role of the Experiential Core in Paul Tillich's Systematic Thought*. Studia Philosophiae Religionis. Vol. 14. Ser. ed. Dick Haglund and Hans Hoff. Stockholm: Almqvist and Wiksell, 1987.

Riswold, Caryn. "From a Babylonian Captivity to the Otherworld: Martin Luther and Mary Daly." *Currents in Theology and Mission* 24 (1997): 50-58.

Robbins, Jeffrey. *In Search of A Non-Dogmatic Theology*. Contemporary Religious Thought. Ser. ed. Clayton Crockett and Jeffrey Robbins. Aurora, CO: Davies, 2003.

—. "Introduction: After the Death of God." In *After the Death of God* by John Caputo and Gianni Vattimo. Ed. Jeffrey Robbins. Insurrections: Critical Studies in Religion, Politics, and Culture. New York: Columbia UP, 2007. 1-24.

—. Rev. of *Derrida and Religion: Other Testaments* ed. by Yvonne Sherwood and Kevin Hart. *Journal of the American Academy of Religion* 74.3 (2006): 776-778.

—. "Terror and the Postmodern Condition: Toward a Radical Political Theology." *Religion and Violence in a Secular World*. Ed. Clayton Crockett. Charlottesville, VA: U. Virginia P, 1996. 187-205.

Roberts, David. "Tillich's Doctrine of Man." *The Theology of Paul Tillich*. Library of Living Theology 1. Ed. Charles Kegley and Robert Betalles. New York: Macmillan, 1951. 108-130.

Robinson, John. *In the End God: An Invitation to Explore the Grounds of Hope Within Us*. Religious Perspectives. Vol. 20. Ser. ed. Ruth Anshen. New York: Harper, 1968.

—. *Honest to God*. 40th Anniversary Ed. Louisville: KY: Westminster, 2002.

Rodkey, Christopher. "A Polemic Against the 'Festival of the Christian Home.'" *Sacramental Life* 17.2 (2005): 7-9.

—. "The Existential Notion that 'God is Dead' in Industrial Music." *Exordium* 8 (1999): 17-27.

—. "Form, Fragmentation, and Theonomy: Noise as an Expression of Reality." M.Div. thesis, University of Chicago, 2002.

—. *In the Horizon of the Infinite: Paul Tillich and the Dialectic of the Sacred*. Ph.D. diss., Drew U., 2008.*

—. "Is Bad Theology Good Philosophy?: Revisiting Paul Tillich's Problem of Philosophy and Theology." *Bulletin of the North American Paul Tillich Society* 31.2 (2005): 18-23.
—. "Nietzschean Christology." *The Fractal Self.* Ed. Douglas Shrader. Oneonta, NY: Oneonta Philosophical Studies, 2000. 155-174.
—. "The Practice of Youth Ministry and the Mystery of the Divine." *Journal of Youth and Theology* 5.2 (2006): 47-62.
—. "Reality Check: Confirmation *is* Graduation." *The Education Connection* (Winter 2008): 4+.
—. "Reconsidering Noise in Theology and in Praxis." *Doxology* 21 (2004): 72-91.
—. Rev. of *Approaches to Auschwitz*, rev. ed., by Richard Rubenstein and John Roth. *Journal of Cultural and Religious Theory* 5.3 (2004): 86-88.
—. Revs. of *The New Gospel of Christian Atheism* and *Godhead and the Nothing* by Thomas Altizer. *Bulletin of the North American Paul Tillich Society* 31.2 (2006): 7-9.
—. Rev. of *Thinking Through the Death of God*, ed. Lissa McCullough and Brian Schroder. *Journal of Cultural and Religious Theory* 6.3 (2005): 109-115.
—. Rev. of *Tillich and the Abyss* by New York: Palgrave Macmillan/Springer, 2016. American Academy of Religion, Reading Religion, online, 2018.*
—. *The Synaptic Gospel.* D.Min. diss., Meadville Lombard Theological School, 2007.
—. *The Synaptic Gospel: Teaching the Brain to Worship.* Lanham, MD: UP America, 2012.*
Rollins, Peter. *How (Not) to Speak of God.* Brewster, MA: Paraclete, 2006.
Roman Catholic Church. Fourth Lateran Council (1215) documents. English. Online. [http://www.Raphael.net/Church/Lateran4.htm]. Accessed 21. August 2007.
—. First Vatican Council (1870) documents. English. Online. [http://www.intratext.com/IXT/ENG0063/_P5.HTM]. Accessed 21. August 2007.
Ross, Robert. "A Form of Ontological Argument." *Harvard Theological Review* 70.1/2 (1977): 115-135.
—. "From World Negation to World Affirmation: A Study in the Development of the Theology of Thomas J. J. Altizer." *Journal of the American Academy of Religion* 37.4 (1969): 353-359.
—. "God and Singular Existence." *International Journal for Philosophy of Religion* 8.2 (1977): 127-141.
—. "The Non-Existence of God: Tillich, Aquinas, and The Pseudo-Dionysius." *Harvard Theological Review* 68 (1973): 141-166.
Roth, John. "The Silence of God." *Faith and Philosophy* 1.4 (1984): 407-420.
Rowe, William. "Atheism." *The Shorter Routledge Encyclopedia of Philosophy.* Ed. Edward Craig. London: Routledge, 2005. 73.
—. "The Meaning of 'God' in Tillich's Theology." *Journal of Religion* 42.4 (1962): 244-286.
—. *Religious Symbols and God: A Philosophical Study of Tillich's Theology.* Chicago: U Chicago P, 1968.
Rowland, Robyn, and Renate Klein. "Introduction." *A Reader in Feminist Knowledge.* Ed. Sneja Gunew. London: Routledge, 1991. 305-307.

Rubenstein, Richard. *After Auschwitz: Radical Theology and Contemporary Judaism.* 1966.

—. "Thomas Altizer's Apocalypse." *The Theology of Altizer: Critique and Response.* Ed. John Cobb. Philadelphia: Westminster, 1970. 125-137.

—, and John Roth. *Approaches to Auschwitz: The Holocaust and Its Legacy.* Rev. ed. Louisville, KY: Westminster, 2003.

Ruether, Rosemary. "Renewal or New Creation? Feminist Spirituality and Historical Religion." *A Reader in Feminist Knowledge.* Ed. Sneja Gunew. London: Routledge, 1991. 277-289.

"Rumors are Flying." *The Episcopalian* (May 1960): 38-39. Thomas Altizer Archive, Syracuse University, Box 1, Folder 15.

Runyon, Theodore. "The Death of God: One Year Later." *Christian Advocate* ns 10.22 (17. Nov. 1966): 7-8. United Methodist Archives, GBHA/Drew University, Madison, NJ. Accessed 24. Oct. 2007.

Russell, John. "Tillich's Implicit Ontological Argument." *Asian Journal of Theology* 22 (1988): 485-495.

Ryan, John. *The Awareness of God in the Thought of Paul Tillich.* Ph.D. diss., Drew U., Madison, NJ, 1973.

Ryu, Kee Chung. *Naharjuna's Emptiness and Paul Tillich's God: A Comparative Study for the Dialogue Between Christianity and Buddhism.* Ph.D. diss., Drew U., Madison, NJ, 1984.

Sabatino, Charles. "The Death of God: A Symbol for Religious Humanism." *Horizons* 10.2 (1983) 288-303.

Sabin, Raymond. *Tillich's Concept of God.* Unpublished B.D. thesis, Meadville Theological School (Chicago, IL), 1944.

Saddoris, Benjamin. *Timely Meditations: The Making of the American Nietzsche.* Ph.D. diss., Drew U., 2006.

Sands, Kathleen. "Ifs, Ands, and Butts: Theological Reflections on Humor." *Journal of the American Academy of Religion* 64.3 (1996): 499-523.

Santaniello, Weaver. *Nietzsche, God, and the Jews: His Critique of Judeo-Christianity in Relation to the Nazi Myth.* Albany, NY: SUNY UP, 1994.

Sartre, Jean-Paul. *Truth and Existence.* Trans. Adrian van den Hoven. Chicago: U Chicago P, 1992.

Scban, Jean-Loup. "Jakob Boheme." *The Shorter Routledge Encyclopedia of Philosophy.* Ed. Edward Craig. London: Routledge, 2005. 106.

Scharlemann, Robert. "Critical and Religious Consciousness: Some Reflections on the Question of Truth in the Philosophy of Religion." *Kairos and Logos: Studies in the Roots and Implications of Tillich's Theology.* Ed. John Carey. New ed. Macon, GA: Mercer UP, 1978. 63-82.

—. *Reflection and Doubt in the Thought of Paul Tillich.* New Haven, CT: Yale UP, 1969.

—. *Religion and Reflection: Essays on Paul Tillich's Theology.* Ed. Erdmann Sturm. Tillich-Studien. Vol. 16. Ser. ed. Werner Schüßer and Erdmann Sturm. Münster: LIT, 2004.

—. "Tillich's Method of Correlation: Two Proposed Revisions." *The Journal of Religion* 46.1.ii (Jan. 1966) 92-103.

Schelling, F. W. J. Von. "Ages of the World." 1813 second draft. Trans. Judith Norman. *The Abyss of Freedom/Ages of the World* by Slavoj Žižek and F. W. J. Von Schelling. Ann Arbor, MI: Michigan UP, 1997. 107-182.

Schilling, S. Revs. of *Christ the Representative* by Dorothee Sölle and *God-Talk* by John Macquarrie. *Religion in Life* 37.2 (Summer 1968): 312-313. United Methodist Archives, GBHA/Drew U., Madison, NJ. Accessed Sept. 24, 2007.

Schleiermacher, Friedrich. *On Religion: Speeches to Its Cultured Despisers*. Treans. John Oman. Louisville: Westminster, 1994.

Schneider, Laurel. "The Courage to See and Sin: Mary Daly's Elemental Transformation of Paul Tillich's Ontology." *Feminist Interpretations of Mary Daly*. Ed. Sarah Lucia Hoagland and Marilyn Frye. Re-Reading the Canon. Ser. ed, Nancy Tuana. University Park, PA: Pennsylvania State UP, 2000. 55-75.

—. "From new Being to Meta-Being: A Critical Analysis of Paul Tillich's Influence on Mary Daly." *Soundings* 75:2/3 (1992): 421-439.

Schonenberg, Piet. "From Transcendence to Immanence: Part II." *Transcendence and Immanence: The Papin Festschrift: Essays in Honor of Joseph Papin*. Ed. Joseph Armenti. 2 vols. Vol. 2. Villanova, PA: Villanova UP, 1976. 273-282.

Schrift, Allan. "Putting Nietzsche to Work: The Case of Gilles Deleuze." *Nietzsche: A Critical Review*. Ed. Peter Sedwick. Oxford: Blackwell, 1995. 250-275.

Schroeder, Brian. "Absolute Atonement." *Thinking Through the Death of God: A Critical Companion to Thomas J. J. Altizer*. Ed. Lissa McCullough and Brian Schroeder. SUNY Series in Theology and Continental Thought. Ser. ed. Douglas Donkel. Albany, NY: SUNY UP, 2004. 65-87.

—. "Preface: Forward to a Future Thinking." *Thinking Through the Death of God: A Critical Companion to Thomas J. J. Altizer*. Ed. Lissa McCullough and Brian Schroeder. SUNY Series in Theology and Continental Thought. Ser. ed. Douglas Donkel. Albany, NY: SUNY UP, 2004. vii-xi.

Scott, Nathan. "On the Fallacies of a 'Close Reader:' A Reply." *Journal of the American Academy of Religion* 39.1 (1971): 76-82.

—. "The Presidential Address: The House of Intellect in an Age of Carnival: Some Hermeneutical Reflections." *Journal of the American Academy of Religion* 55.1 (1987): 3-19.

The Sea of Faith Network. Online. Accessed Sept. 15, 2007. [http://www.sofn.org.uk]

Sedwick, Peter. "Nietzsche's Institutions." *Nietzsche: A Critical Review*. Ed. Peter Sedwick. Oxford: Blackwell, 1995. 1-11.

Shute, G. "'God' at the Edge of Language." *The Expository Times* 84 (1973): 187.

Smedes, Lewis. "Theology and the Playful Life." *God and the Good: Essays in Honor of Henry Stob*. Grand Rapids, MI: Eerdmans, 1975. 46-62.

Smith, Steven. Rev. of *The New Gospel of Christian Atheism* by Thomas Altizer. *Journal of the American Academy of Religion* 73.3 (2005): 890-893.

Sölle, Dorothee. *Against the Wind: Memoir of a Radical Christian*. Trans. Barbara Rumscheidt and Martin Rumscheidt. Minneapolis: Fortress, 1999. Trans. of *Gegenwind: Erinnerungen*. Hamburg: Hoffman and Campe, 1995.

—. *Atheistichan Gottglauben.* Fribourg: Walter, 1967.
—. "Breaking the Ice of the Soul: Theology and Literature in Search of a New Language." *The Theology of Dorothee Soelee.* Ed. Sarah Pinnock. Harrisburg: Trinity, 2003. 31-41.
—. *Christ the Representative: An Essay in the Theology After the Death of God.* Trans. David Lewis. Philadelphia: Fortress, 1967. Trans. of *Stellvertretung: Ein Kapitel Theologie nach dem >>Tode Gottes<<.* Kreuz, 1965.
—. *Creative Disobedience.* Trans. Lawrence Denef. Cleveland: Pilgrim, 1995. Trans. of *Phantasie und Gehorsam: Überlegungen zu einer künftigen Christlichen Ethik.* Stuttgart: Kreuz, 1968.
—. *The Mystery of Death.* Trans. Nancy Lukens-Rumscheidt and Martin Lukens Rumscheidt. Minneapolis: Fortress, 2007. Trans. of *Mystik des Fodes: Ein Fragment.* Stuttgart: Krenz, 2003.
—. *Die Warheit ist Konkret.* Fribourg: Walter, 1965.
Solomon, Robert, ed. *Existentialism.* New York: Modern, 1976.
—, and Kathleen Higgins. *What Nietzsche Really Said.* New York: Schocken, 2000.
Sontag, Frederick. "Ontological Possibility and The Nature of God: A Reply to Tillich." *Journal of Religion* 36.4 (1956): 234-240.
"Southeastern Bishops Condemn Altizer Theology." *Christian Advocate* ns 11.4 (24. Dec. 1966): 3. United Methodist Archives, GBHA/Drew University, Madison, NJ. Accessed 24. Oct. 2007.
Spong, John. *Here I Stand.* New York: Harper San Francisco, 2001.
—. *Why Christianity Must Change or Die: A Bishop Speaks to Believers in Exile: A New Reformation of the Church's Faith and Practice.* New York: Harper San Francisco, 1998.
Sprague, Joseph. *Affirmations of a Dissenter.* Nashville: Abingdon, 2003.
Stahl, Roland. "Some Reflections on the Death of God." *Religion in Life* 37.4 (1968): 602-611. United Methodist Archives, GBHA/Drew University, Madison, NJ. Accessed Sept. 24, 2007.
Stenger, Mary. "A Critical Analysis of the Influence of Paul Tillich on Mary Daly's Feminist Theology." *Encounter* 43 (1982): 219-238.
—. "The Limits and Possibilities of Tillich's Ontology for Cross-Cultural and Feminist Theology." *God and Being: The Problem of Ontology in the Philosophical Theology of Paul Tillich/ Gott und Sein: Das Problem der ontologie in der philosophischen theologie Paul Tillichs.* Ed. Gert Hummel. Theologische Bibliothek Töpelmann. Vol. 47. Ser. ed. K. Aland et al. Berlin: Walter de Gruyter, 1989. 250-268.
—. "Paul Tillich and the Feminist Critique of Roman Catholic Theology." *Paul Tillich: A New Catholic Assessment.* Ed. Raymond Bulman and Frederick Parrella. Collegeville, MN: Liturgical, 1994. 174-188.
—. "Troeltsch and Tillich: Christians Seeking Religion Outside the Churches." *The North American Paul Tillich Society Newsletter* 29.3 (2003): 9-18.
Stevens, William. "Paul Tillich and the Postmodern Self." *Encountering Transcendence: Contributions to a Theology of Christian Religious Experience.* Ed. Lieven Boeve, Hans Geybels, and Stijn Van den Bossche. Annua Nuntia Lovaniensia. Vol. 53. Leuven: Peeters, 2005. 83-92.

Stiegler, Bernard. *Technics and Time, 1: The Fault of Epinetheus*. Trans. Richard Beardsworth and George Collins. Meridan Crossing Aesthetics. Ser. ed. Warner Hamachow David Wellberg. Stanford, CA: Stanford UP, 1998. Rpt. *La technique et le temps, 1* (1994).

Stob, Henry. "The Apologetic Stance of Christian Atheism." *The Reformed Journal* 16 (Nov. 1966): 7-11.

—. "Christian Atheism." *The Reformed Journal* 16 (Sept. 1966): 19-21.

—. "The Death-of-God Theology." *The Reformed Journal* 16 (Mar. 1966): 23-28.

Stoker, Wessel. "The Paradox of Complementarity in Tillich's Doctrine of God." *The Theological Paradox: Interdisciplinary Reflections on the Centre of Paul Tillich's Thought/ Das Theologische Paradox: Interdiszipliniare Reflexionen zur mitte von Paul Tillichs Denken*. Ed. Gert Hummel. Theologische Bibliothek Töpelmann. Vol. 74. Ser. ed. O. Bayer, W. Härle, H. Müller. Berlin: Walter de Gruyter, 1995. 104-121.

Stone, Ronald. *Paul Tillich's Radical Social Thought*. Atlanta: John Knox, 1980.

Suber, Peter. "Metaphilosophy Themes and Questions: A Personal List." Philosophy Department, Earlham College. Online. Accessed 18. April 2008.

Suchocki, Margorie. "The Idea of God in Feminist Philosophy." *Hypatia* 9.4 (1994): 57-68.

Suhonen, Marja. "Toward Biophilic Be-ing: Mary Daly's Feminist Metaethics and the Question of Essentialism." *Feminist Interpretations of Mary Daly*. Ed. Sarah Lucia Hoagland and Marilyn Frye. Re-Reading the Canon. Ser. ed, Nancy Tuana. University Park, PA: Pennsylvania State UP, 2000. 112-131.

Surlis, Paul. "The God-World Relationship." *God in Contemporary Thought: A Philosophical Perspective*. Ed. Sebastian Matczak. Philosophical Questions. Vol. 10. Ser. ed. Sebastian Matczak. New York: Learned, 1977. 1043-1052.

Tanner, Kathryn. *The Politics of God: Christian Theologies and Social Justice*. Minneapolis: Fortress, 1992.

—. *Jesus, Humanity, and the Trinity: A Brief Systematic Theology*. Minneapolis: Fortress, 2001.

Taubes, Jacob. "On the Nature of the Theological Method: Some Reflections on the Methodological Principles of Tillich's Theology." *Journal of Religion* 34.1 (1954): 12-25.

—. Rev. *Love, Power, and Justice* by Paul Tillich. *Journal of Religion* 35.2 (1955): 99-100.

Tavard, George. "The Protestant Principle and the Theological System of Paul Tillich." *Paul Tillich in Catholic Thought*. Ed. Thomas O'Meara and Celestin Weisser. Dubuque: Priory, 1964. 85-96.

Taylor, Mark C. "Altizer's Originality." *Journal of the American Academy of Religion* 52.3 (1984): 569-570.

—. "The Anachronism of A/Theology." *Religion and Intellectual Life* 5 (1988): 22-36.

—. "Betraying Altizer." *Thinking Through the Death of God: A Critical Companion to Thomas J. J. Altizer*. Ed. Lissa McCullough and Brian Schroeder. SUNY

Series in Theology and Continental Thought. Ser. ed. Douglas Donkel. Albany, NY: SUNY UP, 2004. 11-28.

—. *Erring: A Post-modern A/Theology.* Chicago: Chicago UP, 1984.

—. "Forward: The Last Theologian." In Thomas Altizer, *Living the Death of God.* Albany, NY: SUNY UP, 2006. xi-xviii.

—. "Masking: Domino Effect." *Journal of the American Academy of Religion* 54.3 (1986): 547-557.

—. "Text as Victim." *Deconstruction and Theology* by Thomas Altizer et al. New York: Crossroad, 1982. 58-78.

—. "Think Naught." *Negation and Theology.* Ed. Robert Scharlemann. Studies in Religion and Culture. Ser. ed. Robert Scharlemann. Charlottesville, VA: UP Virginia, 1992. 25-38.

—, and Carl Raschke. "About *About Religion*: A Conversation with Mark Taylor." *Journal of Cultural and Religious Theory* 2.2 (2001). Online. Access 26. October 2007.

Taylor, Mark K. *Paul Tillich: Theologian of the Boundaries.* London: Liturgical, 1987.

Taylor, Victor. "Theography: Signs of God in a Postmodern Age." *Secular Theology: American Radical Theological Thought.* Ed. Clayton Crockett. London: Routledge, 2001. 189-197.

Teresa of Calcutta. *Come Be My Light: The Private Writings of the "Saint of Calcutta."* Ed. Brian Kolodiechuk. New York: Doubleday, 2007.

Thatamanil, John. "Against the Mystical as Exceptional: A Response to Rob James's *Tillich and World Religions.*" *Bulletin of the North American Paul Tillich Society* 30.4 (2004): 25-28.

—. *The Immanent Divine: God, Creation, and the Human Predicament.* Minneapolis: Fortress, 2006.

"Theoi Greek Mythology." Online. Accessed 19. March 2008.

"Theologian Paul Tillich Upstaged by a Simple Preacher—Fiction!" TruthOrFiction Online. Accessed 16. December 2007. [http://truthorfiction.com/rumors/t/tillich.htm]

Thistlethwaite, Susan. "God and Her Survival in a Nuclear Age." *Journal of Feminist Studies in Religion* 4.1 (1988): 73-88.

Thomas, George. "The Method and Structure of Tillich's Theology." *The Theology of Paul Tillich.* Library of Living Theology 1. Ed. Charles Kegley and Robert Betalles. New York: Macmillan, 1951. 86-105.

Thomas, J. "The Correlation of Philosophy and Theology in Tillich's System." *London Quarterly and Holborn Review* 184 (1959) 47-57.

—. *Tillich.* Outstanding Christian Thinkers. Ser. ed. Brian Davies. London: Continuum, 2000.

Thomas, O. "Being and Some Theologians." *Harvard Theological Review* 70.1/2 (1977): 137-160.

—. "Tillich's *Systematic Theology*: An Assessment of Major Successes and Failures, On the Occasion of the Fortieth Anniversary of Its Completion (11/16/04)." *Bulletin of the North American Paul Tillich Society* 31.2 (2005): 3-7.

Thomas, Terrance. "Paul Tillich and Mircea Eliade and Their Use of Paradox." *The Theological Paradox: Interdisciplinary Reflections on the Centre of Paul Tillich's Thought/ Das Theologische Paradox: Interdiszipliniare Reflexionen zur mitte von Paul Tillichs Denken.* Ed. Gert Hummel. Theologische Bibliothek Töpelmann. Vol. 74. Ser. ed. O. Bayer, W. Härle, H. Müller. Berlin: Walter de Gruyter, 1995. 242-263.

Thompson, Ian. *Being and Meaning: Paul Tillich's Theory of Meaning, Truth and Logic.* Edinburgh: Edinburgh UP, 1981.

Tilley, Terrance. Rev. of *The Surface of the Deep* by Charles Winquist. *Theological Studies* 66.2 (2005): 495.

Tillich, Hannah. *From Time to Time.* New York: Stein, 1973.

Tillich, Paul. "An Afterward: Appreciation and Reply." *Paul Tillich in Catholic Thought.* Ed. Thomas O'Meara and Celestin Weisser. Dubuque: Priory, 1964. 301-311.

—. "Answer." *The Theology of Paul Tillich.* Library of Living Theology 1. Ed. Charles Kegley and Robert Betalles. New York: Macmillan, 1951. 329-349.

—. *Biblical Religion and the Search for Ultimate Reality.* Chicago: U Chicago P, 1955.

—. *Christianity and the Encounter of World Religions.* Fortress Texts in Modern Theology. Ser. ed. B. Gerrish. Minneapolis: Fortress, 1994.

—. *The Courage To Be.* New Haven, CT: Yale UP, 1980.

—. *Dynamics of Faith.* Harper Torchbooks/Cloister Library. New York: Harper, 1957.

—. *The Eternal Now.* New York: Scribners, 1963.

—. *The Future of Religions.* Ed. Jerald Brauer. New York: Harper, 1966.

—. "The Good I Will, I Do Not." *Rockefeller Chapel Sermons of Recent Years.* Comp. Donovan Smucker. Chicago: U Chicago P, 1967. 165-173.

—. *A History of Christian Thought: From its Judaic and Hellenistic Origins to Existentialism.* Ed. Carl Braaten. New York: Simon, 1968.

—. *The Interpretation of History.* Trans. N. Rasetzki and Elisa Talwey. London: Scribners, 1936.

—. *The Irrelevance and Relevance of the Christian Message.* Cleveland: Pilgrim, 1996.

—. *Love, Power, and Justice: Ontological Analyses and Ethical Applications.* London: Oxford UP,1954.

—. "The Meaning and Justification of Religious Symbols." *Religious Experience and Truth: A Symposium.* Ed. Sidney Hook. New York: New York UP, 1961. 3-11.

—. *The Meaning of Health.* Ed. Perry LeFevre. Chicago: Exploration, 1984.

—. *Morality and Beyond.* Library of Theological Ethics. Louisville, KY: Westminster, 1963.

—. *My Search for Absolutes.* Ill. Saul Steinberg. Credo Perspectives. Ed. Ruth Anshen. New York: Simon, 1967.

—. *My Travel Diary: 1936.* Ed. Jerald Brauer. New York: Harper, 1970.

—. *The New Being.* New York: Scribner's, 1955.

—. *On Art and Architecture.* Trans. Robert Scharlemann. Ed. John Dillenberger and Jane Dillenberger. New York: Crossroad, 1987.

—. *On the Boundary: An Autobiographical Sketch.* New York: Scribner's, 1966.

—. *Perspectives in 19th and 20th Century Protestant Theology.* Ed. Carl Braaten. New York: Harper, 1967.
—. *Political Expectation.* New York: Harper, 1971.
—. *The Protestant Era.* Abridged ed. Trans. James Adams. Chicago: U Chicago P, 1957.
—. *The Recovery of the Prophetic Tradition in the Reformation.* Washington, DC: Christianity and Modern Man, 1950. Will Herberg Archive, Drew University, Madison, NJ.
—. *The Religious Situation.* Trans. H. Niebuhr. New York: Living Age, 1962.
—. "The Religious Symbol." *Religious Experience and Truth: A Symposium.* Ed. Sidney Hook. New York: New York UP, 1961. 301-321.
—. Rev. H. Wienman, *The Growth of Religion. Journal of Religion* 20 (1940): 69-72.
—. "Symbols of Eternal Life: The Ingersoll Lecture, 1962." *Harvard Divinity Bulletin* 26.3 (1962): 1-10.
—. *Theology of Culture.* Ed. Robert Kimball. London: Oxford, 1964.
—. *Theology of Peace.* Ed. Ronald Stone. Louisville, KY: Westminster, 1990.
—. *The Socialist Decision.* Trans. Franklin Sherman. New York: Harper, 1977. Rpt. *Die Socialistiche Entschsidung* (Pottsdam: Alfred Protte, 1933).
—. *The Spiritual Situation in Our Technical Society.* Ed. J. Thomas. Macon, GA: Mercer UP, 1988.
—. *Systematic Theology.* Vol. 1. 3 vols. Chicago: U Chicago P, 1951.
—. *Systematic Theology.* Vol. 2. 3 vols. Chicago: U Chicago P, 1957.
—. *Systematic Theology.* Vol. 3. 3. vols. Chicago: U Chicago P, 1963.
—. "Systematic Theology, First Part: Preliminary Draft for the Private Use of My Students." Unpublished manuscript, c. 1944. Carl Michalson Archive, Drew University, Box 16, Folio 12.
—. *What is Religion?* Ed. James Adams. New York: Harper, 1969.
—, et al. *To Live as Men: An Anatomy of Peace.* Santa Barbara, CA: Center for the Study of Democratic Institutions, 1965.
Todorov, Tzvetan. *The Fantastic: A Structural Approach to a Literary Genre.* Trans. Richard Howard. Cleveland: Case Western Reserve UP, 1973.
Tolkien, J. R. R. "On Fairy-Stories." *Essays Presented to Charles Williams.* Ed. C. S. Lewis. Grand Rapids, MI: Eerdmans, 1968. 38-99.
—. *The Lord of the Rings.* Collector's ed. Boston: Houghton Mifflin, 1987.
—. *Tree and Leaf.* London: Unwin, 1964.
"Toward a Hidden God." *Time* (8. April 1966). Online. Accessed 19. June 2008.
Towne, Anthony. "Excerpts from the Diaries of the Late God." *Motive* 28.7 (Apr. 1968): 46-48. United Methodist Archives, GBHA/Drew University, Madison, NJ. Accessed Sept. 24, 2007.
—. "God is Dead in Georgia." *Motive* 26.5 (Feb. 1966): 74. United Methodist Archives, GBHA/Drew University, Madison, NJ. Accessed Sept. 24, 2007.
Towne, Edgar. "Tillich's Postmodern View of the Actuality of God." *The North American Paul Tillich Society Newsletter* 29.3 (2003): 24-29.
Turner, Denys. *The Darkness of God: Negativity and Christian Mysticism.* Cambridge, England: Cambridge UP, 1995.

Tracy, David. *The Analogical Imagination: Christian Theology and the Culture of Pluralism.* New York: Crossroad, 1981.
—. *Blessed Rage for Order: The New Pluralism in Theology.* 1996 ed. Chicago: U Chicago P, 1996.
—. *Dialogue with the Other: The Inter-Religious Dialogue.* Louvain Theological and Pastoral Monographs. Vol. 1. Louvain: Pecteus, 1990.
Trinkle, Joseph. "Christology and Linguistic Analysis." *Sciences Ecclesiastiques* 17 (1965): 135-142.
Tulip, Marie. "Introduction." *A Reader in Feminist Knowledge.* Ed. Sneja Gunew. London: Routledge, 1991. 259-269.
Unhjem, Arne. *Dynamics of Doubt: A Preface to Tillich.* Philadelphia: Fortress, 1966.
Vahanian, Gabriel. *Anonymous God.* Trans. Noëlle Vahanian. Contemporary Religious Thought. Ser. ed. Clayton Crockett and Jeffrey Robbins. Aurora, CO: Davies, 2002. Trans. of *Dieu anonyme ou la peur des mots.* Org. pub. Paris: Desclée de Brower, 1989.
—. "Beyond the Death of God." *The Meaning of the Death of God.* Ed. Bernard Murchland. New York: Vintage, 1967.
—. "The Death of God: An Afterword." In *After the Death of God* by John Caputo and Gianni Vattimo. Ed. Jeffrey Robbins. Insurrections: Critical Studies in Religion, Politics, and Culture. New York: Columbia UP, 2007. 163-178.
—. *The Death of God: The Culture of Our Post-Christian Era.* New York: Braziller, 1961.
—. "Introduction." *Living Questions to Dead Gods* by Jacques Durandeaux. New York: Sheed and Ward, 1968. 7-25.
—. "Theology and the Secular." *Secular Theology: American Radical Theological Thought.* Ed. Clayton Crockett. London: Routledge, 2001. 10-25.
—. "Theology at the End of the Age of Religion." *Concilium* 6.2 (June 1966): 51-65.
—. *Tillich and the New Religious Paradigm.* Contemporary Religious Thought. Ser. ed. Clayton Crockett and Jeffrey Robbins. Aurora, CO: Davies, 2004.
—. *Wait Without Idols.* New York: Braziller, 1964.
Van Buren, Paul. "Anselm's Formula and the Logic of 'God.'" *Religious Studies* 9 (1973): 279-288.
—. *The Edges of Language: An Essay in the Logic of Religion.* London: SCM, 1972.
—. "The Meaning of the Gospel." *Toward a New Christianity: Readings in the Death of God* Theology. Ed. Thomas Altizer. New York: Harcourt, 1967. 283-300.
—. Rev. of *Naming the Whirlwind* by Langdon Gilkey. *Theology Today* 27 (1970): 225-227.
—. *The Secular Meaning of the Gospel: Based on an Analysis of Its Language.* New York: Macmillan, 1966.
—. "Theology and the Philosophy of Religion From the Perspective of Religious Thought," *Union Seminary Quarterly Review* 15.4 (Summer 1969) 467-476.
Van Ness, Paul. *Death of God Theology and Freud: An Examination of the Meanings of Death.* Ph.D. diss., U. Chicago, 1972.

Vattimo, Gianni. *After Christianity.* Trans. Luca D'Isanto. Italian Academy Lectures. New York: Columbia UP, 2002.
—. *Belief.* Trans. Luca D'Isanto and David Webb. Stanford, CA: Stanford UP, 1999.
—. *Beyond Interpretation: The Meaning of Hermeneutics for Philosophy.* Trans. David Webb. Stanford, CA: Stanford UP, 1997.
—, and Richard Rorty. *The Future of Religion.* Ed. Santiago Zabala. New York: Columbia UP, 2005.
Vaught, Carl. "Confronting Paul Tillich: Being, God, and Categories." *Bulletin of the North American Paul Tillich Society* 31.5 (2005): 5-9.
Wainwright, William. "Paul Tillich and Arguments for the Existence of God." *Journal of the American Academy of Religion* 39 (1971): 171-185.
Waits, Jim. "An Inquiry into the Death of God." *The Mississippi Methodist Advocate* ns 19.8 (9. Feb. 1966): 6-7. United Methodist Archives, GBHA/Drew University, Madison, NJ. Accessed 24. Oct. 2007.
Weaver, Mary Jo. "Daly, Daly, Sing to Mary." *Cross Currents* 14 (1985): 111-115.
Wehr, Demaris. "Fracturing the Language of Patriarchy." *New York Times* (22. July 1984): 14.
Weissman, Steve. "New Left Man Meets the Dead God." *Motive* 27.4 (Jan. 1967): 20-30. United Methodist Archives, GBHA/Drew University, Madison, NJ. Accessed Sept. 24, 2007.
Wendte, Martin. "Contradiction and the Living God: On the Contemporary Significance of Hegel's Meditation of Religious Experience with an Onto-Theological Concept of God." *Encountering Transcendence: Contributions to a Theology of Christian Religious Experience.* Ed. Lieven Boeve, Hans Geybels, and Stijn Van den Bossche. Annua Nuntia Lovaniensia. Vol. 53. Leuven: Peeters, 2005. 257-274.
Wesley, John. *John Wesley's Sermons: An Anthology.* Ed. Albert Outler and Richard Heitzenrater. Nashville: Abingdon, 1991.
Wesley, John, and Charles Wesley. *John and Charles Wesley: Selected Writings and Hymns.* Ed. Frank Whaling. The Classics of Western Spirituality. Ser. ed. Richard Payne et al. New York: Paulist, 1991.
Williamson, Clark. "Paul M. van Buren." *A New Handbook of Christian Theologicans.* Ed. Donald Musser and Joseph Price. Nashville: Abingdon, 1996.
Winn, Albert. "Holy Spirit and the Christian Life." *Interpretation* 33 (1979): 47-57.
Winquist, Charles. *Desiring Theology.* Religion and Postmodernism. Ser. ed. Mark C. Taylor. Chicago: U Chicago P, 1995.
—. "Eschatology in the Thought of Paul Tillich: Metonymical Figuration." *New Creation or Eternal Now: Is there an Eschatology in Paul Tillich's Work?/ Neue Schöpfung oder Ewiges Jetzt: Hat Paul Tillich Eine Eschatologie?* Ed. Gert Hummel. Theologische Bibliothek Töpelmann. Vol. 54. Ser. ed. K. Aland et al. Berlin: Walter de Gruyter, 1991. 195-204.
—. "Heterology and Ontology in the Thought of Paul Tillich." *God and Being: The Problem of Ontology in the Philosophical Theology of Paul Tillich/ Gott und Sein: Das Problem der ontologie in der philosophischen theologie Paul Tillichs.* Ed. Gert Hummel. Theologische Bibliothek Töpelmann. Vol. 47. Ser. ed. K. Aland et al. Berlin: Walter de Gruyter, 1989. 48-58.

—. "Postmodern Secular Theology." *Secular Theology: American Radical Theological Thought.* Ed. Clayton Crockett. London: Routledge, 2001. 26-36.

—. "The Sacrament of the Word of God." *Encounter* 33 (1972): 217-229.

—. *The Surface of the Deep.* Contemporary Religious Thought. Ser. ed. Clayton Crockett and Jeffrey Robbins. Davies: Aurora, CO: 2003.

—. Rev. of *The Self-Embodiment of God* and *Total Presence* by Thomas J. J. Altizer. *Religious Studies Review* 8 (1982): 337-342.

—. "Theology beside Itself: Desiring Theology." *The Theological Paradox: Interdisciplinary Reflections on the Centre of Paul Tillich's Thought/ Das Theologische Paradox: Interdiszipliniare Reflexionen zur mitte von Paul Tillichs Denken.* Ed. Gert Hummel. Theologische Bibliothek Töpelmann. Vol. 74. Ser. ed. O. Bayer, W. Härle, H. Müller. Berlin: Walter de Gruyter, 1995. 9-19.

—. "Theology: Unsettled and Unsettling." *Journal of the American Academy of Religion* 62.4 (1994): 1023-1035.

—. "Untimely History." *Truth and History: A Dialogue with Paul Tillich/ Warheit und Geschichte: Ein Dialog mit Paul Tillich.* Ed. Gert Hummel. Theologische Bibliothek Töpelmann. Vol. 95. Ser. ed. O. Bayer, W. Härle, H. Müller. Berlin: Walter de Gruyter, 1998.

Wyschogrod, Edith. "Crucifixion and Alterity: Pathways to Glory in the Thought of Altizer and Levinas." *Thinking Through the Death of God: A Critical Companion to Thomas J. J. Altizer.* Ed. Lissa McCullough and Brian Schroeder. SUNY Series in Theology and Continental Thought. Ser. ed. Douglas Donkel. Albany, NY: SUNY UP, 2004. 89-103.

Yoon, Dong Cheol. *The Protestant Principle: A Study on Paul Tillich.* Ph.D. diss., Drew U., Madison, NJ, 1998.

Young, Julian. *The Death of God and the Meaning of Life.* London: Routledge, 2003.

Young, Katherine. "Rejoinder to Rita M. Gross." *Journal of the American Academy of Religion* 67.1 (1999): 195-198.

Zabala, Santiago. "Introduction: A Religion Without Theists or Atheists." *The Future of Religion* by Gianni Vattimo and Richard Rorty. Ed. Santiago Zabala. New York: Columbia UP, 2005.

Zietlow, Harold. *The Living God: The Existential Systems of F. W. J. Schelling and Paul Tillich.* Ph.D. diss., U. Chicago, 1961.

Žižek, Slavoj. "The Abyss of Freedom." *The Abyss of Freedom/Ages of the World* by Slavoj Žižek and F. W. J. Von Schelling. Ann Arbor, MI: Michigan UP, 1997. 1-104.

—. "Christ's Breaking of the 'Great Chain of Being.'" *Writing the Bodies of Christ: The Church from Carlyle to Derrida.* Ed. John Schad. Aldershot, England: Ashgate, 2001. 105-110.

—. "Defenders of the Faith." *New York Times* (March 12, 2006). Online. Accessed March 13, 2006.

—. *On Belief.* Thinking in Action. Ser. ed. Simon Critchley and Richard Kearney. London: Routledge, 2001.

—. *The Fragile Absolute, or Why is the Christian Legacy Worth Fighting For?* Wo Es War. Ser. ed. Slavoj Žižek. London: Verso, 2000.

—. *The Puppet and the Dwarf: The Perverse Core of Christianity*. Short Circuits. Ser. ed. Slavoj Žižek. Cambridge, MA: MIT UP, 2003.

Zuck, John. "Religion and Fantasy." *Religious Education* 70.6 (1975): 586-604.

INDEX

A

absolutism, 154; absolute beginning, *see under* creation; absolute ending, *see under* eschatology.
abyss, 134-135, 137, 138n, 141; of being, *see under* being
actuality, actualization, 136, 137; self-actualization, 106, 131
After the Death of God (Caputo and Vattimo), 153
afterlife, *see* heaven, hell
Altizer, Thomas, *v, vii, viii*, 1-4, 21, 23, 25, 26, 43-44, 83, 85-89; Apocalyptic Creed, 159-160; archive, *v*, 85-86, 131; Christology, 70, 85-86, 90, 91, 93-115, 143, 148n, 149-152; death, *viii*; and death of Tillich, 86; and M. Eliade, 86, 122-127, 143-144, 155, 157; and the Episcopalian Church, 85, 86; and *kenosis*, 3, 79, 95-101, 106, 108-112, 114-115, 117-119, 121, 124-125, 130-134, 136, 139, 141, 149-152; transcendence and immanence, 91, 117-141, 148; and *Time* magazine, 87; Satanology, 85-86, 153
The Altizer-Montgomery Dialogue (Altizer and Montgomery), 88-89, 95, 97, 98, 108n, 109-111, 149n, 150n
Amazon Grace (Daly), *viii*
American Academy of Religion, 150, 152-153, 154
American Industrial Group, *v*
angst, 68, 111

animism, 15
annihilation, 113, 131; self-annihilation, 101-102, 109n, 110
Anselm of Canterbury, *viii*, 15-20, 31-39, 45-46, 65, 146, 155-157
Anti-Christ, 114
apocalypse, apocalypticism, 31, 73, 91, 99-102, 106-107, 108n, 109-110, 113, 118, 119, 121, 124-126, 128-129, 130, 130-131n, 133-134, 135-136, 138-140, 145-147, 150n, 151, 155, 156; and ethics, 3, 68, 130-131n; prophets, 158; and reconciliation, 109; and salvation, 102n, 131n; Apocalyptic Creed (Altizer), 159-160
The Apocalyptic Trinity (Altizer), *viii*
apologetics, 95, 96
apophasis, 123
Arjuna, in Hinduism, 93
ascension, of Christ, 99-100, 107n, 109n
atheism, 25, 46; Christian, 21, 27-31, 83, 91, 94-95, 99, 115, 118, 136, 145, 151, 154; and theism, 80-81
atonement, apocalyptic, 107, 110-112, 121, 124-125
aufhebung, 52-53
Augustine of Hippo, 35, 46, 126; *massa sancta*, 80

B

Bales, James, 85
Barth, Karl, *vii*, 23

Battle of the Hills, World War I, 44
Beardslee, William, 148n
Bec Abbey, France, 16
Becker's Postulate, 33-34
becoming, 52, 133
begin, as a word, 137-138; *see also* creation
being: abyss of, 50-51, 53, 134; being-itself, 3, 4, 23, 29, 35-40, 47-48, 50, 51-53, 55-56, 58, 63. 70, 77, 139; depth of, 50-51, 59; and first potency, 51; ground of, 50, 53, 63-64; and *ideal-realismus*, 51;and meonic freedom, 51; and *mysterium tremendum*, 51; New Being, 70-71, 143, 155; and the Now, 137-138; as Nothing, 133; power of, 50, 51-53, 62; structure of, 50, 53; unground, 51; *see also* esse-ipsum
benedictio, 146
Bent, Charles, 148n
Berdyaev, Nikolai, 51
Bhagavad-Gita, 93
Biblical Religion and the Search for Ultimate Reality (Tillich), 50-51, 80
Black Mass, 104
Blake, William, 83, 90, 96, 112-115, 126-127, 139, 141-142
Boesel, Chris, *v*
Boheme, Jacob, 51
Bonhoeffer, Dietrich, 149; "world come of age," 93n, 129
Braaten, Carl, 26
Brown, Norman, *vii*
Bruggeman, Walter, 90
Bruno, Giordano, 122-123
Brunswick, Georgia, 153n
Butler, Charles, 148n

C

The Call to Radical Theology (Altizer), *viii*
Caputo, John, 117, 153, 154
Catholicism, 44, 88
Chicago, Illinois, 85
Christ, Spirit of, 108-109
Christian Advocate, 87-88
Christian atheism, *see under* atheism
Christology, 3, 70, 85-86, 90, 91, 93-115, 143, 148n, 149-152; anointedness, 104n; and atheism, 94-95; and *kenosis*, 3, 79, 95-101, 106, 108-112, 114-115, 117-119, 121, 124-125, 130-134, 136, 139, 141, 149-152; the Son, 136
Clyburn, David, 83
Cobb, John, 55, 86, 127
Cogito, 37
coincidentia oppositorum, 85-86, 91, 101, 121-130, 132, 134-136, 141, 146, 148-150, 152, 156-158, 160
conception, ontological, 6, 15-20, 56
conjectio oppositorum, 123
The Contemporary Jesus (Altizer), 111, 132
correlation, method of, 145-146
Corrington, Robert, *v*, 43-44, 58-59, 62
cosmology, 79; Ptolemaic, 68-69
Cosmopolitan magazine, 78
courage, existential, 4, 13, 29, 32, 45, 54, 62-63, 65-66, 70, 77, 79-81, 137, 140-141, 143, 147, 160
The Courage to Be (Tillich), 27, 32, 45, 51-52, 65, 77-78, 81
Cox, Harvey, 1-2
creation, 71, 102n; absolute beginning, 134, 136-137; *ex nihilo*, 131

A Critical Analysis of C. G. Jung's Understanding of Religion (Altizer), 121, 157
Crockett, Clayton, 75, 79, 89
crucifixion, 76; apocalyptic, 99-100, 118; of Christ, 107-109, 121, 124; Dionysian, 145; of the Kingdom of God, 159-160; and self-sacrifice, 101, 107-108, 152
Cyril of Alexandria, 104

D

Daly, Mary, *v, vii*, 25; archive, *viii*; death, *viii*; and philosophy, 3; and radical theology, 1-4, 21; and transphobia, *viii-ix*
darkness, as symbol, 141; luminous, 141
de Beauvoir, Simone, 126n
Death of God, Nietzsche, *vi*, 96, 114-115, and Christology, 96-110, divine perishing, 121; *rigor mortis*, 108; and Tillich, 27, 79; theology, *see under* theology.
death, absolute, 139; and emptiness, 150
deconstruction, 79, 146, 153
deism, 53, 55, 64
depth, of being, *see under* being
Descartes, R., 37
The Descent into Hell (Altizer), 100-101, 117-118, 119-120
determinancy, 131n, 133
Dewart, Leslie, 26
diachrony, metaphysical, 3, 73-75
Dionysian theology, *see under* theology
disjunction, logical, 33
Divine Name, 106-107; I AM, 103-106, 107n, 121, 124, 130, 132, 147; I AM NOT, 107n, 130-131
Dostoevsky, F., 96
doubt, and theology, 77-78
Dow Jones Industrial Average, *v-vi*
Dreisbach, Donald, 51-52
Drew University (Madison, NJ), *v, vi,* 50n
dualism, 53-55, 152

E

Ecce Homo (Nietzsche), 69
ecclesia, 145
Eckhart von Hochheim, 27, 131n
ecstatic naturalism, 3, 4, 57, 58-59, 60, 62
The Edge of Language (Van Buren), 4-6, 11-12, 14, 20-21, 39-40, 45, 59, 78, 103, 130, 146
elementalism, 4
Eliade, Mircea, *vii*, 30, 86, 91, 122-127, 143-144, 155, 157; *see also* coincidentia oppositorum
Emory University, 87-88, 131
emptiness, 134-135
enfleshment, 121, 124; and theosis, 85-86; enfleshed immanence, 3, 90, 119-120, 129-130, 136, 146
epiphany, apocalyptic, 102n, 109-110n, 111
Episcopal (Anglican) Church, 4, 85, 86
eschatology, 110n, 120; absolute ending, 136-137; apocalyptic, 109-110n, 113, 119-120, 137-138, 158; and Christ, 100, 119-121; eschatological movement, 117; eschatological process, 120; Dionysian, 69;

esse-ipsum, 3, 4, 34n, 35-36, 38-42, 45-46, 47-58, 60-63, 65, 69, 70-71, 73, 77-78, 80, 139, 147; *see also under* being
estrangement, 108, 127
Eternal Now, 66-68, 70, 102, 125
The Eternal Now (Tillich), 70, 125-166
eternity, 137; eternal recurrence, eternal return, 23, 65-68, 71, 134, 136-139
ethics, 3, 38, 68, 130-131n, 136-137, 139, 149; and heresy, 90; meta-ethics, 3
Europe, and secularization, 72
evangelicalism, 29, 87, 94n, 149
The Everlasting Gospel (Blake), 90
evil, 71-72
ex nihilo, 133
exile, of self-transcendence, 106-107
exitus, 146, 147
Exodus, exodic theology and narrative, 144, 153
The Expulsion of the Triumphant Beast (Bruno), 122-123

F

fantastical, the, 81
fantasy, 95, 154-160
Father, symbol of God, 101, 136, 151, 152n
Ferre, Nels, 29-30, 59-60, 78
filiation, trinitarian, 151
first potency, 51
flesh, *sarx*, 120, *see also* enfleshment
Flew, Anthony, 13
The Flight of Peter Fromm (Gardner), 47
Ford, Lewis, 61-62
Foster, Durwood, 52-53

fundamentalism, Christian, 85
The Future of Religions (Tillich), 30-31, 50, 56, 71-74, 76, 86, 148

G

Gardner, Martin, 47
The Gay Science (Nietzsche), 20-21, 65-66
generation, trinitarian, 151
Genesis and Apocalypse (Altizer), 101, 119, 132, 134, 137-138, 145-146
The Genesis of God (Altizer), 88, 90, 128-129, 158-160
gesture, and reality, 55, and thinking, 81n
Gier, Nicholas, 86
Gilkey, Langdon, 1, 47
Gnosticism, 125
God-above-God, 25, 27, 39, 42, 48-49, 50, 54-55, 56
Godhead and The Nothing (Altizer), 100, 118-119, 125, 131-132, 136-137, 144-145, 160
Godselfhood, 108-109; *Deo ipse*, 131, 132
The Gospel of Christian Atheism (Altizer), 93n, 94, 97n, 98n, 99n, 107-114, 115n; *see also The New Gospel of Christian Atheism* (Altizer)
grace, apocalyptic, 140, 159-160; gestalt of, 80
Graham, Billy, 85
Greenfield, Trevor, 146
Griffin, David, 55
Grigg, Richard, 26, 65
ground, of being, *see under* being
Guðmarsdóttir, Sigríður, 50n

H

Hamilton, Kenneth, 23
Hamilton, William, 1-2, 143, 144, 149n
Hammond, Guy, 53
Harkness, Georgia, 152-153
Hart, Ray, 102
Heaven, 90, 99-101, 113, 120, 129, 139, 140-141, 149; and ascension, 107n; New Heaven and New Earth, 42n, 74n; heavenly spirit, 159
Hegel, G., 4, 36, 46, 91, 107, 121, 126-127, 132-134, 136-137, 149, 155
Hell, 90, 140; descent into, 100-101, 107n, 113-114, 118, 119-120, 139; harrowing, 100
Heraclitus, 65, 67n
Hinduism, 93
History as Apocalypse (Altizer), 101, 106-107, 147
A History of Christian Thought (Tillich), 4, 31-32, 34-35, 39, 45-46
Holocaust, Nazi Shoah, 149
holiness, 41, 71
The Holy, 30-31, 41, 56n, 59, 60, 62, 71-75; *see also under* not-yet symbols.
Holy Spirit, 104n
honest indignation, theological, 90-91
humanism, 53
hypostasis, 53

I

I AM; I AM NOT: *see under* Divine Name
ideal-realismus, 51
Igrek, Apple, 136
immanence, 2-4, 15, 25, 27, 31, 50, 56-57, 59-61, 74-78, 80-81; absolute, 119, 121, 124, 128-129, 137, 138; and absolute nothingness, 138-139; and abyss, 136; actual, 118n, 130; apocalyptic, 99-100m 136; and Altizer, 91, 117-141; and atheism, 160; and being, 3; and *coincidentia oppositorum*, 121-130; and creativity, 60-61, 118; and the death of God, 89, 117; and diachrony, 75; and elementalism, 3; enfleshed, 4, 90, 120, 129, 146; eschatology, 70, 108n, 109n, 119-120, 128-129; as eternity itself, 137; exile of, 119, 120; and fantasy, 154-160; and gender, 126n; and homecoming, 153; immanence of immanence, 100; implicit, 146; and the Kingdom of God, 128-129; metonymical, 75-80; and models of divinity, 14-15, 56-57, 59; of the Nothing, 147; othering of, 118-119; plane of, 78-79, 80-81, 89, 147; plurality of, 77-78; and postmodernity, 136; present, 132, 136, 155, 157, 158-159; and primordiality, 100, 133-134; progression of, 89, 91, 99-101, 103-104, 108-109, 119-120, 121-130, 138, 153; pure, 118-119, 124-125; as pure transcendence, 137; radical, 61, 62, 66-70, 80-81, 120; and Religion of the Concrete Spirit, 31, 145, 147-148; and ritual, 139; and sorrow, 139; and thinking, 91, 147; and Tillich, 25, 27, 31, 50, 56-57, 59-60, 67, 68, 75-78, 80-81; total, 100, 102, 136,

138; and transcendence, 2-3, 14-15, 50, 53, 55-61, 70, 91, 97, 100, 109, 117-118, 120
Incarnate Word, *see* logos
incarnation, 3, 91, 96, 97-101, 109n, 114, 118n, 119-121, 123-128, 130-131; incarnational theology, 73-74; preincarnation, 151; as theophany, 123-124
indeterminancy, 131n
Inelimanable Mystery, 61
The Inoperative Community (Nancy), 83
ingeneration, trinitarian, 151
Intersubjective Transcendence (Rodkey), *ix-x, 1, 2*
The Irrelevance and Relevance of the Christian Message (Tillich), 27, 28-29, 45, 71, 76
Israel, as symbol, 119, 129

J

Jasper, David, 88-89, 122
Jennings, Theodore, 148n
Jesus, 108, 110-115, 150, 154; language of, 152n; passion, 121; and eschatology, 127, 135; and ethics, 150n; *see also* Christology
Journal of Religion, 58
Journal of the American Academy of Religion, 150, 152-153
joy, apocalyptic, 67-68, 110, 138-139, 141, 147, 159-160
Judaism, 153
Jung, C. G., 122

K

Kabbalah, 102, 133-134
Kairos, 74

Kant, I., 65, 126
Keller, Catherine, *v*
kenosis, 3, 79, 95-101, 106, 108-112, 114-115, 117-119, 121, 124-125, 130-134, 136, 139, 141, 149-152; and ethics, 130-131n
Kierkegaard, S., 62, 149
Kingdom of God, 79-80
Kuntz, Paul, 155-156

L

language, dismembering of, 129-130; ontology and, 147; violation of, 146; theology, *see under* theology
Leahy, D. G., *v*, 104n, 131n, 137-138, 157n
Lehman Brothers, *v*
liberalism, Christian, 31, 95n, 152
life, absolute, 134; life-itself, *see* vita-ipsum
light, as symbol, 141
liturgy, liturgical speech, 103-104; *massa sancta*, 80
Living the Death of God (Altizer), 85-87, 99, 102, 104, 113, 122, 138, 140, 144, 158-159
logical symbols: existence, as existential quantification, 33; square (modal necessity), 33-34, 157; diamond (modal possibility), 33-35, 65, 77, 157; right arrow (material condition), 33-34, 157; descending wedge, as logical disjunction, 33; parentheses, as precedence grouping, 34-35
logos, logocentrism, 93-94, 95-6, 108-109n; Word, 95-96,

107-108, 110-111; *see also* kenosis.
Long, Charles, 148n
Love, Power, and Justice (Tillich), 38-41
luminous darkness, 141
Luria, Isaac, 133-134
Luther, Martin, 126

M

madness, 21, 69, 75-77, 137, 128-129, 159; and Nietzsche, 69; and Plato, 75-78
Manicheanism, *massa perditionis*, 79-80
Mariology, *viii*
Marriage of Heaven and Hell (Blake), 83, 139
Marty, Martin, 49
Marx, Karl, 26
material condition, logical, 33-34, 157
McCullough, Lissa, 101-102, 113-114, 130
McCutcheon, Russell, 49
Meister Eckhart, *see* Eckhart von Hochheim
meonic freedom, 51
The Merv Griffin Show, 87
metamorphosis, kenotic, 111
metatheology, *see under* theology
Methodism, 87-88
metonymy, 75; metonymical immanence, 75-80
Meyer, Eric, 101-102
Midway Plaisance, Chicago, 85
Miller, Jordan, *viii*
Mircea Eliade and the Dialectic of the Sacred (Altizer), 143-144, 154-155, 122n
modernity, 79, 136, 140-141
Moore, G. E., 44-45
Morton, Nelle, 1
Murchland, Benard, 148n

My Search for Absolutes (Tillich), 42, 62, 72
mysterium tremendum, 51
mysticism, 20, 53, 132, 149n

N

Nancy, Jean-Luc, 83
naturalism, 59-60; neo-naturalism, 58; supernaturalism, 59-60, 63-64; supranaturalism, 62; *see also* ecstatic naturalism, non-naturalism
Nature and Grace in the Theology of Saint Augustine (Altizer), 126
Nazism, 25-26, 149
necessity, logical, 33-34, 157
negation, self-negation, 29, 45, 65, 97, 98n, 101, 103-108, 109n, 110-112, 125, 130-131, 134-135, 150, 152; negative theology, *see under* theology
Neoplatonism, 54-55, 127n
The New Apocalypse (Altizer), 126
New Creation, 119-120, 130, 132, 138, 155; New World, 136; power of, 133-134; self-transfiguration, 103; and Tillich, 70, 73-74; total, 98, 109n; 130, 134-136, 158; and transfiguration, 103, 119, 121, 137, 158; of Satan, 158; *see also* eschatology.
The New Gospel of Christian Atheism (Altizer), 99-100, 118-120, 136-137, 154-155; *see also The Gospel of Christian Atheism* (Altizer)
The New Nietzsche (Allison, ed.), 138-139

New York Philosophy Club, 44-45
New York Stock Exchange, *v-vi*
Nicholas of Cusa, 122, 127n
Nietzsche, Friedrich, *vi*, 20-21, 23, 25-26, 65-70, 87, 88, 93-94, 96, 136-137, 146-147, 149
Nihil, 132, 134-135, 146; nihilism, 118, 131-132, 137, 146; *see also* Nothing, nothingness
Nominalism, 38-39, 45
non-being, 39, 62, 133
non-naturalism, ethical, 44
No-saying, 114
Notebooks (Blake), 90
Nothing, nothingness, 3, 4, 91, 131-136, 138-139, 147; and Hell, 140-141; linguistic nothingness, 6n; *see also Nihil*, nihilism.
not-yet, symbolism, 45-46; not-yet-God, 127-128; not-yet-holy, 31, 45-46, 58-59, 71-75, 127-128
Novalis, 65

O

Of Learned Ignorance (Nicholas of Cusa), 122
Ogletree, Thomas, 148n
omnipresence, 124
On the Boundary (Tillich), 45, 74
ontology, 75; etiological, 143; ontological argument, *viii*, 15-20, 31-39, 45, 57, 155-157; and the Psalms, 16-18, 34
ordination, 85
Otto, Rudolph, 51, 53, 71

P

paganism, 15

Palgrave Handbook of Radical Theology (Rodkey, Miller), *viii, ix*
panentheism, 3, 15, 53, 55-57, 60, 61-62
pantheism, 3, 15, 53, 57-58, 59
paternity, trinitarian, 151
Patricca, Nicolas, 44
Paul, the Apostle, 13, 42n, 96
Pennsylvania, *viii*
perfection, and theology, 33-34
Perspectives in 19th and 20th Century Protestant Theology (Tillich), 27, 80-81
Pfister, Oskar, 51
Phaedrus (Plato), 9-10, 75-76
Philosophy, 3, 25, 27, 41, 45-46, 71-72, 114; ancient Greek, 67n; Continental, *vii-viii*; philosophical anthropology, 63-64, 68, 78; of religion, 25, 45, 50
piracy, theological method, *ix*
Plantinga, Alvin, 33-34
Plato, 9-10, 35, 54, 75-76; Platonism, 38, 54-55
pneuma, 120; Pneumatology, *see* Holy Spirit
popular religion, 128n
possibility, modal, 33-35, 65, 157; and theology, 81
post-modernism, 79
power of being, *see under* being
prayer, 104n
precedence grouping, logical, 34-44
predestination, *massa perditionis*, 79-80; and *massa sancta*, 80
preincarnation, 151
Proslogium (Anselm), 15-20, 31-39
The Protestant Era (Tillich), 86
providence, 71, 104n
Psalms, 6n, 16-18, 34
Pseudo-Dionysius, 27

Q

Qoheleth, 21
quasi-religion, 72

R

radical theology, *see under* theology.
Radical Theology and the Death of God (Altizer and Hamilton), 94, 95n, 108, 109n, 111-112, 149n, 150n
Raschke, Carl, 150-151
The Recovery of the Prophetic Tradition in the Reformation (Tillich), 73-74, 76-77
redemption, 95-96, 110, 126, 150; universal, 98; *see also* redemption
The Religious Situation (Tillich), 53
Religious Studies (journal), 15
The Republic (Plato), 54
reputo-ipsum, 3, 4, 90, 138-141, 147, 155, 157, 160
resurrection: of the body, 159-160; of Christ, 3, 91, 107n, 109n, 119-121, 124, 129, 138-139, 140, 146, 160; of the profane, 109n; and theological method, 146
Revelation, book of, 66
Robbins, Jeffrey, *v*
Rockefeller Chapel, Chicago, 95n
Ross, Robert, 124-125
Rowe, William, 35-37, 39-40, 54
Rubenstein, Richard, 1-2, 133-134
Russell, John, 36-38
Ryu, Kee Chung, 51

S

Sabatino, Charles, 148n
sacrifice, 134-135; self-sacrifice, *see under* crucifixion
Saints: St. Anselm, *see* Anselm of Canterbury; St. Augustine, *see* Augustine of Hippo; St. Cyril, *see* Cyril of Alexandria; St. Paul, *see* Paul, the Apostle
salvation, 102, 131n; salvation history, 107, 111, 150; *see also* redemption
sarx, flesh, 120; *see also* enfleshment
Satan, 85, 141; as Messiah of Nature, 126n; devil, 90; theosis of, 153; Satanology, 85-86; *see also* Black Mass
Satan and Apocalypse (Altizer), *viii*
Scharlemann, Robert, 43, 47-48, 77, 79
Schelling, F., 51
Schlegel, F., 65
Schleiermacher, Friedrich, 36, 57
Science of Logic (Hegel), 121, 132-134
Scott, Nathan, 152-154
secular, the, 71-75; secularism, 89
self-actualization, *see under* actuality
self-affirmation, 147
self-alienation, 108
self-annihilation, *see under* annihilation
self-consciousness, 108
self-creation, 131
self-division, 133-135
self-embodiment, 91, 98-110, 118n, 120, 130, 159-160
The Self-Embodiment of God (Altizer), 102-105, 107n, 130
self-emptying, *see* kenosis
self-expression, 110n

self-fulfillment, 110n
self-integration, 70
self-naming, 131
self-negation, *see under* negation
self-realization, 106, 110n, 120
self-sacrifice: *see under* crucifixion
self-silencing, 107n
self-subversion, *see under* subversion
self-transcendence, 3, 4, 45, 58-59, 63n, 65-66n, 70, 72-75, 79, 81, 148; and eschatology, 131; exile of, 106-107; and hearing, 103-104; and immanence, 3, 57, 81; and liturgical speech, 103-104; and nature, 63n; and radical transcendence, 61-65; and Religion of the Concrete Spirit, 147-148; and self-negation, 131; and speaking, 130; *see also* transcendence.
self-transfiguration, *see under* transfiguration
The Shaking of the Foundations (Tillich), 27, 51, 52, 55-56, 65
Sheen, Fulton, 78
Smith 52-College, *viii*
Smith, Steven, 101, 138-139
The Socialist Decision (Tillich), 26
Socrates, 27, 54, 67n, 75
Soliloquies (Augustine), 35n
Southern Jurisdiction of Bishops, United Methodist Church, 87-88
sovereignty, 134
Spinoza, B., 57, 87
spiration, apocalyptic, 117, 136; trinitarian, 151
spirit, *pneuma*, 120
The Spiritual Situation in Our Technological Society (Tillich), 62, 68

Stability amid Change (Harkness), 152-153
State University of New York at Stony Brook, 85
Stoicism, 65, 67n, 138
Stone, Ronald, 44
structure, of being, *see under* being
subjectivity, and transcendence, 103-104
subversion, 90, 130-131n, 146-147, 155, 157; self-subversion, 7, 12, 53, 59, 130-131n
supernaturalism, *see under* naturalism
symbols, symbolism, 29, 34n, 40-46, 48-49, 51-52, 54, 57, 58-60, 76-77, 79-81, 94, 107n, 114-115, 138n, 157; apocalyptic, 120-121, 123; apophatic, 123; Dionysian, 69-70; eschatological, 132; feminine and patriarchal, 97, 101, 126n; and gender, 3-4; and logic, 33-39, 157; and nothingness, 140-141; reconciliation of, 121; in Nietzsche, 138n; non-symbolism, 25, 34n, 39-40; of nothingness, 131; not-yet symbols, 45-46; objects as, 74; unification of, 120-121;
symbolic logic, *see* logical symbols
Syracuse University, *v*, 131
Systematic Theology (Tillich), 26, 28-29, 55, 58, 59, 60-61, 63-64, 77, 80-81

T

Taubes, Jacob, 59, 69-70, 145
tautology, 43-44
Taylor, Mark C., 89, 103, 148n, 150-151

Temple University, 4
Tetragrammaton, 106
Thatamanil, John, 46, 61
theism, 15, 53, 64; and atheism, 80-81; theological theism, 6n, 32, 46
theological anthropology, 76-77, 78
The Theology of Altizer (Cobb, ed.), 149
Theology of Culture (Tillich), 27, 62
theology: apophatic, 123; constructive, 2, 143,145, 160; death of God theology, *vii*, 2, 4-5, 30, 144-145, 152; Dionysian, 59, 67n, 68-71, 145; and doubt, 77-78; exodic, 144; expatriate, 143, 156; and gender, 126; incarnational, 73-74, 114, 119, 124, 130-131n; and language, 4-20, 39-41, 89-90, 102-103, 146-147; metatheology, 4-5, 145, 148; negative, 29, 44, 53, 65, 81, 119; 138n; and modal possibility, 81; and perfection, 33-35, 122-123; post-Christian, , 21, 25, 64-65, 75-76, 89, 141, 153; post-theology, 145; process, 110; public, 25, 87; radical, *vii*, 1-4, 21 25-46, 88, 94, 95n, 96, 128-130, 145-146, 149-; systematic, 143
Theology of Culture (Tillich), 27-28, 34n, 35-36, 38, 58, 62, 80
theonomy, 59, 62, 64, 65, 71, 74, 123-124
theosis, 85-86, 144, 153, 159
thinking, 89, 126-141, 145-147, 150, 156; and symbol, 81n; and theonomy, 75n, 79; the death of God, 79-80; "oriental," 122-123;

thinking now occurring, thinking itself now occurring, 3, 90, 139, 147, 155-156, 160; *see also* reptuo-ipsum
This Silence Must Now Speak (Altizer), *viii*
Thomas, Owen, 53, 54-55
Thus Spoke Zarathustra (Nietzsche), 114, 138
Tillich, Paul: and Absolute Faith, 81; influence, *vi*, *ix*, 1-4, 21, 25, 143-148; and crucifixion, 76-77; death, 25-26, 30, 83, 86; and death of God theology, 26, 27; and doubt, 77-78; and M. Eliade, 86, 143-144; eschatology, 73-74; models of divinity, 2-4, 23, 25-46, 47-81; and philosophy, *vii-viii*, 25, 27, 41, 45-46, 71-72; Religion of the Concrete Spirit, 30-31, 45, 73, 81n, 145, 147-148; and technology, *ix*; and transcendence, 25, 27, 31, 50, 56-57, 59-60, 67, 68, 75-78, 80-81
To Live as Men (Tillich, et al), 53
Torah, 102
Total Presence (Altizer), 107, 129, 160
totality, 108, primordial, 99, 100, 101-102
Toward a New Christianity (Altizer, ed.), 94-96, 114
Tracy, David, 88, 122, 155
transcendence, 3-4,14-15, 25, 45-46, 58, 59-61, 64-65, 70, 78, 119-120; absolute, 91, 99-100, 117-120, 128, 130, 134-135, 137; alien, 102-104, 109, 117-120, 134; and Altizer, 117-141, 148; of being, 137-138; and

coincidentia oppositorum, 121-130; collapse, 101, 119, 126; and creativity, 118; death of, 79, 89; and death of God, 91, 119-120, 138; destruction of, 127, 130-131; disappearance of, 128; and gender, 126n; and Godselfhood, 109-110, 131; and immanence, 2-3, 14-15, 50, 53, 55-61, 70, 91, 97, 100, 109, 117-118, 120; inactual, 129; and liturgical speech, 103-104; and models of divinity, 14-15; and nature, 57-59; negation, 103-104, 106, 109n, 119, 130; passive, 129; primordial, 91, 107n, 117-120, 121, 124, 132, 133-134; progression of, 89, 91, 99-101, 103-104, 108-109, 119-120, 121-130, 138, 153; pure, 137; radical, 61-65; reversal, 91, 103, 117, 134-135; and speaking and hearing, 103-104, 130; transcendence of transcendence, 101
transphobia, *viii-ix*
trinity, trinitarianism, apocalyptic, 136, 150, 151

U

ultimate concern, 40-41, 49-50, 69, 77
ungurd, 51
Union Theological Seminary, New York, 44
United Church of Christ, *vi*
United Methodist Church, 87-88
United States, economy, *v-vi*, War on Terror, *vi*
University of Chicago, 1, 30-31, 85-86, 95n, 126

V

Vahanian, Gabriel, *v*, 1-2, 45, 73-75
Van Buren, Martin, 4
Van Buren, Paul, 1-2, 4-21, 31-32, 39-40, 45, 59, 78, 103, 130, 146, 156
Van Ness, Paul, 126-127
Vanderbilt University, 87
Vattimo, G., 153
vita-ipsum, 3-4, 25, 65-66, 68-70, 74-75-, 77-81, 91, 139-141, 147-148, 155, 157-158, 160
voice, 107n; and transcendence, 104-105, 130; and preaching, 146-147
von Hardenberg, G.P.F.F., *see* Novalis

W

War on Terror, U.S., *vi*
Weil, Simone, 96
Wesley, John, 9
Winquist, Charles, 49, 70, 77-78, 79, 81, 141
Wittgenstein, Ludwig, 13
Word, *see* logos
World War I, 44

X

X, as ontological conception, 5n, 7, 17-19, 32-35

Y

Yahweh, 106
Yes-saying, 67n, 79, 114, 139

Z

Zarathustra, Nietzschean character, 65-66, 67n, 114

Zohar, 133

AUTHOR

Christopher D. Rodkey is a United Church of Christ pastor and educator who teaches itinerantly at Penn State's York campus and online for Lexington Theological Seminary.

also by Christopher D. Rodkey

The Synaptic Gospel:
Teaching the Brain to Worship (2010)

Too Good to Be True:
Radical Christian Preaching, Year A (2012)

The World is Crucifixion:
Radical Christian Preaching, Year C (2014)

Coloring Lent (2017) and *Coloring Advent* (2017)
with Jesse Turri and Natalie Turri

Coloring Women of the Bible (2018)
with Natalie Turri

The Palgrave Handbook of Radical Theology (2018)
edited with Jordan Miller

The Bonhoeffer Chrism Mass (2020)

I Know Why There's Blood in The Nile: A Chapbook (2023)

A Kazoo Christmas:
A Comedic Intergenerational Christmas Pageant (2023)

St. Paul's United Church of Christ, Dallastown, PA:
An Interpretive and Confessional History (2024)

Intersubjective Transcendence:
Mary Daly and the Baptism of Imagination (2025)

Barber's Son Press books are manufactured using Forest Stewardship Council certified, buffered paper free from lead and acid and made from wood-based pulp.

Barber's Son Press
York, Pennsylvania

www.ingramcontent.com/pod-product-compliance
Lightning Source LLC
Chambersburg PA
CBHW030650230426
43665CB00011B/1024